How the Futures Markets Work

Second Edition

Jake Bernstein

NEW YORK INSTITUTE OF FINANCE

NEW YORK • TORONTO • SYDNEY • TOKYO • SINGAPORE

CIP data is available from the Library of Congress.

NYIF and NEW YORK INSTITUTE OF FINANCE are trademarks of Executive Tax Reports, Inc. used under license by Prentice Hall Direct, Inc.

This publication is designed to provide accurate and authoritative information in regard to the subject matter covered. It is sold with the understanding that the publisher is not engaged in rendering legal, accounting, or other professional service. If legal advice or other expert assistance is required, the services of a competent professional person should be sought.

—From the Declaration of Principles jointly adopted by a Committee of the American Bar Association and a Committee of Publishers and Associations.

Printed in the United States of America

10 9 8 7 6 5 4 3

ISBN 0-7352-0129-3

Attention: Corporations and Schools

Prentice Hall books are available at quantity discounts with bulk purchase for educational, business, or sales promotional use. For information, please write to: Prentice Hall, 240 Frisch Court, Paramus, NJ 07652. Please supply: title of book, ISBN, quantity, how the book will be used, date needed.

 NEW YORK INSTITUTE OF FINANCE
An Imprint of Prentice Hall Press
Paramus, NJ 07652

On the World Wide Web at http://www.phdirect.com

Contents

Chapter 6
Getting Started in Trading Futures   81

Chapter 7
Hedging with Spreads   125

Chapter 8
Fundamental Analysis   147

Chapter 9
Technical Analysis: Chart Patterns   163

Chapter 10
Technical Analysis: Timing Indicators 191

Chapter 11
Managing Risk 221

Chapter 12
Computers and Electronic Trading 231

Acknowledgments

This book would not have been possible without the assistance, input, patience, tolerance, and suggestions of the following friends, associates, helpers, editors, and assistants: Marilyn Kinney, Nan Martin Barnum, Patty Lomax, Mary Kinney, Elliott, Rebecca, Sara and Linda Bernstein, Mike Steinberg, Ellen Schneid Coleman, and all the others who helped make this book possible. Special thanks to the good people at CQG Inc. and Omega Research for permission to reproduce charts from their trading software programs.

What This Book Can Do for You

Although the futures markets have existed in one form or another since the 1500s, it was not until the early 1960s that futures trading became a popular speculative and investment vehicle in the United States. Now futures trading has spread to virtually all countries in the world. New contracts and new exchanges have been developed due to a growing need for markets that will allow producers, consumers, investors, traders, speculators, manufacturers, and financial institutions to buy and sell the goods and products they need in order to protect profits and control costs.

THE FASTEST GAME IN TOWN

Futures trading is, in many respects, one of the last frontiers of capitalism. It is one of the few remaining investment-related vehicles requiring relatively low capital input that offers virtually unlimited profit potential to those with motivation, persistence, and skill.

1

Armed with information, sufficient starting capital, discipline, and time, the average investor can generate large profits. Yet there is a losing side to the equation as well. Investors who are not adequately capitalized or funded will most often lose at this fast-paced, high-stakes game.

Few ventures are as speculative, promising, misunderstood, maligned, risky, or basic as futures trading. Those of us who have been involved in the futures industry for many years know that, on the surface, the "game" seems simple, offers the promise of virtually unlimited wealth, and requires only a minimum in start-up capital. This is at one and the same time the lure and the danger of futures trading. Those of us who have traded futures for many years also know that it is impossible to speak of the potential profits without also speaking in even more forceful terms about the potential losses.

Although it is true that futures trading can be learned by almost everyone, it is also true that:

1. *Futures trading is not purely scientific* (nor is any form of investing).
2. *There are no shortcuts or cookbook formulas for success* in futures trading. It takes time and effort to learn the business.
3. *One can lose more than one's original investment* or speculative capital in trading the futures markets.
4. *There are as many as nine losers for every one winner* in the futures markets. In fact, people lose money regardless of their educational background, profession, or social status.
5. *Lasting success is a function of skill, knowledge, and persistence.*
6. *In spite of its seeming simplicity, futures trading is one of the most difficult and demanding endeavors* an investor can undertake.

WHY TRADE FUTURES?

When I first began trading in the futures markets in 1968, my motivation was purely financial. I was in search of the path to quick riches. The promise of wealth and the attraction of low starting capital motivated me, as it did so many other newcomers. I knew that futures speculation (or commodity trading as it was then called) was a game that required a minimum of start-up capital, no major investment in equipment, no lease or space requirements (other than perhaps a desk, telephone, and quotation equipment), and no fixed location from which my work had to be done. I could speculate for the short term, the long term, or the intermediate term. Best of all, I had the potential to use the powerful leverage of the futures markets to my advantage. The ability to control more than $50,000 in goods for less than $1,000 in margin (earnest money) was a most attractive proposition.

Unfortunately, I was blissfully unaware of the risks. Not very long after I began my trading career, I realized the odds of success were not at all in my favor. It was not until many years later that I realized how to tilt the odds in my favor and how to rectify many of the errors and loss-producing behaviors that were part of my trading repertoire. It was also unfortunate that my initial venture into speculation met with success, for it was not until my virtually immediate success turned into abysmal and total failure that I realized clearly the two-sided nature of futures speculation.

In view of the risks involved and the discipline, organization, and commitment that futures trading requires, the question naturally arises, "Why trade futures?"

It is a good question indeed, one that must be answered before an individual decides to become a futures trader. Some valid answers are:

1. *Futures trading offers the independent individual a career that can lead to great wealth,* provided you are clearly in touch with the underlying risk of loss and you can put forth the effort and exercise the discipline necessary to achieve success.

2. *The futures industry has grown rapidly.* There are many career paths to follow. You need not become an independent speculator. Careers in brokerage, market analysis, computerized trading, computer software and hardware support, accounting, law, advertising, and other services related to futures trading offer excellent opportunities.

3. *The futures markets are, in many respects, leading economic indicators.* They can tell you many things about current and projected economic trends. To understand the futures markets and their current status is to understand the economy.

This can be a valuable tool in maximizing the success of your other investments.

4. *Learning how to trade futures can help you develop the discipline necessary for success* in many other investment areas (and in your personal life).

5. Last but certainly not least, *the ability to make profits beginning with a small amount of risk capital* is one of the most obvious and cogent reasons for trading futures. Yet, paradoxically, it should not be your first or only reason.

Profits in futures trading are the outcome of having fulfilled numerous prerequisite conditions. If you are disciplined, attentive, and consistent in your trading system or method, then you will benefit in the long run and profits will be yours.

PRELIMINARIES

Before you read the rest of this book, consider the preliminary statements and suggestions enumerated here. Please read them carefully so that you will not have any prejudices or misconceptions about what this book can do for you or about futures trading in general.

*   *This book will not provide you with a complete education in futures trading.* To cover the topic completely and to learn the necessary skills to trade or to acquire professional certification will require much more reading or structured course work.

*   *If you decide to become a futures trader, remember, above all, that futures trading involves the risk of loss as well as the potential for reward.* Although profits are alluring, the potential for losing more than your original investment must always be foremost in your mind. Always practice good risk management and keep losses to a "reasonable" level.

*   *Because this book is intended for beginners, many topics are only touched on.* If I have piqued your interest, I urge you to continue well beyond what this introductory book can provide. This book can serve only as a starting point. If after reading this book you find that futures trading or the

futures industry are of interest to you, there are many avenues you can pursue to further your education. Do not make the grievous error of thinking that you know all there is to know after you read this book.

- *Take notes.* Where I have presented material in anecdotal form, I suggest that you extract the basic concepts and make appropriate notes.

- *If you do not understand a given topic or concepts,* please reread them until you do understand them. If you are still at a loss, then you may wish to consult one of the sources cited in Appendix I.

- *Application of the concepts can assist in your understanding and learning.* Get a copy of the *Wall Street Journal* or *Investor's Business Daily.* Do some reading. See how well you understand the futures talk in these publications. You may be pleasantly surprised at how much you've learned, and you'll get leads on what you still need to learn. When you understand the basics, expand your reading to some of the industry publications.

- *Don't be afraid to "get your feet wet"* once you feel confident in your knowledge. However, remember to be conservative and, above all, never to take a risk that you cannot afford.

- *Ask questions.* If you're unsure about a concept or term, call someone who knows (brokers can be helpful) or log on to the Internet and search for your topic. There are thousands of Web sites that contain trading information. One caveat, however: Beware of the claims you may read at some Web sites. Don't be fooled into believing the plethora of unrealistic claims you will find on-line. Most are specious.

It is my sincere hope that this book will fulfill the needs you identified when you decided to let me be your teacher. I hasten to add that the knowledge this book will convey is far from complete, but it is certainly more than enough to get you started in the right direction. I can be contacted via E-mail at: jake@trade-futures.com.

Jake Bernstein

CHAPTER 1

The Journey Ahead

This book will take you on a journey that may radically and profitably change your understanding of investing, trading, and speculation. I will assume that you know little or nothing about futures trading, and that you have previously formed general or vague conceptions about the nature of speculation and investing. I will begin the journey at a very basic level.

Before concentrating on such things as the definition of futures trading or the organization and structure of the futures markets, some basic concepts must be understood. Specifically, they involve both the philosophy and the psychology of speculation and investing. Without a firm intellectual footing in these components of futures trading, our travels will lack depth, true meaning, and direction. The core concepts of all futures trading are related to speculation, trader psychology, and the intended purpose of the futures markets. Overriding these concepts are the philosophical and psychological issues.

Prepare to abandon many ideas that may have come to you through the educational system or through your own readings or observations. Fear not; I have no intention of stripping away all of your present ideas. Some of them may, in fact, correlate well with what I have to tell you. My goal is to give you a realistic view of the markets, their purpose, their philosophical underpinnings, the psychological conflicts involved, and how to handle those conflicts.

MYTHS AND MISUNDERSTANDINGS

Language brings with it value judgments that are associated with words—their usage, their implied meanings, and even their intonation. Words conjure up mental pictures, some of which bring with them positive thoughts; some, neutral thoughts; and others, negative thoughts. Consider, for example, the perceived differences between investing, speculating, and gambling. What do you think about when you hear each of these words? What are your mental images for each word? If you are like most people, then you may conjure images like these:

Investor

You picture a well-dressed man or woman, seated at a large expensive desk, perhaps in a bank, studying earnings reports, possibly adding figures on a computer or examining stock prices in the *Wall Street Journal*. If you're not oriented to the business world, you may imagine an everyday person seated in his or her study, analyzing business reports, perhaps looking at stock price charts or talking to a stockbroker. In any event, your mental picture is likely to attribute the following characteristics to the "investor": some degree of affluence, intelligence, logic, studiousness, organization, skill in selecting investments, discipline, and confidence.

Many individuals would not picture a woman, a very young person, a very old person, a foreigner, a disorganized or disheveled individual, or someone who is uneducated, highly emotional, or poor.

In reality, there is no one set of characteristics that can describe the majority of investors. Investors come from all walks of life, all levels of education, all races, both sexes, and virtually every age group. Yet, it is not common for the human mind to think in such general terms. We generally construct or stereotype a given notion of the investor. This is both good and bad. It is good because it allows for mental organization, but it is bad inasmuch as it distorts reality.

Speculator

When asked to construct a mental image of someone who is a speculator, many of us imagine a middle-aged individual, usually male (perhaps more often so than in the case of the stereotyped investor). We think of an aggressive, impulsive individual, perhaps on the trading floor of the stock or futures exchange. He might be holding several telephones at once, buying on one telephone while selling on the other.

Many individuals suspect that the "speculator" seeks to capitalize on the misfortunes of others, taking advantage of short-term imbalances in the equilibrium of the markets. Generally, the image that appears is one of greed, aggression, and youthful wealth without consideration for the welfare of or financial consequences to others. In reality, however, the majority of speculators do not fit this stereotypical image. There is, as you will see, no global or all-inclusive description of the speculator as distinguished from the investor.

Gambler

This group of individuals is generally held in the lowest regard. When we think of a gambler, we often imagine a person driven by compulsion to "play the horses" or to visit casinos in Las Vegas or on a gambling boat. We assume that the gambler is addicted to his behavior, whether he makes money or not.

We may conclude that the gambler suffers from a mental disorder, that he may also be prone to excessive use of alcohol or drugs, and that he will rarely be a consistent winner. He is most often destined to lose and suffer. We tend to think of gamblers as less educated than investors, with the speculator falling somewhere between the two in terms of education, intelligence, and skill.

In other words, the common misconception is that it takes skill and intelligence to invest, intuition and brawn to speculate, and greed to gamble. In fact, none of that is necessarily true.

Furthermore, it is generally believed that investors are apt to be socially conscious individuals whose involvement in the markets is economically productive, whereas speculators serve little or no economic function and gamblers detract from society and the economy by their behavior. In reality, virtually none of that is true.

The purpose of our exercise in exploring perceptions has been to highlight three facts:

1. The human mind must, for the sake of its own organizational needs and integrity, engage in stereotypical or generalized thinking.
2. Such generalized thinking may distort reality, leading to a host of irrational or counterproductive assumptions.
3. What we have been led or educated to believe is not necessarily true, productive, or beneficial.

If what you have learned is not based in truth or reality, then you will be prone to make decisions that not only may affect friendships and other relationships, but also can have a significant impact on your career and financial future. For example, if you've been prone to think of the investor as an individual very different from yourself in skill, intellect, or social class, then you may mentally close the door to opportunities. You effectively shut your mind to the possibility of success as an investor. If you consider the speculator to be an individual who capitalizes on the misfortune of others but of yourself as a sensitive and caring human being, then you will never allow yourself to venture into an area that could bring you large profits, a considerable challenge, and great excitement. Finally, if you think that speculators and investors are nothing more than erudite gamblers, then you may never allow yourself the opportunity to find out what investing in the capital markets can do for you.

For many years, I worked in a psychiatric hospital with patients of every age, social status, and intellectual level. My patients were black, white, Hispanic, Asian, American Indian, and more. Virtually all religious groups were represented, as were many professions. I learned well that perceptions are the ultimate force behind most human behaviors. *What we tell ourselves has a direct and even predictable outcome on behavior.* The implications of this statement are vast, and they are no less applicable to the areas of investing and speculating than they are to any other area of human behavior.

For all too long, the role, function, behavior, and psychology of investors and speculators have not been fully understood. In fact, they have been grossly distorted. This has resulted in a variety of misconceptions, all of which tend to dissuade many individuals from considering a career in these fields or from pursuing a part-time venture as investors or speculators.

Investors in stocks, futures, real estate, or other capital-intensive ventures must begin with sufficient funds to achieve success. You must have money in order to make money. However, it is possible to begin with limited funds. In the futures markets, the more capital you begin with, the better your odds of success. In today's volatile markets the new trader with minimal funds is doomed to failure. Although some promoters will tell you that you can begin with as little as a few hundred dollars, this is *not* true. You will need at least several thousand dollars, preferably at least $5,000, to begin your trading adventure (although $5,000 is minimal today and it may take more money to begin, depending upon market volatility).

How Misunderstandings Perpetuate Fear about the Futures Markets

You may have heard the story of the man who bought wheat futures and ended up with five thousand bushels of wheat being dropped off on his front lawn. Don't believe it. Taking delivery on a futures contract doesn't work that way. Or perhaps you've heard a story about a person who started trading futures with only a thousand dollars and parlayed it into millions, only to lose it all back and more. If this did happen, it was extremely rare. Furthermore, if someone lost more than the profit that was made, the individual was either getting bad advice or practicing bad trading habits. Yes, you can lose more than what you put in, but sensible money management and conservative trading practices will minimize the possibility of this happening.

COMMODITY TRADING VERSUS GAMBLING:
COMPARISONS AND CONTRASTS

It has been said by many, and believed by too many, that trading in the futures markets is nothing more than gambling. Here are some of my thoughts regarding this issue. After reading my comparisons and contrasts, the final decision will be yours.

Let's first begin with dictionary definitions of the terms *gamble* and *speculate. Funk and Wagnall's New Comprehensive International Dictionary* defines these terms as follows:

- **Gamble**—to risk or bet something of value on the outcome of an event, a game of chance, to wager or bet ... to take a risk to obtain a desired result
- **Speculate**—to make an investment involving risk, but with the hope of gain

So, what's the difference between the two? As you can see, the distinction is subtle. As I see it, speculation in its ideal form is a more educated type, a higher level, of gambling. If the purpose of speculation in the stock and futures markets is to take a risk in the expectation of a positive outcome, then speculation should be entered into seriously and with considerable study and analysis.

Gambling may involve a great deal of skill; however, the outcome is theoretically less predictable in spite of the fact that the gambler is able, in some cases, to rely upon certain systems that make the outcome of the gamble more predictable.

Gambling is what the public does
Speculation is what professionals do

I make a very important distinction between gambling and speculation, based on the individual's approach to the action. The general public, the new trader, the uninformed, and the tyro are usually gamblers. We can often know intentions by their actions and verbalizations. The new trader often uses terms like "take a shot" at the market, "take a little gamble," "take a flyer," "roll the dice," or other similar phrases. The gambler in commodities is like the gambler in Las Vegas. He or she puts money into a slot machine and plays the odds. The odds of success are slim to none for most new traders and for most slot machine gamblers. One difference is, of course, that the slot machine gambler won't have to pay commissions or fees, and probably has just as good a chance of success as does the uninformed or the misinformed commodity trader.

The truth is that most new traders are no better than gamblers. They don't study the markets, they have no method, they don't care to know the odds, they pick trades willy-nilly, they follow hunches, and they keep putting quarters into the slots until their money is gone. Every now and then they have a winning streak that keeps them in the game, but they learn nothing and they will never be more than gamblers. The fact is that they'll never even be good gamblers. The good gambler is more of a speculator than a pure gambler and just as the accomplished Blackjack player will follow a method that tilts the odds in his or her favor, the successful commodity trader usually follows a system or a method or a technique or an indicator or an approach. Therefore, I consider the Blackjack player who uses a system, to be a professional gambler, and this is closer in definition to a commodity speculator. I also consider the expert poker player to be somewhat of a speculator inasmuch as knowing how to effectively bluff is a skill that tilts the odds in one's favor, often regardless of what cards are dealt. One major difference between the expert poker player and the commodity trader is that traders have to play with the cards they're dealt; they can't bluff the markets!

The horse race player can be a gambler or a speculator. The good horse player has a system that is logical and well thought out. The expert horse player plays the odds based on various statistical methods, very similar to what the successful commodity speculator does.

Hence, I consider the good horse player to be more of a speculator than a gambler and, in fact, very similar to the informed commodity trader.

The House Almost Always Wins

One of the similarities between gambling and speculation is that in almost every case, the house comes out way ahead. At the race track or the casino, the house maintains the pool of money, paying costs and more than covering its losses with winnings taken from the vast majority of players, who are losers. In commodity trading, commissions must always be paid. While the house doesn't make the money you lose, the house draws interest income on the free capital in your account (known as "float") and the house collects commissions as well as some fees. Another bite is taken by the National Futures Association (NFA) (for the supposed purpose of regulating the industry).

What Can Be Learned from Taking a Loss?

One of the benefits that a trader can derive from taking a loss is to learn from it by finding out what he or she did wrong. The only thing a gambler can learn from his or her losses is not to gamble. The trader or speculator who follows a system can learn where he or she went wrong in implementing the system or method. The trader who has no system learns nothing from losses. The key determinant is whether one is systematic and organized in the financial venture. A venture without a method or system is a gamble from which one will learn nothing. A venture with a method or system can help us learn from our losses. Most traders don't follow a system. Hence they can learn nothing from their losses other than not to trade at all.

Technicals and Fundamental Systems

As I have noted, there are methods and systems that can be applied to gambling that can tilt the odds in one's favor. This, I believe, is also the case in commodity trading. There are thousands of systems, methods, and indicators, all designed to achieve one end: profit.

Sports gamblers have also devised methods for analyzing their game. They follow rules, systems and methods. Hence, the individual who is committed to such studies is, in my estimation, no longer a pure gambler but more of a speculator. Some methods of gambling are based on statistics (i.e., like technical analysis in the markets) while other methods are based on an understanding of the horse, the breeder, the jockey, the opponent in a poker game, or the skill of a baseball player. Futures traders use a host of analytical tools and methods to improve their odds and minimize their risk of loss.

One Big Difference

A major difference between gambling and commodity trading is margin. A slot machine asks for a certain amount of money as a minimum bet. If it's a 25-cent slot machine, then only 25 cents will allow you to pull the lever. If it's a one-dollar machine, you must deposit one dollar to get into the game. You can't play the one-dollar machine with 3 cents unless you've borrowed the money.

In commodity trading, you *can* play a one-dollar slot machine with 3 cents, due to the nature of margin. That's both good news and bad news. Playing a one-dollar slot machine is like buying futures options. The most you can lose is the amount you placed into the slot machine. The good news is that you can't lose more than you put into the machine. The bad news with both slots and options is that most of the time you will lose it.

Why? Because both the slot machine and futures options lose time value. The slot machine thrill is over in a few seconds. You pull the handle, the wheels spin, they stop, you have hope, but you lose. With options the cost is much higher, the thrill lasts longer, you have hope, but it's over as soon as the wheels stop turning, which is when the option expires worthless.

The good news with futures options is that sometimes you are given the opportunity to get out at a profit. Sometimes you can even make money (if you follow the right methods). With the slot machine the thrill is much cheaper, but you can't get out unless you hit the jackpot.

Therefore, the options buyer has an advantage over the slot gambler. Note that the options buyer who takes a "shot" without research or methodology is, in my estimation, a gambler. The result will be about the same as the result for the slot machine player. But the informed options trader can, I believe, achieve success, as long as a few very basic but very important rules are followed. We also know that the options writer or seller has a much better chance of profiting than does the options buyer or the gambler.

Rules and Regulations

The commodity speculator is also limited by the house rules. The gambling house is limited by existing state and federal laws regarding gambling The brokerage house in commodities as well as professional speculators and newsletter writers are limited by a plethora of Draconian rules and regulations that often interfere with rights of free speech and freedom of the press.

Brokerage houses and trading advisors must state categorically that "there is a risk of loss in futures trading." They must give as much weight to the risk of loss as they give to the potential for profit. It's the law!

Gambling houses can and do make all sorts of claims with impunity. And they don't have to state "there is a risk of loss in playing this machine," or "there is a risk of loss in playing poker," or "past performance in playing this Blackjack system is no guarantee of future results."

As an aside, it's rather ironic that our government will allow people to gamble, to buy lottery tickets and to pay psychics for advice that involves finances, all with minimal regulation. The odds of success for the public in any of these ventures are slim to none since they involve blatant gambling.

On the other hand, regulation of the financial markets, trading advisors and newsletter writers is aggressive and running rampant in spite of the fact that the odds of success are considerably better. Seems to me that our priorities are somewhat cockeyed. But, that's no surprise!

REALITIES AND NECESSITIES OF RISK
AND REWARD

It is impossible to trade futures without taking risks. It is impossible to make a commitment to any financial venture without taking a chance that you will lose money. That's the nature of the beast. Where there exists the potential for profit, there also exists the potential for loss. The greater the potential for profit, the greater the possibility of loss. The reality of today's markets is that unless an individual is willing to take the necessary risk to trade, the potential for profit will not be there.

In the 1950s and 1960s, when markets were considerably less volatile and the price of many stocks was lower than it is today, the amount of money needed to get started in futures trading was considerably less than it is today. Along with the increased volatility in so many markets nowadays, the risk as well as the rewards of futures trading have increased substantially. You must accept this fact of market life. Look askance at anyone who tells you that you can achieve success in futures on a shoestring budget. The reality of futures trading in the new millennium is that price moves are volatile. And volatility means you will need to risk more money at the start.

Before I begin my discussion of futures trading in detail, let me assure you that the futures markets are not intended to serve as gambling pits. Although it is true that speculation is, to a certain extent, an educated gamble, futures trading is far more scientific than gambling and must be approached from that perspective. The ultimate intent and purpose of futures trading is to provide a marketplace where buyers and sellers can come together to either protect their existing assets, attempt to increase their profits, or attempt to buy or sell in advance (i.e., hedge) their need or production in given commodity items.

Now that your journey into futures trading is about to begin, I suggest you keep the following points in mind:

- Futures trading is a solitary endeavor, one that each individual must attempt in isolation and that will likely work best when practiced with only minimal interference from the rest of the world.

- Futures trading is perhaps the single most difficult undertaking any individual can attempt.

- Futures trading will be a challenge to anyone who attempts it, regardless of how successful you have been in other professions.

- A commodity trader can be a gambler or a speculator, but most commodity traders are gamblers.

- Profitable futures trading requires more brains than brawn and more psychology than methodology. Futures trading is more a mind game than it is a game of technique.

- Trading commodities can be a gamble or it can be speculation. It all depends on how one approaches trading, how the game is played, how risk is managed, and whether the trader can learn from his or her losses and profits.

- Success in futures trading rests upon only a handful of time-tested, validated methods that are not difficult to learn, not costly to obtain, but extremely difficult to implement due to limitations inherent in the human psyche.

Armed with the understandings and preliminaries presented in this chapter, let us go on to some basic definitions, terms, and procedures.

CHAPTER 2

Beginning with the Basics

This is the story of a fictional character named Woody Carver. Mr. Carver is a very talented person. Since he was a young child he has been able to create delicate, lifelike figures from small bits of wood, using only a set of knives that he inherited from his grandfather, Woodrow (Woody) Carver I. Woody produces an impressive array of miniature animals and people—squirrels, horses, toy soldiers, and historic personalities. Recently, he began carving miniature wooden versions of exotic cars, which are very popular with some of his professional friends.

A few years ago, Jack Merchant saw some of the marvelous toys that Woody had created, and he asked Woody if he could offer some of them for sale in his trendy little boutique at the local mall. Woody agreed, and the hand-carved figures quickly became a favorite of Jack's customers, who bought all of the original consignment within a week, paying very high prices for them. Jack knew he was onto something and asked Woody for more of his products.

Having sold the little toys for far more than he ever imagined possible (this was, after all, only a hobby to Woody before Jack came along), Woody excitedly agreed to sell Jack some more carved figures. This time, however, he did not have a ready supply, as Jack had bought most of his collection the first time. So he agreed to deliver some of the figures immediately and the rest in two months. By working in the evenings and on weekends, Woody was able to fulfill his agreement with Jack, who in turn sold the popular little carvings as quickly as he put them on display. A number of customers, in fact, began ordering specific figures that they particularly liked, and Jack in turn began placing special orders with Woody.

To meet the demand for his little creatures, Woody hired a neighborhood youth to work with him on some of the simpler models, and he began teaching him the art of woodcarving. Within a year, Woody had quit his job and was overseeing a workforce of five assistants, three of whom were learning Woody's craft as apprentices. Jack, on the other hand, was marketing Woody's creations through a mail-order catalog he had established a few months earlier, and the orders were flooding in. Hundreds of customers wanted toy soldiers for Christmas, while hundreds more were eager to purchase a miniature Ferrari or Lamborghini. Jack quickly discovered that he should have placed larger orders for certain items many months ahead of time, as he ran out of some of the more popular items after filling only a fraction of the orders.

Realizing that he must plan better for his second catalog, Jack met with Woody and they agreed that Woody's shop, now known as Mini-Carve, would produce 10,000 wooden soldiers by the next September and 5,000 each of the Lamborghini and the Ferrari by the coming July, to be delivered to Jack's warehouse in good condition and of the same quality as Woody's past products. Woody was pleased when Jack paid him 5 percent of the agreed-upon price as a binder to the deal. Jack was confident that he would make a killing on the resale of Woody's popular handmade toys, judging from the response to the prior catalogue.

Only rarely, usually just before falling asleep, did Jack consider the risk he had taken. After all, he had agreed to pay more money than he could possibly raise for thousands of little toys that might not sell. At those moments, Jack remembered how fickle many of his boutique customers could be. He recalled the few times he had bought large quantities of items that he just knew his clientele would snap up, only to have them sit unsold on his shelf, ultimately to be disposed of to a discount store at a loss.

One day, a few weeks after the signing of the contract with Jack, Woody got a telephone call from Mr. Harvey Watts, who identified himself as the buyer for a huge Midwest mail-order conglomerate. Harvey wanted to know whether Woody would be interested in selling his carvings through their catalog, which had a very large distribution and clientele. Woody was flattered but was forced to tell Harvey he already had a delivery contract with Jack Merchant as well as an agreement that Jack would have exclusive distribution rights to his creations.

Upon hearing this news, Mr. Watts called Mr. Merchant to inquire whether Jack might be willing to relinquish his distribution rights and sell the toys he had ordered. "Jack," said Harvey, "how much did you agree to pay for those little hand-carved beauties?"

"Well, Harvey, I have a contract to buy 10,000 toy soldiers in September at a price of $2.00 each and a contract to buy 10,000 wooden cars in July at a cost of $5.00 each."

"Tell you what, Jack; I'll take those contracts off your hands. I'll pay $2.20 for the soldiers and $5.50 for the cars. You get the difference in cash up front."

Jack quickly figured in his head what he could make on this deal. At 20 cents a piece for the toy soldiers, he would receive $2,000, and at 50 cents each for the cars, he would get $5,000. He had already paid Woody $3,500 as earnest money, so he would profit handsomely on his original investment if he sold the contract. On the other hand, he had planned to resell the figures through his own catalog at a 30 percent profit, which would net him $21,000. To sell the contract now would deprive him of $14,000 in potential profits. If the items didn't sell, though, he faced a potential $70,000 loss.

"Harvey," Jack said, "I just can't let those little guys go. I really love those little carvings, and so do my customers. My little girl would never forgive me if I sold off my stake in Mini-Carve."

"Jack, I'll give you 20 percent on each item—forty cents for the soldiers and a buck for the cars—cash up front. "

"You got a deal, Harvey."

At that moment, Jack and Harvey completed a transaction involving two futures contracts—contracts established originally between Jack and Woody. Each contract specified that a certain quantity (10,000) of a commodity (hand-carved wooden soldiers and hand-carved wooden cars) would be delivered to a certain place (Jack's warehouse) on a specified date (September and July) in good condition and of the same quality as past toys had been. Because all of these criteria were included in the original contract, it could easily be transferred to a third party (Harvey). Of course, Harvey would probably change the delivery site, but that change would likely cost him only a small amount of additional money in freight charges.

Who benefited from the transactions? Woody, of course, was the beneficiary of a contract that assured him a price for his toys before he ever manufactured them. Thus, he could plan his production and control his costs so as to guarantee himself a profit. He would not have to speculate about the market for his toys several months hence. Thus, he transferred the risk of financial losses to Jack by making the contract with him.

After some initial euphoria, Jack began to realize that he had taken on a lot of risk. He had speculated that the market for wood-carved toys would remain as strong as it had been in the past, and he had bet a lot of money on that prediction—money he did not have. All he had risked initially was $3,500, but if he was wrong about the demand for the toys, he stood to lose as much as $70,000.

Along came Harvey. He was the biggest speculator of all. He was willing to predict not only that the toys would sell well, but also that they would bring even higher prices than they had previously. Perhaps he knew something that Jack didn't. Maybe he was relying on the resources of his company to advertise the toys heavily and thus raise the chances of successfully selling them. Maybe he just had a gut feeling about the toys. No matter. Whatever his reason, he was willing to pay Jack $14,000 on the possibility that hand-carved wood cars and soldiers would sell very well even at a high price.

Jack transferred his risk to Harvey, and in so doing he locked in a fair profit for himself—not the profit he envisioned when he first made the deal with Woody, but enough to compensate him for escaping the risk of huge losses. Harvey stood to make a lot of money on the deal if his predictions were correct, but in the end he was left with all the risk if he was wrong.

DEFINITION OF A FUTURES CONTRACT

A futures contract is an agreement between a seller and a buyer. The agreement calls for a seller to deliver a specified quantity of a particular grade of a certain commodity or its cash equivalent to a predetermined location on a certain date. That's simple enough. A rancher could sign an agreement with a meat packer to deliver 44,000 pounds of 600- to 800-pound steers, to a particular packing-house, on a date six months in advance. This constitutes a futures contract, or a contract for future delivery, just like the contract between Woody and Jack in our example.

Tradable Contracts

Neither of the example contracts, however, is a futures contract capable of being traded at a commodity futures exchange. Each is a unique contract with specifications unique to that transaction. Each calls for delivery of goods at a future date. However, only a limited number of individuals would have an interest in becoming a party to either contract. Who, other than Harvey, for example, would want to speculate on wooden toys? What each of these contracts lacks is standardization. To be traded on the floor of a commodity futures exchange, a contract must be standardized so that the only negotiable part of the contract is price. All other aspects are predetermined by regulation.

A typical futures contract—one that is traded presently at the Chicago Mercantile Exchange—is a contract for frozen pork bellies (slabs of bacon). This contract calls for 40,000 pounds of "green, square-cut, clear, seedless bellies with 75 or fewer minor defects, cut from barrows, gilts, and smoother sows (no stags or boars permitted), to be delivered from a federally inspected packing plant in Chicago during the months of February, March, May, July, or August" (the trader chooses the delivery month). Anyone who trades in pork bellies at the Chicago Mercantile Exchange will trade only that particular contract, abiding by the specifications if delivery is made or taken. Only the price per pound will be negotiated on the trading floor.

There are many contracts negotiated (traded) every day, like the one between Woody and Jack, that could be called futures contracts. The only characteristic they share, however, is that they all have a future element—that is, they call for future delivery of a commodity. Therefore, because the commodity is different from contract to contract, or the quantity or the delivery point or the quality varies, each contract has a very limited appeal to speculators, who might otherwise be interested in buying such a contract on the assumption that conditions in the future might change the value of the commodity.

In Harvey's case, once he bought the contract from Jack, he was virtually stuck with having to take delivery of the toys, because the chances of finding someone else interested in speculating on the price of wooden toys was next to nil. In the futures industry, we call that a lack of liquidity. What separates a futures contract at a futures exchange from a contract for future delivery, then, is the element of standardization. All commodity futures contracts traded on the trading floor of a commodity futures exchange are standardized according to quantity, grade, delivery month and delivery point, like the contract for pork bellies at the Chicago Mercantile Exchange.

WHAT IS RISK TRANSFER
AND WHY TRANSFER IT?

Contrary to the perception of many who are only marginally familiar with futures trading, standardized futures contracts were not established simply because a group of speculators was eager to take a chance on making a killing and needed a vehicle for that purpose. Certainly, the popular misperception of the modern commodities trader, romanticized to near-mythical status as a self-made person of great wealth—the wearer of a Rolex watch, the driver of a Rolls Royce, BMW, or Mercedes-Benz—perpetuates the mistaken impression that speculation is the sole purpose for trading futures contracts and that no legitimate economic or social benefit accrues from the buying and selling of commodity futures. Nothing could be further from the truth. The fact is that standardized commodity futures contracts were established in response to the economic risk inherent in dealing with certain perishable or seasonal commodities.

Ask any farmer about the risks involved in growing a crop of corn. If the weather during the growing season is ideal, the farmer may have a bumper crop, but so will many other farmers. Consequently, corn supplies may be large and supply may exceed demand. Prices will fall if demand does not increase with supply. On the other hand, if the weather during the growing season is too dry or too wet or too windy, the farmer may have a poor crop, but so will other farmers. Consequently, there won't be enough corn to meet the demand and prices will go up.

How can farmers predict the price they will get for their corn at harvest time? The answer is, they can't, and so the very act of planting corn is a speculation. But most farmers don't enjoy being speculators. They want to know they will get a fair price for their product, enough to make a fair profit to provide support for their families. If they could transfer some of the risk involved in their business, they would be happy to do so in exchange for a degree of security in the way of a confirmed price.

Ask contractors about the risk involved in building a house. When they bid a price for the home, they know the price of lumber at that moment. They can only speculate, however, on the price they will have to pay for lumber when it comes time to purchase the materials for constructing the house. They would be very happy if they could accurately predict that price and lock it in. Although not as volatile as the farmer's risk, there is, nevertheless, a risk factor.

Thus, for both producers and end users of many commodities, risk and speculation are inherent and inescapable aspects of doing business. Consequently, the higher the risk that must be assumed by either party, the higher the price of the product will be to the consumer to cover that risk.

The standardized futures contract provides a vehicle whereby business risk can be transferred from producers and users of commodities to speculators, who are willing to take a chance in exchange for the possibility of huge profits. As the producers and users are able to transfer their risks, like Woody Carver, they are able to plan more efficiently and thus reduce the cost of doing business. The ultimate beneficiary of the futures exchange, therefore, is the consumer, who pays lower prices for the commodity. But who is the loser in this equation? Is the benefit one-sided?

Who Benefits from the Transfer of Risk?

The transfer of risk using a futures contract can benefit the buyer, or the seller, or both. Much depends on the intent of the buyer or seller when the contract is made. A seller who is selling a corn futures contract at $3 and has a production cost of $2 per bushel has locked in a profit of $1 on the sale. The trader who took the other side of the corn transaction is unhappy (provided he or she still holds the contract) to be losing $1 on the trade.

The risk in this case has been transferred from the producer (seller) to the buyer. Assume that the farmer sells the corn at $3 and the market goes up to $3.50. Since the cost of production is $2, the farmer has made $1 profit per bushel and is happy to have locked in the cost of production. The speculator who bought the $2 contract and sold it at $3.50 has made money as well. The farmer may not have made the most money possible, but has still made money and has had the option of buying back the contract well before it went to $3.50. In this case, both the buyer and the seller have made money.

On a broader scale, the consumer or end user benefits as well, since producers or manufacturing firms that use the futures markets wisely can control their costs, thereby (hopefully) passing on some of the cost savings to the consumer. In part, the effective use of futures markets can spell the difference between running a highly profitable company or a losing company. The ability to hedge currencies, interest rates, and stock prices in recent years has expanded the use of futures trading to virtually all areas of business.

MARKET PARTICIPANTS

There are four broad categories of market participants in futures trading:

Producer

This group of market participants manufactures, grows, mines, or otherwise produces the goods that are contracted for in a futures transaction. These goods can be anything from grain to livestock to Swiss francs to silver. The producer may be a seller of goods as well as a buyer. A farmer, for example, may sell soybean futures against his or her own production, but may also be a buyer or seller of petroleum futures to hedge the cost of fuel, or may also be a buyer of T Bond futures in order to hedge the cost of money to run the farming operation.

End User

This group often consists of manufacturers or large users of raw products. As an example, an automobile producer would be a buy hedger of items like copper, platinum, currencies, and perhaps other metals. This end user might also hedge in the interest rate markets to defray the cost of borrowing operating capital.

Speculator

The speculator is neither producer nor end user. The speculator can be either a buyer or a seller, depending on his or her analysis of and orientation to the markets. The speculator is often willing to take a position contrary to the current market trend in the hope of making a profit.

Floor Trader or Pit Broker

The purpose of the floor broker is to facilitate the transactions between buyers and sellers by matching buy and sell orders. Often the floor broker takes the role of a speculator; but most often the floor broker merely fills orders (known as "paper"). Due to the advent of electronic order matching, the floor trader may be a vanishing breed.

PRICE RISK

Price risk occurs as a result of time intervention in a transaction. In a complex international market, the time between production and end use of a product can often be very long, ranging from months to years. During that intervening time lag, the price of the commodity is vulnerable to change. If the producer holds the commodity during the interval, prices could drop precipitously in the interim, creating a huge loss of income. On the other hand, prices could rise significantly, creating an additional expense for the buyer. Either way, one party to the transaction stands to lose a significant amount of money while the other stands to gain unexpected profits, all because of circumstances that neither has control over.

Time alone, of course, does not create the risk. In an international market, conditions can transpire anywhere in the world that directly affect the price of a commodity: drought, flood, war, political upheaval, storms—the list could go on. An individual or a company holding large amounts of that commodity can suddenly find that the value of the stores has decreased (or increased) by substantial amounts, almost overnight. Thus, a grain buyer who purchased 500,000 bushels of corn from Midwest producers, utilizing credit to finance up to 90 percent of the transaction, could find itself in serious financial difficulty if the price were to drop 20 cents per bushel before it resells the corn to a mill.

In a complex international market, furthermore, there is often intense competition that can bid a price up or down very quickly, resulting in broad price swings in a relatively short period of time. Other risk factors, related to supply and demand, are seasonal harvests and seasonal demand for some products.

Ultimately, the factor of time combined with unpredictable circumstances related to supply and demand creates potential price risk that is untenable to a buyer or a seller of a commodity. Some means to reduce risk is essential to the orderly transaction of business in any market subject to such volatile price changes. The standardized commodity futures contract is the instrument whereby risk can be transferred.

The Early History of the Futures Contract
in Europe and Japan

In medieval Europe, most business was transacted at regional market fairs, often by barter. These fairs turn up quite often in the nursery rhymes, stories, and songs we hear as children. The fair is where Jack traded the family cow for a bunch of magic beans, where Simple Simon met the pie man, and where Johnny, who stayed so long at the fair, was to have bought a bunch of blue ribbons for his love, so she could tie up her bonny brown hair.

To facilitate the orderly and honest transaction of business, the market fairs through the years became more specialized and organized, with rules that the merchants were expected to follow. If Jack had dealt with more scrupulous merchants who followed the fair regulations, he never would have incurred his mother's intense wrath. But then, neither would he have discovered the goose with the golden eggs, and we would have been denied the wonderful fantasy of the magic beanstalk.

Unlike Jack's swindling traders, most medieval merchants found that adhering to the regulations established by the fairs reduced the risk of doing business, and so they were quite willing to follow the rules. At the fairs, for example, commodities were traded at scheduled times and places, so that buyers and sellers could find each other more easily. All traders were confined to the fairgrounds, so that side deals could not be made apart from the open market, where bids and offers were required to be public. Under such conditions, it was much more difficult for unscrupulous buyers or sellers to cheat one another or to corner the market on a particular commodity.

As open market fairs grew, there developed a sort of currency called a fair letter, which established a future cash settlement date for a transaction. With fair letters, merchants could travel from fair to fair, using the letters as a medium of exchange in the transaction of business. Fair letters were the crude forerunners of the modern futures contract and, like the futures contract, were born out of legitimate business demands.

The first recorded example of actual futures trading occurred in Japan in 1697. Whereas the European fairs had developed the structure and rules presaging a modern futures market, they were, nevertheless, cash markets. No attempt was made to take the next step and develop an actual futures contract. Evidently, the market fairs did not present a set of circumstances that made the trading of futures contracts beneficial.

In Japan, however, the feudal system did just that. Japanese landowners found that they could use certificates of receipt against their rice crops as a sort of currency. As these certificates found their way into the economy, various individuals discovered that the

value of the certificates could rise or fall as the price of rice fluctuated. Thus was born the Dojima Rice Market—the world's first
futures market—where speculators traded the certificates of
receipt, which were actually contracts for the future delivery of rice.

The practice of transacting these certificates of receipt, however, was little more than gambling, because there was no
allowance for physical delivery of the rice. When no delivery can
take place, then a futures contract has little relationship to the
underlying cash value of the commodity, and its value on an open
exchange can fluctuate wildly and unpredictably. As a consequence, the Japanese government prohibited futures trading for a
while in the seventeenth century. Later, with increased regulation
that made physical delivery possible, the government allowed
futures trading exchanges to reopen.

The History of the Futures Contract in the United States

During the nineteenth century, the industrial growth of the
United States resulted in the steady increase of production capabilities for farmers and a greater degree of specialization in the
marketplace. Local self-sufficiency gave way to regional and
national markets. The time lag between the production of a crop
and its end use became greater. No longer could a farmer simply
take a wagonload of corn to the local miller, have it ground into
meal and bagged for use during the coming months, and leave
some for the miller in payment for the processing. Rather, small
local millers gave way to larger regional mills; small local farmers
gave way to larger enterprises. Intermediaries established grain
elevators, where the farmer's produce could be purchased and
stored for transportation to larger regional distribution and storage centers.

As the country's population moved westward, new markets
opened up for industrial products, resulting in further expansion
of production facilities. For the farmer, the market progressed from
local to regional to national, and finally to international, as production capacity grew and transportation and communication systems expanded and improved.

Chicago became a booming center of transportation and commerce, with most of the agricultural and industrial products that

were headed for larger markets passing through the city. Midwest farmers in the 1830s and 1840s, however, experienced problems in marketing their grains. Railroads, which would later facilitate the movement of large quantities of grain to many far-flung markets, had not yet been built. There were few storage facilities, which made it impossible to store the grain for future sale. As a consequence, at harvest time, farmers arriving in Chicago with their crops often created a great oversupply of grain.

This flood of grain caused prices to drop and resulted in very little return to the farmers: They were forced to accept whatever price they could get for the grain. It also caused vast spoilage, as the market could not absorb the supply of grain being brought in. Immense quantities of spoiled grain were often dumped into Lake Michigan.

A few enterprising farmers, however, began to avoid the rush to market by arranging for future sales of their crops. They would contract with a buyer for an agreed-upon price on delivery of the grain at the market, perhaps two weeks hence. Later, these "to-arrive" or "forward" contracts were extended to longer periods, say, 30 to 60 days hence. Such a contract effectively transferred a degree of price risk from the farmer to the buyer. It also tended to smooth out the occurrence of alternating gluts and shortages during the year.

With forward contracts, buyers could schedule grain deliveries at more convenient intervals. Grain elevators were able to plan the utilization of storage space more effectively. Processors could expect a steadier supply of grain without the extreme price swings that had resulted from the earlier oversupply and undersupply situations. Forward contracts seemed to be the perfect solution to the extreme problems of the 1830s and 1840s.

Nevertheless, some problems remained. It was not difficult, for example, for a farmer who was able to get a better price at the time of delivery to renege on a deal. Likewise, a buyer might try to renegotiate the deal if prices had dropped in the interim.

Speculators entered the market along with the development of forward contracts. They were individuals who were not in the grain trade, but would enter a contract in anticipation of a price change by the time of delivery. A speculator who contracted to buy a load of grain naturally expected that the price on the cash market at the time designated for delivery would be higher, so the speculator could immediately sell the grain at a profit.

Likewise, a speculator might agree to sell a load of grain, expecting that when the contract came due, the trader could buy grain at a lower price and sell at the contracted price. By so doing, some of the risk that would have been transferred to the buyer from the farmer was now transferred to the speculator. It was not uncommon for a forward contract to change hands several times before delivery actually took place.

In the absence of a regulated market, however, transacting business via forward contracts remained a difficult and risky endeavor. A buyer might hold a contract for delivery of corn at an established price, for example, but because there was no standard for quality, the buyer was never sure exactly what was being bought until delivery took place. It was very possible that the corn being delivered would be of inferior quality.

Furthermore, there was no way for a buyer or a seller to be sure the negotiated price of the forward contract was fair, because prices were often kept secret. For the speculator who traded forward contracts, each transaction was a unique business deal because the size of the contracts varied as did the terms of payment and delivery. All of these shortcomings led to a loose association of grain merchants in Chicago who attempted to standardize contracts and provide some organization to the chaos of the Chicago grain market.

In 1848, the Chicago Board of Trade was established as a place where grain merchants could meet and attempt to solve some of the problems they encountered. By 1865 the Chicago Board of Trade had established standards for contract size, quality, and delivery, as well as a set of rules for trading contracts. This date marks the beginning of futures trading in the United States. The "to arrive" contract had become a commodity futures contract.

REGULATION OF THE FUTURES INDUSTRY

Through the centuries, the practice of futures trading has always been somewhat suspect. After all, how can someone sell what he or she does not own? In the original Japanese Dojima Rice Market, the government temporarily halted trading because of irregularities, as well as the fact that, with no cash settlement being allowed, futures trading was little more than gambling.

As commodity futures trading became more popular in the United States, various attempts were made to regulate the process and to control manipulative and fraudulent practices. Because the futures market is in many ways the essence of a free-market capitalist economy, attempts to regulate and restrict the business have met with solid resistance through the years. The struggle has always been to provide a balance between protecting the unwary from unscrupulous tactics and placing undo restrictions on a free-market economy.

The earliest government regulation of futures trading in the United States occurred in 1916 with the enactment of the Cotton Futures Act. This was followed in 1922 with the Grain Futures Act, which was amended in the 1930s and changed to the Commodity Exchange Act. With this act, administered by a division of the Department of Agriculture called the Commodity Exchange Authority, the government outlawed some of the most blatant manipulative practices of the futures markets and established rules whereby customers' money would be kept safe from unscrupulous brokers.

In 1974, Congress passed the Commodity Futures Trading Commission Act, which established governmental authority over all commodities, rights, and services traded on futures contracts. The Commodity Futures Trading Commission (CFTC) was established, with two goals in mind: 1) to foster competition and 2) to protect the participants in the futures markets from fraud, deceit, and abusive practices. To accomplish these goals, the CFTC requires that every person involved with the execution of orders or in dealing with the public be registered. Registration involves demonstration of a basic understanding of the business through standardized testing and a personal record that is clear of involvement in illegal or unethical practices. For this purpose, fingerprinting is a required part of the registration procedure.

The CFTC has established a number of specific categories of individuals in the futures business, each with its own set of requirements and regulations. These include the Introducing Broker (IB), who introduces business through a Futures

Commission Merchant (FCM), who may or may not be a clearing member of an exchange. Other categories include the Commodity Trading Advisor (CTA), the Commodity Pool Operator (CPO), and the Associated Person (AP) working for any of the above persons.

National Futures Association (NFA)

The National Futures Association (NFA) is a self-regulatory organization established in 1982 under provisions of the CFTC Act of 1974. Anyone in the futures business who is required to register with the CFTC must also become a member of the NFA.

The primary purpose of the NFA is to assure "high standards of professional conduct and financial responsibility" on the part of its members. To accomplish this, the NFA conducts periodic audits of members' financial and other records. In addition, the NFA monitors the sales practices of its members, requiring, among other things, that certain disclaimers appear on all published documents and that all claims regarding profitability in the futures business be accompanied by statements that describe the risks associated with such investments. The NFA also provides a mechanism for arbitrating disputes arising from futures-related business between NFA members and their customers.

Who Is Required to Register with the CFTC?

The individuals who must register with the CFTC are listed here. The CFTC is very specific regarding who must register with them. (The descriptions given here are taken directly from the National Futures Association Application Guide for NFA memberships and CFTC registration.)

Futures Commission Merchant (FCM)

Generally, an FCM is an individual or organization that does both of the following: 1) solicits or accept orders to buy or sell futures contracts or commodity options, and 2) accepts money or other assets from customers to support such orders.

Introducing Broker (IB)

An IB is a person or organization that solicits or accepts orders to buy or sell futures contracts or commodity options but does not accept money or other assets from customers to support such orders.

Commodity Pool Operator (CPO)

A CPO is an individual or organization that operates or solicits funds for a commodity pool; that is, an enterprise in which funds contributed by a number of persons are combined for the purpose of trading futures contracts or commodity options.

Commodity Trading Advisor (CTA)

A CTA is a person who, for compensation or profit, directly or indirectly advises others as to the value of or the advisability of buying or selling futures contracts or commodity options. According to the CFTC, providing advice, even indirectly (as in a newsletter or hotline), is considered exercising trading authority over a customer's account.

Giving advice through written publications or other media is also considered to be an activity that requires registration. In 1999 the courts reversed this requirement. Hence a newsletter writer, trading system seller or developer, Internet publisher, or hotline provider are no longer required to register. This may change because the decision is likely to be appealed by the CFTC; check with your attorney or the CFTC to be certain.

Associated Person (AP)

An AP is an individual who solicits orders, customers, or customer funds (or who supervises persons so engaged) on behalf of an FCM, IB, CTA, or CPO.

Protection for the Individual Investor

The CFTC seeks to protect the public who are involved in the futures business by establishing extensive regulations, maintaining effective surveillance procedures, and rigidly enforcing the rules. Potential abuses in the futures industry fall into three broad categories: unfair trading practices, credit and financial risks, and sales practice abuses.

Unfair trading practices include price manipulation, prearranged trading, and trading ahead of a customer. The CFTC has stringent surveillance practices in place to detect these abuses.

To guard against the risk of insolvency, the CFTC enforces strict net capital requirements and position limits on firms doing business in the futures industry. Moreover, the CFTC requires that customers' funds be maintained in segregated accounts, separate from the operating capital of the firm.

Sales practices are closely regulated and monitored. Brokers are required to disclose the risk involved in futures trading and are prevented from making wild claims of profitability. Any claim regarding profit must be accompanied by the disclaimer that loss may also occur; any reporting of past profitability must also state that past profits are not necessarily indicative of future profits.

A Commodity Trading Advisor or a Commodity Pool Operator must file a disclosure document with the NFA and include a three-year track record in the disclosure. Brokers are required to know their customers, so that unsuitable recommendations are not made, and are prohibited from furnishing false or misleading information, engaging in high-pressure sales tactics, and employing unqualified or unsupervised sales personnel. Any customer who has experienced fraudulent practices or other illegal activities on the part of a futures broker is entitled to file for money damages under the reparations program operated by the CFTC.

TRADING THE FUTURES CONTRACT

At this time, you should have a good idea of what a futures contract is and how it has evolved historically. You now know that the reason futures contracts are traded is to transfer risk from producers and users of a commodity to speculators, who hope to reap great profits. What you have yet to learn is how that transfer of risk takes place.

As stated previously, a futures contract is standardized by quantity, quality, delivery date, and delivery point. This is done to encourage liquidity, which simply means a lot of traders exchanging a lot of contracts of that commodity. By now, these thoughts have probably crossed your mind: "If I choose to enter a contract as a buyer or a seller, what happens if the contract expires and I have to make good? Where will I find all those pork bellies to deliver? What if I'm a buyer? Will my freezer hold 40,000 pounds of frozen bacon?"

The fact is, you have nothing to worry about. Fewer than 5 percent of all futures transactions result in delivery. The vast majority of contracts are offset or liquidated prior to delivery. As a trader, you simply make sure that you liquidate your position prior to the delivery date of the contract.

Perhaps, though, another question has occurred to you: "What happens if a seller of livestock futures chooses to make delivery and there are no cattle around of the grade specified in the contract?" If that happens, then a different grade is delivered and a premium is charged or subtracted, depending on whether the cattle to be delivered are superior to or inferior to the grade specified by the contract. Likewise, if delivery is to a different location, the cost of transporting the cattle from the contract delivery point to the requested delivery point is added to the settlement cost.

So how do speculators make money on futures contracts if no delivery ever takes place? A commodity futures trader enters into a futures contract by agreeing to sell a commodity or buy a commodity according to the precise contract specifications established by the exchange. By entering into the contract, the speculator has also agreed to a specified price. For example, if I choose to trade a contract for corn, I may agree to sell 5,000 bushels of corn at $2.11 per bushel to be delivered in July of the current year. The position I have established is a "short" position. I could now say that I am a "short seller" or that I am "short" one contract of corn. The linguistic root of this expression is the same as if I were to say I am short of money to buy a pair of shoes. In the shoe example, short means I do not have all the money required to buy the shoes. "Short" in the commodities market means I will be a seller and thus be short of the commodity if delivery is taken.

Now that I have a short position in corn, I have two alternatives. One is to hold the position until the contract expires. At that time, I can arrange to buy 5,000 bushels of corn for cash and then deliver them to the buyer of my contract. If I buy the corn at less than $2.11 per bushel on the cash market, I will make money when I sell it for $2.11 per bushel to the contract buyer. On the other hand, if I have to pay more than $2.11 on the cash market, I will lose money. For example, if I pay $2.15 per bushel, I lose $0.04 per bushel times 5,000 bushels, or $200.

The other alternative available to me as a short seller is to offset, or liquidate, my position, hopefully when the futures price of corn will allow me to make a profit. I can liquidate by taking the opposite position. Since I am a seller (short), I can liquidate by becoming a buyer (going long). If this is confusing, just remember what happened when I chose to hold my position until expiration: I offset my short position by buying corn on the cash market, which I then deliver to the buyer of my contract. The same occurs here: If I have a long position and a short position, they cancel each other out, and I am out of the market.

Did I make money? If I went short at $2.11 per bushel and then went long, or liquidated, at $2.05 per bushel, I made $0.06 per bushel times 5,000 bushels, which equals $300. Don't get confused: If I buy at $2.05 and sell at $2.11, I make a profit of $0.06, regardless of the order in which I do it. The rule is always "Buy low, sell high," but it can be reversed to "Sell high, buy low." The point is to buy for a lower price than the price at which you sell a commodity, no matter which transaction (buy or sell) comes first.

Electronic Trading and Electronic Order Entry

The open outcry system of futures trading is slowly but surely being replaced by an electronic system of order entry and execution. The floor broker is no longer used at some exchanges. The London International Financial Futures Exchange (LIFFE) market in London, for example, has instituted some fully electronic markets in which the floor broker is not involved at all. Orders are matched electronically by computer. As computer technology improves, the number of markets that will be traded electronically will increase. The role of the floor broker will continue to diminish and the markets will likely become more efficient over time.

Where Futures Contracts Are Traded

Futures trading has expanded to virtually every nation of the world. There are even futures exchanges in Russia and China. Literally hundreds of different contracts and commodities are traded. You can trade everything from cocoon futures in Japan and pepper futures in India to pork bellies in the United States and French bond futures in Paris. Note, however, that not all futures contracts are actively traded. In addition, be aware of the fact that different commodity exchanges have different rules and regulations, particularly those in Asia. I urge new traders to participate only in the U.S. markets before trying to play the international game. More specifics are given on where markets are located and what is traded in Chapter 5.

Defining Margin

When I decide to sell a contract of corn on the futures exchange, I don't actually sell the corn. I only agree to sell the corn at a later date. It would be the same if I were to sell my house. Usually, when a house is sold, the seller signs a sales contract agreeing to deliver title to the house at a closing, which normally occurs 60 to 90 days later. When the title is delivered, payment is made from the buyer to the seller. In the meantime, the buyer puts up earnest money to indicate the intent to honor the contract and actually buy the house when the closing date arrives. Remember the $3,500 that Jack deposited as earnest money with Woody when they signed their contract? Although the actual transaction would take place later, the deposit indicated Jack's intention to follow through on the deal.

Likewise, a futures contract is only an agreement that a transaction will take place later. Consequently, no money changes hands until the transaction occurs at its scheduled date. All parties to the transaction, however, must put up earnest money to guarantee that they will live up to the terms of the contract. In the case of the house, only the buyer puts up earnest money. In the futures market, both parties to the transaction put up earnest money, which is called margin. Margin usually amounts to approximately 1 percent to 5 percent of the contract value, depending upon requirements of the futures exchange(s). This is called initial margin.

The Purpose and Function of Margin

If a trade moves against you, that is, if prices change so that you are losing money on your position, you might have to put up additional money. The futures exchange requires traders to maintain a certain amount of margin in their accounts. This is called maintenance margin for each trade. Thus, it may be that you have to put up $2,000 in initial margin money to make a trade, with the understanding that you will maintain at least $1,500 in margin if the trade moves against you.

Margin requirements are intended to protect you from taking too much risk by trading with too much leverage. The futures exchanges that set the margin requirements attempt to strike a good balance between margin that is high enough to keep the market from being too speculative, and margin that is small enough to attract traders. Your brokerage firm is required to charge the minimum margin as determined by the exchange; however, they may, at their discretion, charge more than exchange minimums.

In the event that a trade or trades move so far against a customer as to use up the capital in the customer's account, the brokerage house will issue a "margin call," which requires that the customer post an additional amount of money by a specified time. Should the money not be sent, the brokerage house may, at its discretion, close out the client's positions in order to reduce additional risk exposure to the broker and the brokerage house.

Who Sets Margin Requirements and Why

Margin requirements are determined by and set by the various futures exchanges. They set requirements in order to curb excessive speculation and to protect the trader from price swings that are too large for the required margin. As the price of a commodity increases, so does the margin. Whereas the margin on corn futures might be $700 when corn is at $1.75 per bushel, it could be as high as $5,000 when corn futures are at $3.75.

You would do well to pay attention to the margin requirements set by the various exchanges. If margins are raised suddenly and by a substantial amount, this is often an indication that the given futures exchange is concerned about the high price level of a market or about its volatility. Act accordingly to reduce your risk. Note that there is no one-to-one relationship between the level of margin and the potential for profit in any given market.

"Marked to Market" Margins

When risk is deemed to be relatively low, the brokerage firm may decide to mark margins to the market. In other words, there will be no specific dollar margin amount. Rather, the profit or loss at the end of the day will be considered your margin. If your trade(s) show an open loss, your liability will be the amount of the open loss.

"Marked to the market" margins are usually charged on spread positions that are deemed to be lower in risk. Such spreads are usually intracommodity (i.e., in the same market) spreads. (Spread trading is discussed in Chapter 7.)

Margin and Customer Protection

The purpose of margin is not only to assure that the buyer or seller has made a commitment of "earnest money," but also to protect the customer and the broker in the event of a market move contrary to the existing long or short position. Margin is a buffer designed to afford some degree of protection. If you buy corn futures, for example, and are charged a margin of $1,000, then corn futures would need to decline $1,000 in value, or 20 cents, before your margin is in jeopardy and you are asked to put up more margin (unless there is already sufficient money in your account). The more margin you are required to post for a given trade, the larger the move will need to be against you before your initial margin is in jeopardy.

Margin and Broker Protection

The purpose of margin is to protect the broker and the brokerage house as well as the customer. By keeping margins reasonably high, the broker is protected in the event that a trade moves against a customer. Since the broker is often liable in the event that a customer cannot meet a margin call, the house must set margins high enough to minimize the risk of the broker being liable for losses. As you can see, margin is a necessary consideration in all futures trading. Its purpose is to protect broker, client, and brokerage house.

WHAT IS A HEDGE?

Now we know how a speculator makes or loses money in the futures market. Earlier we said that the primary function of the futures exchange is to transfer the risk of the end user or producer to the speculator. This occurs through a process known as hedging. Hedging occurs when a producer or end user takes a position in the futures market that is the opposite of his position in the cash market.

Suppose that a farmer is raising cattle that he intends to bring to market in six months. Since he intends to sell cattle for cash in six months, he can sell a futures contract for cattle now. If the price of cattle goes up in six months, the farmer will make money on his sale of cattle but will lose money on the futures position. Conversely, if the price of cattle declines, the farmer will lose money in the cash market where he sells the cattle, but will make money in the futures market. By hedging, the farmer has cut his profit potential as well as his risk of loss. His cash position and his futures position balance one another, and his price six months hence is "locked in," or pre-determined, at the sell price of his hedge.

How Hedging Transfers Risk

When a hedge is placed, risk is transferred from the hedger to the individual who has taken the other side of the contract. Assume, for example, that a farmer sells corn as a hedge against her production. The price she gets for the sale of corn futures will lock in her profit at the given sell price. Should corn prices move higher than the locked-in price, the farmer will still get the price she contracted for, even though she could have gotten more if she had not hedged or if she had hedged at a higher price. The buyer of the contract will benefit in this case, since he or she bought from the farmer at a given price and sold out at a higher price. The profit the farmer could have made by not hedging now belongs to the speculator.

On the other hand, if a farmer hedges corn at $2.50 per bushel, for example, and if corn prices then decline to $2.00, the farmer has saved 50 cents per bushel. This can be a considerable amount of money. Note that the farmer (hedger) or speculator may close out the position at any time prior to contract expiration in order to take a profit or minimize a loss.

Advantages and Disadvantages of Hedging

Clearly, there are distinct advantages as well as disadvantages to hedging. The main advantage is that of locking in a price whether you are a buyer or a seller. This allows the hedger to plan ahead and to know, in advance, what profit (or loss) will be derived from a given crop or product. For producers who must buy given commodities in order to run their operations, buy hedging can spell the difference between a minor profit, a large profit, or a loss.

The advantage is the ability to lock in costs or profits, which is central to running a successful operation or to effective planning. The disadvantage is that when you lock in costs or profits, you may be doing so too soon and thereby limiting your profit potential. Fortunately, you can exit your futures hedges at any time prior to the delivery date if you feel you have acted too soon or if conditions change.

The use of the futures markets by producers can allow them to limit costs and to lock in profits. As a result, costs to the consumer can also be controlled. This is not to say that all profits from hedging operations will be passed on to the consumer; they will not be. However, effective hedging by producers can be a major factor in limiting price increases at the retail level.

The Abuse of Hedging

All too often an undisciplined hedger will overstep the boundaries of sensible practice by establishing positions that are either too large based on actual needs, or otherwise inconsistent with known needs. As an example, consider the commercial baking firm that takes a buy hedge position in sugar, wheat, corn, and soybean oil to lock in its cost of production. These positions are consistent with its business needs. The firm might even take a hedge position in Treasury bond futures to limit its borrowing costs. However, taking a long position in gold futures as a purported hedge against inflation would be an abuse or misuse of hedging. Rather than a pure hedge, the gold position is really a speculative position that has nothing to do with the production operations of the company.

Consider the case of the cattle producer who runs a feedlot operation raising cattle. The operator will want to lock in his profit by selling short cattle futures if they are at a high enough level to show a profit when compared to the cost of production. The producer, however, decides to be a buyer of cattle futures because he feels that prices will move higher and he does not have enough cattle on the feedlot. This is known as the "Texas hedge" and is not really a hedge at all; rather, it's a speculative position.

For those who abuse hedging by using such strategies, the risks are considerable. There is a real danger that severe losses could result if the hedges are not true hedges either against the cost of production or to lock in a profit.

ESSENTIAL ELEMENTS FOR PROFITABLE TRADING

If you have even the most limited experience as a trader, then you know that the system or method you use is only part of the over-all formula for success. The fact is that lasting success as a trader depends on a combination of three primary ingredients:

1. *An Effective Trading System or Method:* By this I mean a trad-ing system or methodology that has a demonstrated histo-ry of success through all types of markets and that contains definitive, objective operational rules. The longer the sys-tem has been in use, the better.

2. *Risk Management:* I define this aspect of profitable trading as a method that takes you out of losing trades and keeps you in winning trades for as long as possible. Ordinarily this task is part of the trading system; however, traders often override their trading systems, so they need a fail-safe procedure.

3. *Discipline:* This includes all aspects of trader psychology: self-control, persistence, positive attitude, and so on.

If you can master or even come close to mastering all three aspects, then you are apt to achieve consistent success as a trader. Moreover, you will avoid the "boom or bust" syndrome that afflicts so many traders and that can adversely affect your mind-set as a trader.

CHAPTER 3

The Modern Futures Exchange

In Chicago, there is a three-block stretch of LaSalle Street known as "the Canyon." As you walk south along these three blocks, you understand the reason for this popularized appellation. Lining the street on both sides are dark, imposing buildings of stone, concrete, and brick that block the sun from the street during most of the day. Even on relatively mild days, cold, sharp winds rush through the Canyon and threaten the unwary pedestrian.

The buildings along this section of LaSalle Street were built to house the great financial institutions of the Midwest. Up and down LaSalle Street are many foreign bank branches and representative offices to which Chicago is home. Here, too, you can see the main offices of major domestic banks.

Not as well-known in public lore as Wall Street, LaSalle Street is nevertheless a very imposing and quite proper center of international banking and finance. Chicago locals know that when you are on the Lake Michigan shore just north of downtown, you are on the Gold Coast, but when you are here on LaSalle Street in the Canyon, you are near the gold.

As with many canyon formations that occur naturally in mountainous terrain, the LaSalle Street Canyon, here on the plains of Illinois, near the shore of Lake Michigan, is a box canyon. At the southern end of this man-made gorge, blocking any further advance of LaSalle Street, as well as most of the sunlight from the canyon, is a tall, narrow, dark-stained stone edifice, looking very much like an obelisk or a mystical monument. The top of this huge tower is scaled back, forming a sort of pyramid, at whose apex, far above street level, stands an imposing goddess of fertility, looking out on the infertile concrete, brick, and stone of the great city that is spread beneath it. This is the Chicago Board of Trade (CBOT).

Stretching vertically along the north face of the CBOT building are narrow five-story-high windows, behind which is one of the two huge trading floors of the CBOT. Ironically, these windows served an important function when the CBOT first moved into this building in 1928.

At that time, the CBOT was primarily a grain exchange, and sample bags of the various grades of grain were kept around the floor. The windows allowed traders plenty of natural light by which to inspect the various bags of grain. Today, these majestic windows are mostly hidden to the traders on the floor by long blackout shades, and the activity in this north trading floor has been entirely given over to the trading of various financial and interest rate futures rather than grains. Here in the Bond Room of the CBOT, traders trade in U.S. Treasury bond futures and options, municipal bond futures and options, and other financial instruments, none of which would have been recognized as legitimate products of the commodity futures industry in 1928.

Today's CBOT is the world's oldest futures exchange, accounting for a substantial percentage of all the futures trading done in the United States. However, with the proliferation of new contracts being added each year, and with the popularity of financial futures and stock indices eclipsing the more traditional contracts in grains and livestock, the CBOT is no longer the world leader in trading activity. Just down the street and over a few blocks stand the twin towers of the Chicago Mercantile Exchange (CME) building with the two red-stone office towers connected by the ultramodern trading floors. With over 70,000 square feet of trading area, the CME has overtaken the CBOT, gaining an ever-increasing share of the futures business. The two exchanges together account for the majority of the most actively traded futures contracts in the United States.

There are twelve major futures exchanges in the United States. Of the twelve exchanges, five are in New York:

1. The International Securities Exchange
2. The Coffee, Sugar and Cocoa Exchange (CSCE)
3. The Commodity Exchange, Inc. (COMEX)
4. The New York Cotton Exchange (NYCE)
5. The New York Mercantile Exchange (NYMEX)

Four exchanges are in Chicago:

1. The Chicago Board of Trade (CBOT)
2. Chicago Board Options Exchange (CBOE)
3. The Chicago Mercantile Exchange (CME)
4. The Mid-America Commodity Exchange (MidAm)

The other three exchanges are located in:

1. Kansas City (the Kansas City Board of Trade—KCBT)
2. Minneapolis (the Minneapolis Grain Exchange—MGE)
3. Philadelphia (the Philadelphia Board of Trade—PBOT)

Internationally, the number of exchanges has been growing faster than in the United States, as major economic centers have rushed to service the ever-increasing demand for new instruments to hedge against fluctuating interest rates, changing foreign exchange rates, and institutional securities portfolios. There are presently more than 90 foreign futures exchanges.

The countries where they are located are: Argentina, Armenia, Australia, Austria, Bahrain, Bangladesh, Barbados, Belgium, Bermuda, Bolivia, Botswana, Brazil, Bulgaria, Canada, Cayman Islands, Chile, China, Costa Rica, Cote D'Ivoire (Ivory Coast), Croatia (Hrvatska), Cyprus, Czech Republic, Denmark, Ecuador, Egypt, El Salvador, Estonia, Finland, France, Germany,

Ghana, Greece, Honduras, Hong Kong, Hungary, Iceland, India, Indonesia, Iran, Ireland, Israel, Italy, Jamaica, Japan, Jordan, Kenya, Korea (South), Kuwait, Latvia, Lithuania, Luxembourg, Macedonia, Malaysia, Malta, Mauritius, Mexico, Morocco, Namibia, Netherlands, New Zealand, Nicaragua, Nigeria, Norway, Oman, Pakistan, Panama, Paraguay, Peru, Philippines, Poland, Portugal, Romania, Russian Federation, Saudi Arabia, Singapore, Slovak Republic, Slovenia, South Africa, Spain, Sri Lanka, Swaziland, Sweden, Switzerland, Taiwan, Thailand, Trinidad and Tobago, Tunisia, Turkey, United Kingdom, United States, Venezuela, Yugoslavia, and Zimbabwe.

The modern futures exchange exists for the purpose of bringing buyers and sellers together and providing a facility where futures trading can take place. So that business will be transacted in an efficient, fair, and ethical manner, the exchange supervises all trading that is conducted on the trading floor and establishes the rules by which trading is to occur. In addition, the exchange collects and disseminates the price and volume information in order to keep traders fully informed of prices and price changes.

MANAGEMENT AND ORGANIZATION
OF THE EXCHANGE

In order to facilitate the orderly and honest transaction of business, the modern futures exchange is highly organized and operates under a strict set of rules and regulations. Most exchanges are non-profit organizations, whose members serve on various committees and boards to regulate and oversee the operation of the exchange and its paid administrative staff. Members of the exchange, who have paid for their membership, or "seat," also enjoy the privilege of access to the trading floor, where they may operate as floor traders if they choose. Table 3-1 depicts a typical organizational chart of a modern futures exchange.

The daily affairs of the futures exchange are managed by a chief executive officer, usually known as the president. This is a salaried position appointed by the Board of Governors, who govern the exchange by establishing major policies and setting the rules by which the exchange will operate. The Board of Governors is usually comprised of both members and nonmembers, and it is

Table 3-1: Board of Governors (Members and Nonmembers)

Clearing Members	President (Salaried)	Committees (Members)
Members	Staff (paid)	Staff (paid)
	Research	Clearinghouse
	Education	Floor Practices
	Audits and Investigations	Business Conduct
	Quotations	Contract Specifications
	Statistical	Rules
	Public Relations	Pit
		Floor Brokers
		Membership
		Public Relations
		Arbitration

elected by the exchange membership. Nonmembers on the Board of Governors represent both the general public and businesses that have an interest in futures trading.

One of the tasks of the Board of Governors is to establish the number of memberships in the exchange. All memberships are privately held, and a change in membership occurs through a bid-and-offer process. Thus, the price of a seat on the exchange fluctuates depending on demand.

A prospective member applying for a seat on the exchange must pass muster with the exchange members by submitting to a thorough investigation of his or her financial background and personal character. After passing the investigation, the applicant is presented to the Board of Governors for approval. Once approved, the new member may exercise the four privileges of exchange membership:

1. access to the trading floor;
2. the right to function as a floor trader;
3. reduced commissions on trades; and
4. participation in the management of the exchange.

Members become involved in the management of the exchange by serving on one of several committees:

- *The Clearinghouse Committee* determines the required qualifications to be a clearing member and passes judgment on applicants.

- *The Floor Practice Committee* oversees all floor activity and deals with issues of trading ethics and price discrepancies.

- *The Business Conduct Committee* maintains orderly and businesslike trading practices by assuring the integrity of the members.

- *The Contract Specifications Committee* reviews existing contracts and recommends changes to the Board of Governors.

- *The Rules Committee* reviews existing rules and recommends rule changes or new rules to the Board of Governors.

- *The Pit Committee* assures the orderly opening and closing of trading and operates as arbiter regarding price discrepancies that occur during trading.

- *The Floor Brokers Committee* assures the qualifications of all brokers and floor traders.

- *The Membership Committee* reviews the financial background and personal character of all prospective members.

- *The Public Relations Committee* oversees matters pertaining to publicity and public relations.

- *The Arbitration Committee* resolves disputes between members.

The exchange staff under the direction of the president carries out the day-to-day activities of the exchange. The staff is usually organized into departments, of which the following are typical:

- *The Audit and Investigations Department* monitors member firms for financial strength and ethical practices and collects information on prospective members of the exchange and the clearinghouse.

- *The Statistical Department* disseminates daily price data.

- *The Quotations Department* oversees the posting of price data on the trading floor and over the wire services.

- *The Research Department* researches new contracts and possible changes in existing contracts.
- *The Education Department* provides information to hedgers, speculators, brokers, and the public.
- *The Public Relations Department* manages publicity for the exchange.

The Clearinghouse

One of the most important divisions of the futures exchange is the clearinghouse, which is an adjunct to the exchange. All clearing members are members of the exchange, but not every exchange member is a member of the clearinghouse; some clearinghouses are integral divisions of the exchange whereas others are separate corporate entities. All clearinghouses provide essentially the same functions for the exchange, though. One of those functions is to facilitate the exchange of funds as member firms transact business.

Another important clearinghouse operation is to settle all transactions that are executed on the trading floor by matching all purchases and sales. Through a process called trade checking, all transactions are settled daily. The clearinghouse then takes the opposite side of all the contracts traded that day, thereby guaranteeing the contractual obligations of each transaction.

The financial integrity of the futures exchange rests on the solvency of the clearing members. Therefore, exchanges establish minimum capital requirements for clearing members, requiring that they maintain as much as several million dollars on deposit with the clearinghouse, the amount depending on the number of contracts being guaranteed by the clearing members.

The futures exchange closely monitors the financial activities and condition of each clearing member through regular financial reporting, surveillance, on-site audits, and sharing of financial information with other exchanges. The exchange may, in an emergency, call for immediate capital increases in margins on deposit, reductions in positions, or early settlement, thus allowing the exchange to take immediate action on the basis of financial information it may obtain regarding a clearing member firm.

Any exchange member wishing to trade on the exchange must either be a clearing member or have a relationship with a clearing member. All trades must be registered with and settled through that clearing member.

DEFINING A "CLEARED" TRADE

The most important function of the clearinghouse is to "clear" all trades. That is, the clearinghouse takes the opposite side of all trades. At the end of each trading day, all transactions between floor brokers are confirmed. At that time, the clearing member to whom the broker is responsible is then checked by the clearinghouse and tallies all confirmed trades. After all trades have been matched, the clearinghouse becomes the seller to all buyers, and the buyer to all sellers. Thus, the trade is cleared, and the traders no longer have an obligation to the opposite parties in the original transactions.

The activity of clearing trades serves three essential functions for the exchange. First, the liquidity of the market is maintained because a trader can offset all positions simply by taking the opposite position later. That is, if a trader is long in soybeans because he bought one contract, the opposite party to his contract is the clearinghouse. Therefore, if the trader wishes to liquidate his position (get out of his obligation), he simply sells a contract to the exchange. This offsetting position relieves the trader of any further contractual responsibility, and he did not have to look up the original trading partner to accomplish that.

Second, if delivery of the contract is to take place (only 5 percent or fewer of all futures contracts result in delivery), the process is much easier when the clearinghouse is the opposite party. The trader wishing to make delivery simply notifies the clearinghouse, which then notifies the trader with the oldest existing long position (contract to buy) that delivery is to take place. None of the traders who may have handled one side or the other of that contract during its life need to be involved in the delivery transaction in any way.

Third, if one party to a contract defaults for any reason, the fulfillment of the contract is guaranteed by the clearinghouse, which is now the opposite party to the transaction. All clearing members contribute to a special fund to be used to fulfill contractual or financial obligations of members who default.

THE ROLE OF THE EXCHANGE
IN FUTURES TRADING

We have said that there are important sectors in an open market economy in which risk is the result of either a time factor (delivery is to take place much later, when prices have declined) or a distance factor (delivery must take place a long distance away, where prices might be significantly lower or the currency might be different and adversely affect price). We have also said that futures contracts allow the legitimate producer or user (hedger) to transfer that risk to a speculator, who is willing to assume the risk because of the possibility of great profitability if prices move the right way. The role of the exchange is to bring together the buyers and the sellers, the hedgers and the speculators, in an orderly, efficient manner. In the process of bringing the players in a futures transaction together, the exchange performs four vital roles for the open market economy: price discovery, risk transfer, liquidity, and standardization of contracts.

Price Discovery

As sellers offer to sell and buyers offer to buy in the pit, they provide immediate information regarding the price of the futures contract. The price is usually given as a "bid-ask." For example, the price for corn might be $2.40 bid, $2.42 ask, meaning a buyer is willing to pay $2.40 a bushel, but the seller wants $2.42 a bushel.

The exchange does not set prices. The activity on the trading floor, in the pits where price is discovered through open outcry auction, establishes prices. The exchange does disseminate price information so that speculators and hedgers not on the trading floor can know what the market is.

Risk Transfer

In a futures transaction, risk is not created as it is in a gambling situation. A gambler creates risk by choosing to bet money on the roll of the dice or the turn of a card. The only way to eliminate risk is by choosing not to gamble. In a futures transaction, as we have seen, risk is an inherent part of doing business, but the exchange provides a setting in which risk can be transferred from the hedgers to the speculators.

Liquidity

If risk is to be transferred efficiently, there must be a large group of individuals ready to buy or sell. When a hedger wants to sell futures contracts to protect her business position, she can't afford to wait around for a long time for a buyer. She needs to know she can effect the transaction quickly. The futures exchange brings together a large number of speculators, thus making quick transactions possible. Moreover, by clearing all trades, the exchange allows contracts to be bought and sold rapidly.

Standardization of Contracts

The exchange writes the specifications for each contract, setting standards for grading, measurement, methods of transfer, and time of delivery. Some contracts allow settlement in the cash equivalent of the underlying commodity in order to facilitate the delivery and contract fulfillment process. By standardizing the contracts in this manner, the exchange opens the futures market up to almost anyone willing to hedge risk. In the pits, then, the auction process is facilitated because only price must be negotiated. It is important to remember that the exchange does not own or trade contracts. It simply provides a market where that trading can occur.

THE ELEMENTS OF FUTURES TRADING AT THE FUTURES EXCHANGE

Remember that any kind of contract trading can include a futures element. If you're buying a car, you can arrange for future delivery at a specified date, at an agreed-upon location and price, with options you choose, in a color you selected. If you are a commercial buyer, you can order a quantity of merchandise for future delivery at an established price. Futures trading, as we have seen, is more than simply contracting for future consummation of a business transaction. Futures trading, as it is done through an organized futures exchange, involves several specific elements:

1. *All trading is done in a specified area according to an established set of rules.* This area is known as the pit. In the case of fully electronic trading, there is no pit trading. All trades are matched electronically via computer.

2. *All trading is done within specified hours.* No trading may occur outside these scheduled trading times, although different commodities have different trading hours.

3. *Most trading is done by open outcry.* Therefore, all bids and offers are known to all participants, and all transactions are public knowledge. Electronic trading is growing rapidly and may eventually replace the open outcry system

4. *All trading is done in contracts that are standardized* for quality (grade), delivery date, location, procedure, and contract size.

5. *Negotiation in the pit is limited to price and quantity* only (bid-ask).

6. If a contract is to be fulfilled by arranging delivery (which occurs in fewer than 5 percent of the trades), *a premium or discount will be attached to the price* for any differential from the contract specifications.

7. *The exchange clearinghouse assumes the opposite side of all trades.* The buyer and seller negotiate price, after which each has an obligation with the clearinghouse, not with each other. This is important when positions are later liquidated, as it would be very difficult to find the original buyer or seller, who might not be of a mind to cancel the contract at that time or price anyway.

8. *All futures contracts can legally be neutralized by taking an offsetting position.* Therefore, if a trader buys six contracts of December corn, and later sells six contracts of December corn, the original position is deemed liquidated, and there is no more obligation to either contract.

9. *The exchange clearinghouse guarantees all contracts.* To do this, the clearinghouse requires that a member's account have a minimum amount of capital in it (specified by the exchange), from which a preestablished margin amount is obligated as earnest money when a futures contract is entered into.

CHAPTER 4

Life on the Trading Floor

For many years, the business of the modern futures exchange has been transacted on the trading floor, where hundreds of individuals gather each day for the purpose of exchanging futures contracts. Amid a steady din of voices crying out bids and offers, various clerks and runners scurry here and there with orders to be filled and orders to be reported.

The scene is noisy, colorful, frenetic, and exciting—quite unlike anything that most people have experienced. In the 1990s, fully computerized trading was introduced in a number of markets. Although computerized trading may eventually replace floor brokers and the open outcry system, floor trading is still a major aspect of the futures markets and deserves considerable attention.

A friend who worked on the floor at both the Chicago Board of Trade (CBOT) and the Chicago Mercantile Exchange (CME) often told me stories about his experiences there. I remember particularly the vivid description of his first day at the CME (also known as the Merc).

I waited by the reception desk while they paged my new floor supervisor. From the desk, I looked up at two long escalators carrying a steady stream of people up and down. There were people going up the escalator on the right wearing winter coats and jackets, with hats and gloves and purses and bags. They could have been at Sears or any other large downtown department store. Coming down the other escalator, everyone was wearing a bright-colored sports coat. The predominant color was gold, although I saw light green, dark blue, and light blue interspersed among them.

All the men wore ties, although very few were pulled up tightly around their necks. All of the jackets had picture ID cards clipped to the lapels, which the wearer would unclip and run through a slot in the turnstile to gain entrance to what I presumed was the trading floor. It was as if all the people going up the escalator were being processed through a room where their normal street identity was removed and they were issued uniform jackets that made them members of some kind of exclusive club.

As I marveled at this transformation that was occurring to such a multitude of individuals, my new boss approached me. He came from the opposite direction, through one of the same turnstiles that were measuring with mechanical precision the flow of bright jackets from the escalator into the corridors leading to the trading floor. He was wearing a dark blue jacket.

I figured out that dark blue must mean authority. There were very few jackets of that color around, and they came up from the floor below, rather than down with the horde. My new boss had a larger badge, too, with three large letters on it. As I looked, I saw that it was a member's badge. I was impressed.

The boss sent me up the escalator with some papers to look for the processing room. Soon, I was riding the escalator back down with a picture ID clipped to the lapel of my fresh gold jacket. I was in the club.

When I zipped my ID badge through the slot in the turnstile, a small light turned green, granting me entrance. A guard in a smart brown suit watched me push on the metal bar, which gave easily to my shove, clicking softly as it turned. I was inside, headed for the doors that marked the boundary of the trading floor.

As I pulled open the glass door, I was overwhelmed by the noise that suddenly confronted me. I immediately jumped to the conclusion that something quite significant must have happened, and a lot of people were mad about it, because here and there all over this huge room, groups of people were yelling at each other. With some hesitation, I walked in, only to find myself being pushed and jostled by various gold- and green-coated individuals who were hurrying around in what seemed to be a chaotic and disorganized confusion of aimless activity.

I fully expected a fight to break out at any moment.

To the uninitiated, it is totally incomprehensible that millions of dollars worth of business could be transacted every day, in exchanges around the world, in such a primitive manner. In an era of computers, instant worldwide communication, mushrooming technological advancement, ultrasophisticated marketing techniques, international corporate conglomerates, arbitrageurs and proliferating MBAs, the trading floor seems an anachronism. And so it is.

The trading floor at the modern futures exchange is little removed from the open-air auctions and livestock sales of a century or more ago. Although monitored and reported by state-of-the-art electronics, the trading pit is nothing more than a process of offering a price for, or asking a price for, a specific commodity.

Naturally, if business is to be transacted in a fair and consistent manner under such conditions, there must be rules. And rules there are. The procedures are clearly spelled out; the limits are clearly established. The roles of the various characters in this intense daily drama of intrigue, excitement, subterfuge, and deal making are clearly written, and the system works remarkably well.

THE PIT

At the heart of the open outcry market system is the *pit*, a circular construction forming just what its name implies: a hole in the trading floor. Concentric rings form steps, which flow from the outside of the pit toward the center, and upon which the floor traders stand, each a little higher or lower than the trader in front or behind.

The highest step is above the floor level, so that one must first walk up two or three steps before walking down into the pit. On these outer steps, leading down from the top, stand clerks in gold jackets—assistants to the floor brokers. On the inside steps, leading down toward the sunken center of the pit, stand the floor brokers and the

Figure 4-1: Diagram of Lower Trading Floor, Chicago Mercantile Exchange

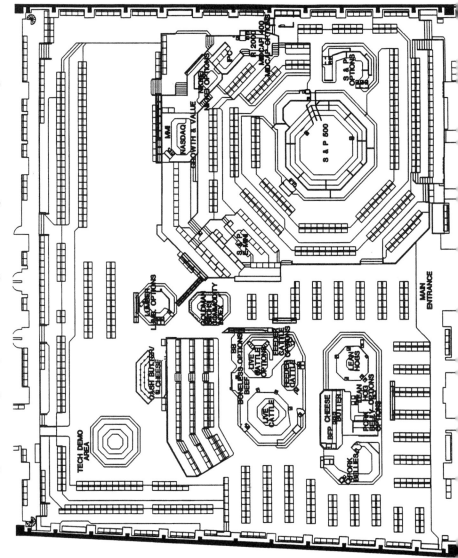

Figure 4-2: Diagram of the Lower Trading Floor, Equity Complex, CME

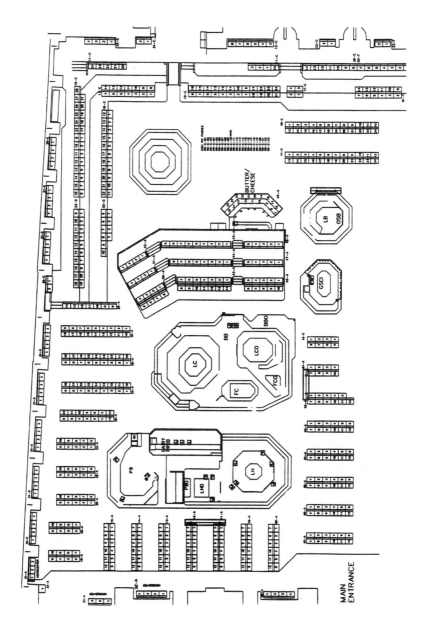

locals—traders who work for themselves—making trade after trade all day long, hoping to scalp a small profit from each trade.

Each pit is divided into pie-shaped wedges, with the nearby contract month always located in a particular area and the back months located in declining order around the pit. When a contract month expires, all the other contract months move up, so that, for example, the area that was formerly February pork bellies becomes March bellies when the February contract expires, and so forth. Figure 4-1 shows the live cattle pit (and other pits) at the Chicago Mercantile Exchange. When the *front month* (or spot month) contract expires, each of the *back months* moves counterclockwise one spot.

The Floor Broker

The *floor broker*, or *pit broker*, is a member of the exchange who has a business relationship with one or more brokerage firms. Most of the trading he or she does during trading hours is to fill orders that are brought into the pit by runners who work for the brokerage houses. At any one time, a pit broker will have a stack of orders in his or her hand, arranged in order of price and divided into buy orders and sell orders.

Many brokers have so many orders that they employ clerks, or deck holders, to help hold the orders and keep them arranged. The deck holders stand on the outside steps of the pit. It is not uncommon for brokers who work the very busy contract months to have three or four clerks working for them.

Each of the pit brokers wears a distinctively colored jacket with his or her ID badge prominently displayed. On the badge are three to five large letters that identify the broker to other traders in the pit. When a trade is completed, these identifying letters appear on the order form as an endorsement, along with the letters identifying the trader who took the other side of the trade. Each set of letters is unique, so there is no mistake as to who made the trade.

Most floor brokers handle orders for only one contract month, particularly if they work in one of the nearby contract months, where volume can be very high. In some of the very high-volume pits, a broker may handle only the buy orders for one contract month while another broker handles the sell orders. Other brokers handle only spread orders. By specializing in this manner, a broker ends up working in one particular spot in the pit day after day, making him or her easy to find when an order needs to be filled quickly.

The Floor Trader

The *floor traders*, or *locals*, are the traders who give liquidity to the market. Trading only for themselves, they make trade after trade, often taking the opposite side of a trade with one of the brokers, then exiting that trade in a few minutes when the price moves a few ticks. Often called scalpers, the locals rarely hold a position overnight, even though they may have made dozens of trades during the day.

In some of the high-volume pits, like the T bonds at the CBOT or the S&P 500 at the CME, a local will stand in the same spot in the pit all day long, shoulder to shoulder with other traders, with still more traders in front and back, using his or her hands to signal a bid or an offer. (A bid to buy is made with the palms turned in, toward the trader's own chest, while an offer to sell is made with the palms turned out, toward the other trader.)

How the Trading Floor Is Organized

Standing in the pit is not unlike being in the middle of a crowd leaving a football game or a rock concert, with people crowding against you, jostling you, pushing you, and breathing down your neck. It can be very warm and quite uncomfortable, as your feet grow tired and sore and your throat becomes dry and hoarse.

Toward the end of a six- or seven-hour day, the job does not seem nearly as glamorous as most people assume it to be. In fact, working in a trading pit is a very physically demanding, emotionally draining, competitive job. Figures 4-1 and 4-2 will give you a good idea of how a typical trading floor is organized.

The trading floor contains pits as well as order desks. Brokers call their orders down to the clerks who sit at trading desks. They, in turn, relay the written orders to runners who deliver the orders to the pit brokers. In some markets, however, orders are hand signalled to the pit, avoiding the runner.

A trader must keep his or her senses sharp even when six hours of tumult, noise, yelling, negotiating, and general confusion have dulled them to the point of being sluggish. Rushing adrenaline must certainly be a factor in maintaining a trader through a brutal trading day. The exchange keeps oxygen handy for the occasional trader who is physically overcome by the entire situation.

LAYOUT OF THE TRADING FLOOR

Figure 4-1, a diagram of the trading floor at the CME, is typical of the layout of a large futures exchange. Notice that the meats are in one area, the currencies in another, and the financials in a third. The space around the pits is often clogged with runners, clerks and assorted other people moving around at a feverish pace. Around the perimeter of the floor and in certain locations around the pits are rows of telephone desks, where phone clerks receive orders from their respective order rooms to be delivered to the pit brokers. At one corner of the floor are located the various news services, such as Reuters and Dow Jones, that are available for the trader's use.

High above the trading floor, on each wall of the trading room, are the quote boards, where the tick-by-tick price appears for each contract of each commodity. On the quote board, the most recent price appears at the bottom of a column of prices, with the previous price above that and the five previous prices in order above that (see Figure 4-3). As a trade is made, the new price appears at the bottom and the other prices move up, with the top price dropping off. The quote board also gives the previous day's settlement price and the high-low of the day's trading, along with

Figure 4-3: Quote Board

10:32	SX9	CZ9	WZ9	SMZ9	BOU9	OZ9	LCV9	LHQ9	PBQ9	2
O	4784	2350	2940	1473	1645	1172	6525	5105	5705	
H	4850	2380	2970	1486	1680	1190	6532	5165	5715	
L	4750	2320	2924	1460	1636	1170	6467	5100	5435	
L	4750v	2336v	2932v	1461^	1642v	1180v	6487^	5155^	5450^	
Δ	-80	-16	-24	-25	-9	+2	-48	+93	-222	
	GCV9	SIU9	PLV9	PAU9	RSU9	RDU9	RJU9	RPU9	RKU9	
O	2585	5345	3515	34800	6718	5483	8717	16060	6670	
H	2595	5395	3540	34800	6720	5490	8737	16068	6684	
L	2583	5345	3515	34500	6698	5476	8701	16010	6650	
L	2590v	5360^	3530^	34500v	6712^	5489^	8713v	16054v	6657в	
Δ	+7	-52	+10	-225	-38	-27	-48	-60	+4	
	CPZ9	CCU9	CFU9	CTV9	RBU9	VIU9	EUU9	OJX9	DFU9	
O	7880	955	9300	5230	11403	10437	107310	8425	10750	
H	7880	963	9470	5275	11405	10518	107360	8450	10765	
L	7840	938	9290	5225	11322	10437	107090	8325	10705	
L	7860^	948v	9430^	5235	11327^	10518^	107340^	8450^	10765^	
Δ	0	-17	+140	+26	-12	+28	-530	+105	+35	
	NGU9	HOU9	HUU9	CLU9	SUV9	SPU9	LBU9	FCQ9	EDU9	
O	2715	5450	6570	2090	600	130470	36500	7657	94440	
H	2770	5470	6595	2098	604	131450	37100	7685	94440	
L	2680	5425	6530	2076	594	130380	36500	7650	94410	
L	2745в	5450v	6545v	2088^	601v	131080v	36600v	7665^	94420^	
Δ	+47	-3	-38	0	+2	+380	+310	+8	-40	

08/09/99 10:32

(C) Copyright 1999 CQG INC.

the opening range, the year's high and low, and the net difference between the last price and the previous day's settlement prices.

HOW AN ORDER IS FILLED

To the uninitiated, it seems almost miraculous that one small order for one futures contract from a trader somewhere in Idaho could actually be filled a good price and in a reasonable time in the midst of all the chaos on the trading floor. And yet, that's exactly what happens, day in and day out. The trader in Idaho may call his or her broker with an order to buy one contract of live hogs at the market. The broker may be a discount broker in Chicago or a local broker in the trader's Idaho hometown. That broker then relays the order to a phone clerk on the trading floor. The process for relaying the order varies from one brokerage firm to another. Some have central order rooms to whom the broker gives the order. Others have a direct hotline to the floor. At each stage, the order is taken on a recorded phone and time stamped. When it arrives at the trading floor, the phone clerk there writes the order and hands it to a runner, who quickly carries the order to the appropriate pit broker. The order is given directly either to the broker or the broker's clerk (the deck holder).

Because the order is a market order, the broker will bid the appropriate price, depending on the price at which live hogs have been trading. If he or she does not get a response at that price, the bid is made at a higher price, until the order is filled.

The runner, knowing the order is a market order, has waited for the fill, so as soon as the pit broker endorses the order, he or she returns it to the runner, who carries the filled order immediately to the phone clerk, who in turn calls the broker who phoned in the order to give him or her the price fill. At each step of the fill confirmation, the order is again time stamped.

If the order is a price order, it is simply delivered to the broker or the clerk, who then places it in the appropriate spot in the deck. Later, if the order is filled, it is returned to a runner, who carries the order back to a phone clerk, who then confirms the fill with the broker. At the end of the day, all unfilled orders that have not been designated "good till canceled" are voided.

In many of the currency and financial pits, orders are filled in a somewhat different manner. When the order is phoned in, the phone clerk, through a set of hand signals called *arbing* or *arbitrag-*

ing, flashes the order to an arb clerk, who then conveys the order orally to the broker in the pit. As soon as the order is filled, the arb clerk flashes the signal back to the phone clerk, who often still has the retail broker on the line and confirms the fill immediately. A runner then carries the written order into the pit so that the broker can endorse it later.

THE BID AND THE OFFER

The first question asked by most people when encountering the trading floor for the first time is, "How does anybody know what's going on in all that confusion?" Fortunately, a set of rules and procedures—some formal, some informal—govern the activity so that business can be transacted efficiently.

In the open outcry system, a trader in the pit must communicate his or her intentions, because prices move quickly and trades occur rapidly. To accomplish that, a code has been developed that is easily understood and communicated. As we have already learned, the only part of a contract that is negotiated in the pit is price. Everything else is standardized. Therefore, the trader in the pit need communicate only three things:

1. Whether he or she wishes to buy or sell;
2. The number of contracts he or she wishes to trade; and
3. The price. (The contract month is known because of the location in the pit where the trader is standing.)

Let's say a trader is willing to pay $8.30-1/4 for two contracts of November soybeans. All the other traders in the pit know that soybeans are trading at $8.30, so the trader only needs to mention the one-quarter cent. If the trader means to say, "I'll pay $8.30-1/4 for two November soybeans," then all he or she needs to yell is "Quarter for 10." (There are 5,000 bushels of soybeans in a contract, commonly shortened to 5; two contracts would be 10). If, on the other hand, the trader wishes to sell three contracts of soybeans at $8.30-1/2, rather than yell, "I'll sell 15,000 bushels of November soybeans at $8.30-1/2," he or she simply yells "15 at a half."

Along with yelling the bid or offer, the trader also uses hand signals at the same time. With arms outstretched to get attention, the palms face in if the trader wishes to buy and out if the trader wishes to sell.

HOW PRICES REACH THE QUOTE BOARD

At the CME, a *pit observer*, who is an employee of the exchange, stands in the pit with a walkie-talkie. Each time the price changes, the observer radios the information into the CME operator, who enters the information into the CME Quote Entry System. The price immediately appears on the quote board and is simultaneously broadcast on the CME ticker to the public. Thus, traders who have the equipment to receive ticker information and who have paid the necessary subscription fees receive price quotes at the same time they appear on the quote board.

There are times, however, when trading volume is so high that the quote entry system cannot keep up. At those times, the board will note that it is a fast market and will only display four prices rather than the usual seven. Figure 4-3 depicts a quote board listing prices for numerous markets.

At each of the individual brokerage house desks around the floor of the exchange is a *floor manager* or *floor supervisor*. As the name implies, the floor manager is in charge of the operations at the desk, seeing that orders are handled with dispatch and with care. If disputes arise over prices, the floor manager is the first line person to try to resolve the difference. Basically, it is the job of the floor manager to see that everything runs smoothly around the desk.

Many of the larger brokerage houses have *market analysts* on the floor at all times. These are market veterans who watch closely what is happening in the pit, reporting on who's buying and who's selling and why. Often, their reports go out periodically to the retail brokerage offices around the country so that brokers can report up-to-the-minute developments to their clients.

Each of the brokerage houses also employs *out-trade clerks*. At the close of trading each day, it is the job of each trader to match all the trades from the day's activity and to clear them through the clearinghouse. With all the activity that goes on in the pit during trading hours, however, it is not uncommon for errors to be made. One floor broker may claim a trade with another broker, only to find that the second broker has no record of the trade. This is call an *out-trade*. Naturally, the customer has already been given a fill; a match must be found somewhere so that the trade can be cleared. It is the job of the out-trade clerk to find that match. Often the problem is simply that the wrong ID was written on the order form when the broker endorsed it or that the wrong price was noted on a local's trading card. At other times, there is another out-trade on the opposite side that can be matched with the first one. Whatever the solution, it is the out-trade clerk's job to find it, because no outstanding trade can be allowed to remain uncleared until the next day's trading.

Consequently, each day before the markets open, the out-trade clerks from the various brokerage houses meet in one of the pits, computer printouts in hand, taking care of all the trades that the computer has been unable to match. After particularly high-volume days, it is not uncommon for the out-trade clerks to arrive at 3:00 or 4:00 A.M. to take care of all the out-trades before the start of trading.

ELECTRONIC TRADING

The late 1990s witnessed the growth of fully computerized fulfillment of orders that bypasses the open outcry system. This method of trading relies entirely on orders between sellers and buyers being matched by computer. For example, if I have entered an order to sell (i.e., an offer) at 6440 and another trader has entered an order to buy (i.e., a bid) at 6440, the orders are matched by the computer. Although the process is not usually this simple, the manner in which trades are filled is more efficient and equitable than the typical case in the open outcry system. The drawback is that unless there are sufficient orders to balance out volatility, price swings may be very large and erratic.

Only time will tell how the fully electronic system will fare. I am certain that with today's advanced hardware and software, progress will be quick. One concern about electronic trading is that if the computer processing system ceases to operate due to hardware, software, or electrical problems, trades will not be processed and traders will, therefore, be unable to conduct their business. Although some remediative actions have been taken, the systems have not been tested in a situation of very heavy volume.

CHAPTER 5

The Variety of Futures Markets

The modern futures trading industry originally developed in the United States in order to fill a need to transfer risk from the everyday business of buying and selling grain in Chicago. Today, at the Chicago Board of Trade (CBOT), grain futures are still traded much as they have been for over 100 years. The soybean and its derivatives, soybean oil and soybean meal, have joined the traditional grains—corn, oats, and wheat—as popular and heavily traded futures contracts at the CBOT. Although grain futures are still a significant part of the futures industry, the business of trading futures contracts has grown far beyond the grain markets in scope and popularity.

Historically, wherever a high degree of price risk is attached to doing business because of the effect of time or distance on price, futures trading has been likely to develop. In the 1840s, price risk primarily occurred in the grain markets of Chicago, and the CBOT responded in 1865 with the organized trading of futures contracts. (Even though the CBOT was established in 1848, a formal set of rules for trading futures contracts was not written until 1865, which is a more accurate date from which to mark the beginning of futures trading in the United States.) At the same time, other agricultural markets were also flourishing in Chicago, which in the 1850s and 1860s had become the nucleus of the nation's agricultural marketing system. The convergence of canals, rivers, lakes, and railroads in and around Chicago made it the center of transportation for the country and the distribution point for a wide variety of agricultural products.

Grains and livestock were not the only agricultural products marketed in Chicago during the last half of the nineteenth century. Not far from the present downtown location of the Chicago Mercantile Exchange (CME), along the Chicago River, is the site of the old South Water Street Market, Chicago's historic farmers' market. Here, on May 20, 1874, a group of South Water Street suppliers and merchants organized the Chicago Produce Exchange to provide an efficient market for butter, eggs, poultry, and other farm products.

In 1895 a dissident group of dealers, dissatisfied with market quotations, formed a division within the exchange to "establish official quotations." In 1899 this group established a separate organization called the Chicago Butter and Egg Board, which in 1919 became the Chicago Mercantile Exchange. That year, the CME clearinghouse was established to process futures transactions, and on December 1, 1919, the first futures contracts for eggs were traded at the newly formed CME.

From then until 1945, the CME traded futures in eggs, butter, cheese, potatoes, and onions. Later, the exchange added contracts in apples, poultry, and frozen eggs and in 1954 added iron and scrap steel. None of these earlier futures contracts has endured as a viable futures market at the CME. They have been replaced with livestock futures, currency futures, interest rate futures, and stock index futures.

It is significant that these days the successor to the Butter and Egg Board trades only a little butter (the contract is not listed by the CME) and no more eggs (fresh white eggs are listed as an inactive contract at the CME), for it reflects the direction taken by the entire industry since the early 1970s. The futures business is no longer focused primarily on agricultural commodities, and the term "futures trader" has become much more accurate than the former name, "commodities trader."

PROLIFERATION OF FUTURES MARKETS

In the last half of the nineteenth century, a localized economy grew into a regionalized economy, then into a national economy, and finally into an international economy. So the world marketplace continues to expand and to become ever more complex. The traditional commodity futures markets—grains, cotton, and livestock—have been upstaged since the mid 1980s by the burgeoning growth of futures trading in several related, though quite different, markets.

Futures and futures options trading has been growing steadily in volume yearly. Even Russia now have futures exchanges, although they are in their infancy. This explosive growth has been a natural response to increased price volatility, international instability, growing consumer demand, and unstable global weather conditions. All of these factors have increased price risk to the producer, making the use of futures markets more important than ever before.

Explosive Growth

The Chicago Board of Trade had a full-time staff of only 80 people in 1973. In 1987, only 14 years later, the CBOT employed over 450 full-time persons. By 1999 the numbers had increased to approximately 800 employees. In that same time period, the total volume of trading in futures contracts grew from just over 18 million (1972) to more than 184 million (1986), a tenfold increase in 14 years. In 1999, futures trading continued to set records all over the world.

In 1972, of the top ten most actively traded futures contracts, eight were agricultural futures. The other two were silver contracts. In 1977, although the order had changed and live hogs had replaced sugar, the lineup remained eight agricultural and two silver. But only five years later, in 1982, T bonds had risen to the top of the list, only five years after their introduction on the futures market. In its inaugural year, the S&P 500 Index was in tenth place, after having traded less than a full year! Altogether, by 1982 agricultural futures held only six of the top ten places, and silver was no longer on the list.

Four years after that, in 1986, agricultural futures had been nearly eclipsed by financial, stock index, and currency futures. Only three agricultural contracts remained in the top ten, none among the top five. In that year, T bonds alone traded more than twice the total number of futures contracts traded in all markets in 1972. In the late 1990s, the top volume leaders were interest rate futures, stock index futures, energy futures, currency futures, and agricultural futures.

Today, new contracts are being developed so rapidly that it becomes difficult to keep up. Lists are outdated as soon as they are written, as new contracts are continually being developed.

International Markets

As international trade has grown, the relative value of one country's currency against another's has become a critical factor in the profitability of businesses in every part of the economy. The Bretton Woods agreement after World War II attempted to stabilize world currencies by establishing narrow zones within which the U.S. dollar and other currencies could fluctuate. In the early 1970s, however, this agreement began to break down, resulting in increasing volatility in international exchange rates.

This volatility increased the risk of engaging in international trade. Just as with the agricultural markets in the 1830s and 1840s, there were speculators willing to assume this risk from legitimate business people, who were only too happy to transfer that risk through hedging.

As a result of these actions, the futures industry, which had been largely confined to agricultural commodities for more than a century, began in the 1970s to expand into new areas. Money itself became a commodity to be traded, as foreign currencies fluctuated, often wildly, against each other and against the U.S. dollar. The world financial community looked for ways to hedge the risk of doing business in the face of unstable exchange rates, and the futures industry responded.

In 1972 the CME established the International Monetary Market (IMM) division and initiated trading in seven foreign currency futures contracts. Other futures exchanges have followed suit, and most of the world's major currencies are now being traded on the floors of futures exchanges worldwide.

But just what is a foreign currency future? As we saw in Chapter 2, the concept of a futures contract is, in itself, very difficult to comprehend. But as we proceeded through the development from a cash sale of a commodity, to a forward, or to-arrive, contract, to a futures contract, the concept became more understandable. With currency futures, however, we have no underlying commodity to function as part of the exchange. There is no corn that will ultimately be delivered for a cash payment. There is only the cash itself. How do we develop a futures contract from that?

For anyone who has traveled outside the United States, the idea of trading in currencies is rather easy to understand. As you cross the border into one country from another country—let's say, into France from Germany—you must get rid of the money from the country you are leaving (Deutsche marks) and obtain currency from the country you are entering (francs). Otherwise, when you stop to buy lunch later, you may go hungry when you offer Deutsche marks and the restaurant accepts only francs. (In 1998 a unified European currency made this process largely unnecessary, yet there are still a number of European currencies not represented in the union.)

Now, if France has been experiencing an inflationary period, which results in the constantly declining value of the franc (as inflation continues, one franc will buy less of a commodity as the price of the commodity goes up), and Germany, on the other hand, has been enjoying very low inflation, the value of the Deutsche mark in comparison to the franc will increase. When you cross the border into France and stop at the currency exchange, therefore, you will trade Deutsche marks for francs at the current rate of exchange, which may be different at that time than it was the day before or the week before.

Let's say that you originally traveled from France to Germany two weeks earlier and exchanged money as you entered Germany. You bought Deutsche marks using francs as currency. Now, two weeks later, you re-enter France, so you wish to sell the Deutsche marks still in your possession. But in the meantime, the value of the franc has dropped, and you now are able to sell your Deutsche marks for more francs than you paid for them. In this situation, the Deutsche mark is said to be stronger against the franc, and the franc weaker against the Deutsche mark. All you know is that your Deutsche marks are worth more francs than when you left France two weeks ago.

In this simple example, you can readily see how currency can become a commodity to be bought and sold. For the average tourist, the fluctuation of currencies is little more than a mild irritant during the course of a vacation trip. To a merchant who imports or exports products from abroad, however, the shifting values of worldwide currencies can represent a major risk factor over which little control can be exercised.

If I am an automobile distributor, for instance, and I place an order for 20 million dollars worth of German cars to be delivered in three months, I face the risk that when I pay for the cars the value of the Deutsche mark, which I must use to pay the manufacturer, may have gone up in relationship to the dollar. In other words, when I order the cars, my U.S. dollar is worth a certain number of German Deutsche marks, a value we will call X. Three months from now, however, when I draw money from my bank in the United States to pay for the cars, the dollar is worth $X - Y$ dollars, Y representing the amount by which the Deutsche mark has increased in value over the U.S. dollar. In the event that the German mark has decreased against the U.S. dollar the opposite condition will hold true.

To buy the cars from the German manufacturer, I must first buy Deutsche marks, just as you had to when you traveled from France into Germany, but Deutsche marks cost more now. The price of the cars is the same. The cost of the money to pay for the cars has gone up. I must now sell the cars for more money in the United States if I am to preserve my profits. Alternatively, I will have to take less profit.

Of course, the opposite might also happen. The Deutsche mark might drop in value, meaning I could buy more Deutsche marks with my U.S. dollars three months hence. If that happens, I will make a larger profit than I had planned, or I can reduce the price of the cars in the United States. Either way, the risk involved in the transaction is more than I care to assume. I would like to find a speculator willing to relieve me of that risk. That is why futures exchanges offer contracts in foreign currency futures.

With agricultural commodity futures, the hedgers are the producers and the users: the farmers, the mills, and the packinghouses. With foreign currency futures, the hedgers are the banks that must often exchange large amounts of foreign currency; corporations that must do business abroad; and foreign exchange brokers and institutional investors who invest in foreign securities.

AN OVERVIEW OF MARKET SECTORS

There are several major categories of markets. All major American and European markets fall within the general categories or market sectors listed below.

Foreign Currency Futures

In order to hedge against fluctuations in currency relationships, a producer can use foreign currency futures as his or her vehicle. Speculators can also buy and sell currency futures, hoping to capitalize on expected or predicated fluctuations. The most active futures market in currencies is at the International Monetary Market of the Chicago Mercantile Exchange in Chicago.

Interest Rate Futures

The success of foreign currency futures has led to the development of futures contracts in another area of monetary risk: fluctuating interest rates. Anyone who has purchased a house in the last ten years is familiar with the risk associated with unstable interest rates. It is possible, and at times quite likely, for home mortgage rates to change as much as two or three percentage points in the 60 days normally required to close a real estate deal. During particularly volatile periods, a person unable to "lock in" a rate when the mortgage application is filed can sometimes end up paying a lot of extra money each month in higher interest rates.

Likewise, interest rate volatility represents a large risk to businesses and investors who count the interest earned or paid on borrowed money as a source of profit or expense. If I am a banker, for instance, I may want to invest some of my bank's assets in government securities. The amount of interest those securities earn will directly affect the profitability of my bank. Therefore, volatile interest rates represent a major financial risk to me. I don't want to speculate on what interest rates will be three, six, or twelve months from now. But there are speculators willing to assume that risk by trading interest rate futures contracts. Thus, I might want to hedge my government securities with an interest rate futures contract.

The most highly traded interest rate futures contract for several years has been the U.S. Treasury bond contract. Introduced on the CBOT in 1977, T bond futures are now traded worldwide. The first interest rate futures contract was the Ginnie Mae, or Government National Mortgage Association (GNMA) contract at the CBOT, which began trading in 1975. At this writing, interest rate futures are traded at many exchanges worldwide.

Stock Index Futures

A person responsible for the assets of a large pension fund or mutual fund who must maintain a productive, well-balanced portfolio of investments understands the risk involved in owning millions of dollars worth of stocks. After the stock market crash of October 19, 1987, that risk became particularly apparent. In 1982 the futures industry responded to the need to hedge such risks by offering the first stock index futures contract, the Value Line Index, at the Kansas City Board of Trade.

Five years of planning and negotiating solutions to regulatory problems preceded the inauguration of the Value Line Index, which is based on the Value Line Average (VLA), an index of 1,700 stocks. In 1982 the Chicago Mercantile Exchange established the S&P 500 Stock Index futures, and the New York Futures Exchange offered the New York Stock Exchange Index. A new era in trading futures had begun.

In its first year of existence, the S&P 500 Index became the tenth most actively traded contract in the world. By 1986 it was second only to the T bond contract at the CBOT in total volume. In 1999, stock index futures were traded on practically every futures market in the world. Hence stock index futures trading is not only one of the most popular vehicles for traders, but also one of the most volatile. Stock index trading has become so successful that a vast majority of exchanges throughout the world trade in one or more of the many stock indices.

Agricultural Futures

Trading in agricultural commodities such as grains, soybeans, and meats is found on numerous exchanges throughout the world. The vast majority of trading in these markets takes place at the two major Chicago exchanges.

Metal Futures

Silver, gold, copper, platinum, and palladium futures are actively traded in New York, while the London Metal Exchange (LME) trades in base metals such as tin, zinc, lead, and aluminum.

Energy Futures

New York is the primary location for trading in petroleum, natural gas, and electricity futures. The energy markets are traded more actively every year as a result of growing world demand.

Tropical Futures

Coffee, cocoa, sugar, and orange juice are traded in New York; these commodities (with the exception of orange juice) are traded all over the world as well.

Emerging Futures Markets

Numerous markets have emerged in virtually all major capitals of the world. Since the late 1990s, it has been possible to trade in everything from dried silk cocoon futures to freight futures.

Cash Settlement

It is easy to visualize a trader taking delivery on a contract for pork bellies. They are commodities that can be seen and touched. It is not difficult to imagine taking delivery on a contract for U.S. Treasury bills or even foreign currencies. But how does a trader take delivery of a stock index, which has no substance and cannot be seen or touched? The answer is, by cash settlement.

In cash settlement, if a futures contract has come due for delivery, the two parties can settle for the difference between the price of the contract that day and the price on the day they first made the contract. Thus, a trader does not have to go out and buy a share of stock in each of the companies included in the index in order to fulfill the contract. Cash settlement of a futures contract was first implemented with the EuroDollar contract at the CME in 1981. (EuroDollars are U.S. dollars on deposit in European banks.)

A 24-HOUR WORLDWIDE MARKET

Just as new contracts are being added to futures exchanges in the United States, thus expanding the industry exponentially, so too are new contracts and new exchanges being developed around the world in various centers of commerce and finance. The futures industry is at the forefront of the development of a unified, integrated worldwide economy.

On October 19, 1987, as the Dow Jones plummeted, the news was full of disastrous plunges occurring in stock exchanges worldwide: London, Tokyo, Singapore. The panic of that day carried from one economic center to another, just like a tidal wave washing across the face of the world, knocking the foundations from under the great financial institutions of the world as it went. Would such an event have occurred 15 years earlier with such velocity and an international domino effect? Probably not. But as the news of the worldwide economic panic surrounded us all, we became acutely aware of just how thoroughly integrated and interdependent the world's marketplaces have become during the past several decades.

The development of satellite and Internet communication has probably contributed more than anything else to the internationalization of the economy. As the facility for instantaneous worldwide communication became both economically and technologically available, the world's mercantilists and speculators rushed to utilize its full potential. As a result, exchanges around the world can communicate price quotes and other information almost instantaneously with exchanges in any other part of the world.

The Big Markets

The high-volume, high-volatility markets traded overseas are listed here. Compare the indicated trading volume with the S&P, which records about 95,000 contracts daily; T bonds, at about 370,000 contracts daily; the EuroDollar, at about 625,000 contracts daily; COMEX gold, at about 64,000; and crude oil, at 159,000.

Market	Contracts Traded Daily
Notionnel	64,000
FTSE 100	27,000
DAX	68,000
Gilt	55,000
Italian Bond	10,000
Short Sterling	194,000
Euro Swiss	28,000
Japanese Bond	32,000

These are some of the more active markets at the LIFFE. As you can see, they compare favorably to the U.S. futures markets mentioned earlier. They are viable vehicles for futures traders.

The Big Markets

Grains and Oilseeds
Barley
Wheat

Interest Rates
1-Month EuroMark
3-Month ECU
3-Month EuroMark
3-Month Short-Sterling
5-Year Gilt

BTP
Bund
ECU
EuroDollar
EuroLira
EuroMark
EuroSwiss
EuroYen
Italian Government Bond—BTP
Japanese Government Bond—JVG
JGB
German Government Bond—Bund
Long Gilt
Medium-Term German Government Bond—Bobl
Short Sterling
Spanish Government Bond (Bonos)
Indexes
FT-SE-100 Stock Index

Foods

Cocoa
Potatoes
Robusta Coffee
White Sugar

Equity Options

BIFFEX (Dry Freight Futures)
Eurotop
FTSE 100
FTSE 250

CHAPTER 6

Getting Started in Trading Futures

An individual who wishes to trade commodity futures must make several crucial decisions before he or she begins. One of the most critical of these decisions is the choice of a broker.

CHOOSING A BROKER

Only a few years ago, choosing a broker was less difficult than at present. Prior to the 1960s, there were not many firms to choose from, and all seemed to offer about the same service. Then, during the 1960s, brokerage firms tended to develop specialties; some were thought to be particularly adept at metals, for example, while others were especially good at tropicals. Customers expected their brokers to have an inside line on the commodity and therefore gave great credence to the brokers' advice. In fact, most people who speculated in commodities during that era did so on the basis of their brokers' recommendations, believing that a good broker was the key to making profits in commodities.

During the 1970s, two developments occurred that significantly altered the broker–client relationship. The first was the de facto deregulation of brokerage commissions, which led to a brutal commission war and the proliferation of discount brokerage firms. At the same time, an ever-growing number of speculators were relying on their own technical analysis of the markets rather than their brokers' advice. To these individuals, a commission rate that was one-half or one-third that of the full-service broker was very attractive. The second development was the decrease in futures trading volume in the traditional commodities and the corresponding surge of volume in financial and currencies contracts. No longer did firms have specialties and thereby attract and retain a certain loyal clientele.

As a consequence of these developments in the futures industry, the process of choosing a commodities broker has become both complex and confusing. Consider the following scenario.

Alice, an attorney, has lunch with a colleague who spins a gripping tale told her by a friend she spoke with over cocktails at a party the previous Friday night. The colleague's friend, it seems, had been watching interest rates and the T bond market quite closely, and he knew the bonds were ready to make a big move. He opened a small account with a broker, bought a contract for bonds, and five days later had doubled his money.

A week later, Alice is at a cocktail party and strikes up a conversation with a stranger who talks at length about the declining value of the dollar. After a stunning display of financial expertise, he concludes the discourse by saying, "I'm fully invested right now, unfortunately, but if I had some extra cash I'd open an account with a discount firm and buy some Swiss francs."

By now, it has become obvious to Alice that there are people who have an insight into the various markets and that if she can tap into that she might make a lot of money. On her way to the office one morning shortly thereafter, she relieves the boredom of the train ride by glancing through the business section of the newspaper. Sure enough, there are columnists writing with glib confidence about the balance of trade, the deficit, the direction of interest rates, and the value of the dollar on international markets. Just before the train arrives downtown, Alice tears out a coupon from a brokerage firm ad and stuffs it into her purse. Later, at the office, she fills out the ad and mails it.

Less than a week later, Alice receives a phone call from the broker in the ad. He determines that Alice is a novice, with approximately $5,000 to risk, who is interested in speculating in bonds or Swiss francs, depending on how they are doing right now. "Well, Alice," the broker responds, "I'm particularly bullish on soybeans right now. We've been having a dry spring, and I think they could go to $9.00 in the next week or two. The bonds and francs have been too choppy lately, so I don't see a good trade there."

After covering two more good reasons to buy soybeans, the broker agrees to send Alice some account forms, which she receives two days later. Glancing quickly through the disclaimers that caution her about the risk of significant losses, she fills out the forms, makes out a check, and mails the package back to the broker. Two days later, she receives a call from the broker, who confirms that he received the account forms and lets her know that he will call as soon as the right trade presents itself. Alice, of course, has been watching the price of beans on her train ride to work every morning and knows they have indeed been going up.

One day later, the broker calls with a recommendation to buy November beans at a price of $7.60 a bushel. Alice quickly agrees, and the broker places the order. Five minutes later, the phone rings again, and the broker informs her, "You bought 5,000 bushels of November soybeans at $7.65 a bushel." Alice is ecstatic. She was able to make the investment since the required margin or earnest money was only $1800.

Unfortunately, Alice is very likely to have a bad experience in the commodities market because of the haphazard manner in which she selected her broker. It is highly unlikely that she would plunk down $5,000 so easily for any other reason. For example, she would be very careful about buying a used $5,000 automobile, carefully selecting the dealer to buy from, having the car inspected by a mechanic, checking the Blue Book of car prices, reading through the annual used car issue of *Consumer Reports* magazine. Yet, without hesitation, she just sent $5,000 to a voice on the phone.

The Role of the Broker

Many of the problems that occur between broker and client arise from unrealistic client expectations. All too often, customers blame brokers for their losses. In some instances the blame is certainly justified. However, there are also situations in which the broker is not at fault. Frequently problems arise due to a lack of knowledge on the part of the client. Some traders, due to their own egos, refuse to accept personal responsibility for their shortcomings, errors, and failures. The broker often serves as a convenient scapegoat.

In the 1960s when I started trading, a "good" broker was defined as one who was able to give his or her clients profitable trades or profitable trading ideas. This view of the good broker has slowly faded through the years, as clients have realized that brokers are not necessarily any more knowledgeable than their clients when it comes to picking trades and trends. Brokerage houses have developed their own research departments or have contracted with independent trading analysts and advisors to conduct research that will, at least in theory, provide clients with reliable trading advice.

During the last 25 years, the level of client education about market analysis and trade selection has increased. At the same time, the level of broker education about market analysis and trading has either decreased or remained the same. Clients have learned more about how to find trades and how to place orders, how to use orders for effective entry and exit, and how the markets actually work. Brokers, on the other hand, have learned more about the laws and regulations of futures trading, how to be ethical, and what not to say to clients in order to avoid litigation.

The rigid application of licensing requirements and testing developed by the National Futures Association (NFA) has placed a premium on brokers' learning and following the legalities and technicalities of trading as opposed to the actual business of analyzing and understanding markets. The latter role has been left to the Commodity Trading Advisor (CTA), who is also tested on his or her knowledge of the regulations as opposed to his or her knowledge of how to make money trading.

The irony in the NFA's testing requirements for CTAs is that advisors are not tested on their ability to advise. Rather, they're tested on their knowledge of regulations, contract specifications, rules regarding solicitation for business, and practically useless skills such as calculating spread ratios. Hence, registration with the NFA as a CTA is not assurance of one's ability to give clients good recommendations. The same is true of one's registration with the NFA as a broker. Therefore, working with a registered broker or a registered CTA simply means that you're dealing with a person who knows the rules and who, theoretically, won't break the rules or make technical errors in placing your orders or in assisting you with market information such as the dollar value of a tick, opening and closing times, types of orders, and so on.

Do not expect your broker or CTA to make investment decisions for you, unless they have taken the time to specifically develop and acquire the skills to do so. Many brokers have specific systems they follow. Take the time to learn what they're doing, so you'll be informed about their approach and methodology.

How to Find a Good Broker

Being a broker involves an inherent conflict of interest. As you know, a broker makes money when you close out a position. Therefore, the more often a client trades, the more profit for the broker. Commissions are the lifeblood of the futures market and the brokerage business. Without commissions, brokers go broke, brokerage firms go broke, and the NFA won't collect its fees (because they make money every time you trade). Without trading, floor traders can't make money.

A broker who trades customers too often is guilty of "churning," one of the worst offenses a broker can commit. However, if a customer calls the shots and does not give the broker power of attorney to make trades, then the customer can churn all he or she wants without any liability to the broker. Brokers who are experienced in handling clients may have subtle ways of making clients trade, even when a trade is not in the client's best interest.

So how do you find a broker who will be helpful to you in making your investment decisions? The next section provides guidelines for finding and working with a good broker as well as a good brokerage house.

Rules for Selecting a Broker

Rule 1

A would-be speculator in commodity futures must first decide what kind of trader he or she would like to be. In today's market, there are four general categories of traders:

1. *The novice.* This trader has little or no experience or knowledge of futures trading; is probably nervous, uncertain, and insecure; and requires a broker who is patient, not too busy, and familiar with the details that concern the novice trader, such as appropriate placement of orders, margin requirements, understanding purchase and sale statements, contract specifications, reports, and various trading systems.

2. *The experienced short-term trader.* This is usually an individual with considerable experience and market knowledge who is interested in making intraday trades or trades that will last only a few days. This person may want price quotes and other information from the broker, but basically he or she requires a broker who can execute orders promptly, efficiently, and at reasonably good prices.

3. *The long-term trader.* Generally, a long-term position trader uses fundamental knowledge of the commodities he or she trades in to take a position and hold it for a relatively long time. This trader would do well to use a brokerage firm that can provide correct statistical and fundamental data.

4. *The independent trader.* This trader desires absolutely no input from the broker and works best with a broker who is primarily an order taker.

Rule 2

The would-be trader must survey the available brokerage firms and determine what services each provides. There are two broad categories of brokers, the full-service broker and the discount broker, although the difference is growing less distinct as time passes.

1. *The full-service broker.* This is the traditional brokerage firm that provides virtually any financial service including

stocks, bonds, futures, money market funds, tax shelters, options, research publications, and so forth. Some full-service brokers handle both stocks and commodities, while others provide services in the area of futures trading only. A full-service futures broker provides considerable research, offers price quotes, gives trading advice and assists the customer in making trading decisions, and may offer discretionary and managed account programs.

2. *The discount broker.* Discount brokers do not provide costly research and research publications, nor do they help the client develop a strategy or provide trading advice beyond the most basic. They simply fill orders and meet the reporting and financial obligations of a broker, such as trade confirmations and purchase and sale statements. In recent years, however, some discount brokers have begun offering a sliding scale of commissions, based on a selection of optional services such as research and broker assistance, usually at a rate less than the full-service houses charge. Likewise, many full-service firms are offering discounted services to clients who do not require broker assistance, price quotations, and market research.

Rule 3

When selecting a brokerage firm, the speculator must be certain that his or her capital will be safe. Look for a brokerage house that's well-capitalized and avoid a brokerage house that doesn't have a good balance sheet. The more money the firm has, the more stable it is likely to be, and the more clout it will have on the trading floor. Find out how much money the firm has in aggregate accounts and how much money it has behind it.

Rule 4

Determine whether a registered NFA member has had a record of complaints or violations or if there are any disciplinary proceedings currently under way. Find out if the principals of a brokerage firm are reputable individuals or if they've been involved in scams or questionable dealings. The National Futures Association maintains a toll-free number you can call for this information, all of which is public information.

Rule 5

Compare commission rates. It is important, however, not to make a decision based solely on the price of commissions. After deciding on the services required (Rule 1), the trader must be prepared to pay a reasonable fee for those services. Avoid any broker who charges extraordinarily high commissions for options. These charges cannot be justified and you should not pay them.

Rule 6

Interview your broker. Ask questions about his or her trading philosophy. Listen for appropriate statements such as, "I won't tell you what to do unless you ask me," or "I'm here to take your orders and give you information when you need it." If possible, visit the brokers' offices before making a final decision. A great deal can be learned from such a visit.

Rule 7

If you will rely on recommendations from the broker, check the broker's track record. How good is this broker at calling winning trades? How many clients have ended up losing all or most of their money by following this broker's advice? A track record may be difficult to pin down, but asking the right questions can generate useful information. Remember that the vast majority of traders who trade small accounts on their brokers' advice lose money.

Rule 8

Dot not set up unrealistic expectations about a broker. Here is a list of what a good broker should and should not do.

A Good Broker Should:

- Answer the telephone quickly and take your order promptly and professionally.
- Place your order directly to the trading floor, and not through another party.
- Report order executions to you promptly.
- Execute your orders with a minimum of errors.

- Inform you of market-related information that may be important (e.g., first notice day, market closings, new price limits, new rules, etc.).
- Come to your assistance in resolving account-related problems or bad price fills.
- Help you use the correct orders at the right times.
- Help you monitor your equity so that you don't overtrade or encounter margin problems.
- Give you advice only when you ask for it.

A Good Broker Should Not:

- Encourage you to overtrade.
- Talk you into or out of trades.
- Urge you to trade based on emotion, rumor, or tips.
- Add to your insecurity or uncertainty.

Rule 9

Establish a clear agreement with your broker before you begin to trade. The agreement should include such things as what you expect from your broker and what he or she will do or not do in the way of giving advice. Reaching an understanding at the very beginning can help you to avoid potential problems.

Rule 10

Don't hesitate to ask your prospective broker how much experience he or she has had. Try to use a broker who has had considerable experience in all types of markets.

Rule 11

Find out if your broker offers on-line trading and how it works.

Rule 12

Avoid brokers who make fantastic claims. As with many other things in life, the basic rule in futures trading is that if something sounds too good to be true, then it probably *is* too good to be true.

Rule 13

Remember that a broker makes his or her money by commission. The more trades that are made, the more money the broker makes. On the other hand, a broker who recommends too many trades may burn the account out too quickly, thus losing the account. In either case, the client's interests are often at odds with the broker's interests. In conversation with a prospective broker and through recommendations, attempt to ascertain the broker's performance in light of this consideration.

The degree of competition in the brokerage business has increased dramatically as commissions have declined. Some brokers offer numerous free sign-up bonuses at low rates. Other brokerage firms have persisted in keeping their rates extremely high, claiming that they provide services you cannot get at lower rates elsewhere. Sometimes you will indeed get better service if you pay a higher commission rate, but all too often you won't. Take your time and shop around. If you plan to trade only via electronic order entry, make sure your broker has state-of-the-art facilities for such orders. Whereas most brokerage services were essentially similar many years ago, there are distinct differences nowadays. Take time to discover these differences, because some of them are significant.

Now that we know the procedure Alice should have followed in selecting her broker, let's take a look at what happened to her after she sent $5,000 to a firm she knew nothing about.

First, the broker Alice selected was correct in his assertion that soybeans would go up. In fact, less than two weeks after Alice bought her beans at $7.65, the price of soybeans was trading as high as $8.65. Since each one-cent change in soybeans is worth $50 to Alice, because she purchased 5,000 bushels, Alice should have made $5,000 on her trade.

Unfortunately for Alice, though, the day after she bought her soybeans, the price dropped 30 cents, which is the limit that the soybean market can move in one trading day. (This is called a limit move.) The next day, prices stabilized but did not bounce back. Alice's account was now worth only $3,500. In a panic, she called her broker, who assured her that such short-term moves are not uncommon, and that this one occurred because a local weather forecaster predicted rain—a prediction that did not materialize.

The third day of Alice's trading career, a rumor of rain again swept the market and the price once more dropped 30 cents. Alice now had only $2,000 left. Again she called her broker. "What's going on?" she demanded. "You said this was a sure thing, and here I am losing all my money. I was counting on that money for a vacation I'm planning, and now it's almost gone!"

In a calm, reassuring voice the broker told Alice that things should turn around soon, but just in case they didn't perhaps she should put a stop-loss order in. In effect, this stop-loss order instructed the floor broker to liquidate Alice's position if the price of soybeans dropped to $7. Having no one to rely on but the broker, Alice agreed and then waited.

The next day, the price of beans opened unchanged— a good sign. In the next half-hour, the price crept up slowly. When Alice called her broker at 10:00 A.M., the price stood at $7.10. The broker was certain that prices would continue to go up, based on a long-term weather forecast of continued drought. But then, something strange happened. Prices began to fall again. An order to sell a large quantity of soybeans had come into the pit, driving prices down. From $7.10, they went to $7.08, then $7.05, then $7.03. At $6.98, the slide ended, and prices began to rise again. By the end of the day, prices stood at $7.35, a limit-up move. The broker was right! They did recover!

But Alice did not profit from the rise. When prices dropped to $7, the floor broker had dutifully filled her order to sell, thus taking Alice out of the market. Her net loss was $3,250.

The next morning, in shock and depressed, Alice called her broker and asked him to send her the remaining $1,750 in her account, which he did, minus the $125 commission charge. Then she called her travel agent and canceled her vacation plans.

Would things have turned out differently for Alice if she had been more careful in selecting a broker? That is difficult to say. Certainly, there are brokers who would have asked more questions about her investment goals as well as the source of her money, and most brokers would have cautioned Alice not to use vacation money to speculate with.

If Alice had shopped around for a broker, she might have had a better experience in commodities trading, or she might have decided not to trade at all after she had learned the true risks involved. Then again, she might have continued to insist on plunking down her $5,000 and taking her chances. We will never know. The point is that the broker–client relationship is critical to successful commodity trading, and it is essential that every active or would-be commodity trader carefully follow the rules I have presented for choosing a broker.

OPENING AN ACCOUNT

Once an aspiring commodities trader has decided on a suitable broker, the next step is to open an account. The paperwork is fairly simple and straightforward, and the broker will be more than happy to help with it. The forms to be filled out serve two essential purposes: to ascertain whether the individual is financially qualified to trade commodities, and to obtain the individual's signature acknowledging the various risks involved in trading commodities.

In recent years, legislation that established the Commodity Futures Trading Commission (CFTC) and self-regulation by the National Futures Association (NFA) have led to a situation in which every broker must be very concerned about the interests of the potential client. Thus, the process of establishing an account will likely include carefully worded disclaimers, which the client must sign, and a tape-recorded conversation, usually by phone, in which the broker qualifies the client by verifying the information included in the application form and determining that the client understands and acknowledges all the risks involved in futures trading.

When opening an account, the would-be futures trader faces another important decision: What size account should you establish? Is $1,000 enough? Do you need $5,000? Though seemingly a simple decision, research has shown that the size of a trading account has a direct bearing on success in futures trading. The fact is that most accounts of $5,000 or less lose money. In fact, it is not until account size reaches $15,000 that the odds of success become more realistic.

Consider the fact that the best professional futures traders rarely achieve more than 50 percent accuracy in their trading. In other words, most successful traders lose money on more than half of their trades. Their success lies in being able to cut their losses short on each losing trade and in staying with the profitable trades long enough to offset all the small losses and thus show a net profit in the account.

Once this is understood, it becomes apparent why an account of less than $15,000 is very risky. There is little room in such an account to withstand a series of small losses. Often, the account will be depleted before a profitable trade occurs. An account of $5,000 will not allow a trader to stay with a high-conviction trade through a series of short-term opposing moves, whereas an account of $15,000 might allow the investor to place a stop-loss at a point further away from the trading price, thus avoiding being stopped out of the market. Then, a losing trade can be turned into a very profitable trade.

How to Open a Commodity Trading Account

Opening a commodity trading account is as simple as filling out the application and sending in the money. It is now possible to complete the entire process on-line. But the ease of opening an account should not be confused with the trading process. While opening an account is a relatively quick and painless process (provided you meet the financial requirements), the trading experience can prove to be quite the opposite if you are uneducated or unprepared.

Your account applications will request the standard information as well as a basic financial history. You will also be required to read various risk disclosure documents and sign a few statements indicating your awareness of the risk. Read all paperwork carefully and fill out the forms honestly. Do not overstate your income; if you do, you may waive your right to effective litigation in the event that you have a future claim against the firm. Evaluate carefully whether you should be trading futures.

Financial Suitability

Different brokerage firms have different financial suitability requirements and standards. Some allow you to open an account with as little as $1,000 while others require $5,000 or more. The more money you begin with, the better your odds of success. Regardless of what the broker requires, the ultimate burden of determining suitability is yours. Unless your trading capital is 100 percent risk capital, you are advised against futures trading.

Who Should and Should Not Trade Commodities and Why

Although there are many people who want to trade the commodity markets, it is evident that not all individuals are suited for such trading either financially or emotionally. Although a brokerage firm cannot stop you from trading if you have the money and financial suitability to trade, you may still be unqualified due to your lack of discipline, knowledge, and/or trading procedures. Futures trading should only be attempted by those who have risk capital and sufficient income. The brokerage firm you desire to work with will determine your suitability to trade since requirements can vary considerably.

ELEMENTS OF A TRADE

Contract Specifications

In an earlier chapter, the point was made that quantity, quality, and point of delivery standardize futures contracts. Because most futures traders never take delivery of the commodity, they do not need to be concerned with the quality and delivery point, except to understand that they are standardized. The unit size of a contract is of concern, however, if only to avoid confusion when placing orders.

I will not attempt to cover every contract as to size and specifications here. Rather, I have included in Appendix II a complete list of futures contracts, which (as of this printing) provides all the information needed by a futures trader regarding a contract to be traded. For now, I wish to focus on two specific aspects of the standardized contract: the contract size designation and the tick value of the contract.

For hedgers, the size of a contract is of particular interest, because they must trade in sufficient quantities to cover their holdings of the commodity itself. For a speculator, the size of a contract is of little interest, except to note the difference between grain contracts and all other contracts. In the grains, which include oats, corn, wheat, and soybeans, a contract is for 5,000 bushels.

When placing an order in the grains, the trader specifies "Buy (or sell) 5,000 bushels" of whatever grain is being traded. In shorthand, this becomes "Buy five corn" (or wheat or oats or beans). It is important to remember that the number five in that phrase refers to thousands of bushels. In every other contract, the number in the order refers to the quantity of contracts being traded, for example, "Buy one Japanese yen."

The tick value of a futures contract is critical for the futures trader. The tick value is called the dollar value of the minimum fluctuation. For the trader, this simply means how much one tick on the chart is worth.

Thus, if I am trading in cattle and I have a long position (I am a buyer) at $67.50, this means that I have a contract to buy 40,000 pounds of cattle at 6.75 cents per pound. In cattle, the minimum fluctuation (one tick) is worth $10. This simply means that every time the price goes up one tick, I make $10 (because I can then sell for $10 more than I paid). Likewise, every time the price goes down one tick, I lose $10. The tick value varies for each commodity, so it is important for the trader to check the tick value before attempting a trade.

Contract Months

One of the first things a new speculator will notice when attempting to trade commodity futures is that there are several different contracts available for each commodity, each designated by a certain month. The closest month is called the front, or the spot, month, whereas the further months are called the back months. Some contracts may be for as far away as four years, while others may be due for delivery the very next month after the one in which the trade is made.

In a normal market, the further a contract is from the spot month, the higher the price. This higher price represents the carrying charge, or the cost of holding a commodity in storage. Sometimes, however, the back month prices are lower, creating an inverted market.

The highest volume of trading occurs in the front months, creating the most liquid market. Generally, the further a contract delivery date is from the spot month, the less volume there is. For short-term or intraday traders, then, the best month to trade in is the front month because of the liquidity of the market in this month.

When a market lacks volume, or liquidity, it becomes more difficult to get in and out of the market at a desirable price. For longer-term position traders, the back months provide appropriate trading opportunities.

Delivery Points

Many commodity contracts (particularly in the grains and foods) specify delivery points or warehouse locations. None of this should be of concern to you, the speculator, because you will not be holding your contracts into the delivery period.

Cash Settlement

In many cases a seller need not deliver the actual commodity to the buyer but can, as an alternative, fulfill the commitment with the cash equivalent of the given commodity.

Margin and the "Margin Call"

The term "margin" as it is used in commodity trading is really a misnomer that has been carried over from stock trading. When a trader buys stock, he or she can borrow half the purchase amount from the broker and put up the other half in cash. This is called a 50 percent margin, which is the limit brokers are allowed to offer. (In the 1920s, brokers were selling stock on 10 percent margin, which many believe contributed to the 1929 market crash.) In the futures market, a specified amount, also called margin, is deposited with the broker when a trade is made. This margin money, however, does not purchase anything. It simply serves as earnest money.

When a trader enters into a contract to either buy or sell a commodity at a future date, no sale actually occurs, hence no money is spent. If the market moves against the trader, the margin will be used to pay for the loss as the position declines in value. At a certain point, however, the margin money on deposit may be insufficient to cover additional losses, and the trader will be asked to deposit additional margin money or to liquidate the position and take the present loss. Thus, for each commodity, there are two margin values established: initial margin and maintenance margin. Initial margin is the amount that must be on deposit in the account when a trade is initiated. Initial margin requirements vary substantially from commodity to commodity and are subject to change by the exchange, depending on the volatility of the market. For example, in October 1987, immediately following the stock market crash, the margin for the S&P 500 contract was raised from $6,000 to $50,000 nearly overnight. The reason was that the unprecedented price swings that were occurring often caused losses that exceeded the margin money many traders had on deposit.

Maintenance margin is the minimum amount that must be maintained in the account to hold a position. As a trade loses value, it erodes the amount of margin in the account. Once the account balance is below the established maintenance margin, the broker issues a margin call. The trader is obligated to immediately deposit enough money in the account to return the account to initial margin. Otherwise, the broker will liquidate the position.

Minimum margin requirements are established by the exchange. Individual brokers may, and often do, establish higher margins than the minimums, but they may not establish margins that are lower than the exchange minimums. Day trades—trades that will be exited by the end of the day—are not subject to margin requirements. Any position held past the end of the trading session, however, must be covered by the necessary margin amount.

Short Selling

One of the most difficult concepts for the novice commodities trader to master is the idea of selling a commodity first, then buying it back later. "How can I sell something I don't own?" is the common question. Actually, the practice is not unique to futures trading.

To cite a very familiar example, consider what happens when a Girl Scout solicits orders for Girl Scout cookies during the organization's annual fund drive. Essentially, when the Girl Scout takes an order for cookies, she has become a short seller. She has sold cookies she doesn't have, with the agreement that she will deliver the cookies at a later date. The same thing occurs at an automobile dealership when a customer orders a new car for later delivery. This time, however, the salesperson will likely demand a deposit— earnest money—before accepting the order. The salesperson has, however, sold a car he or she does not own, and that has not yet been built. The salesperson is "short" the car (in the same way a person might be "short" of cash). That salesperson, then, has become a short seller in a futures contract.

The difference between the two preceding examples—the Girl Scout and the car salesperson—and futures trading is that delivery of the cookies and the car will likely occur, whereas delivery of a commodity futures contract rarely occurs. To avoid having to make delivery, the short seller can simply become a buyer of the same commodity in the same delivery month and offset the previous short position.

The same thing can happen in our example of the Girl Scout cookies. Perhaps, after the Girl Scout takes our order (she sells short), she turns the order over to the Girl Scout leader, who then arranges for delivery of the cookies and collection of money. By turning in the order (the contract), the Girl Scout has liquidated her position by transferring it to the leader, who is now the short seller. In the futures market, the trader who originally took a short position liquidates that position by taking an offsetting long position.

The exchange functions exactly like the Girl Scout leader, in this case, by assuming delivery responsibility from the trader. The trader's profit or loss is the difference between the selling price and the buying price, minus commissions. The important point to remember, though, is that short selling, or taking a short position, can occur either to liquidate a previous long position or to take a new short position. The procedure is the same.

Commissions

In the world of selling, the charging of sales commissions is a ubiquitous and easily understood practice. When a person sells an item or a service, he or she receives a commission as payment for having successfully completed the transaction. In the same way, a brokerage house charges a commission for facilitating a futures' transaction. In futures trading, however, a transaction is not considered final until the trader's initial position has been closed.

Therefore, a commission is not charged when a trader first enters the market, no matter whether the initial position is long or short. When that position is offset, or liquidated, then a commission is charged. A commodity broker's commission, then, represents payment for two transactions: getting into the market and getting out of the market. This is called, appropriately enough, a round turn or a round trip. Thus, broker's commissions are usually quoted at a price per round. Note that on a spread there are two commissions, one for each side of the spread.

As we noted earlier, the amount of commission paid will vary depending upon the service expected or rendered. Prices may vary from $15 or $20 per round turn (completed trade) for a no-frills discount broker to $125 or more for a full-service broker.

PLACING AN ORDER

In futures trading the timing of a trade is key to determining the success or failure of the trade. In many of the futures markets, there is a great deal of volatility in price movement throughout the day. Thus, a trader who wishes to place an order might need to do so at a certain price in order to make a successful trade.

Knowing how to get an order filled at a reasonably advantageous price is a critical skill for the would-be futures trader. Additionally, because the chance for error is so great in a fast-paced business like commodity trading, following the correct procedure for order placement is one way to avoid costly mistakes.

Many order conversations are recorded, so that in the event of an error or a disputed order the tape can be played back to determine exactly what was said. If the trader made a mistake, he or she is liable for the resulting expenses, whatever they may be. If the broker or order clerk makes a mistake, an adjustment will be made. However, nobody can make up for missed opportunities or disadvantageous fills that occur because of trader ignorance or negligence. In every situation, the trader must insist that the person who takes the order repeat the order back before ending the phone call. Placing the order, then, is simply a matter of calling the broker and giving him or her the instructions. Giving the proper instructions, though, is crucial.

With the advent of electronic trading as well as electronic order placement, there are several additional important considerations. Electronic markets do not necessarily accept all types of orders. In addition, they may have certain rules that differ from those for orders placed in open outcry markets. Make certain you know the rules before you place electronic orders in any market! Electronic orders are either filled by computer or by an actual pit broker. They are confirmed back to you either by telephone or e-mail.

In order to help you get the most out of every single trade you make, you will need to be completely familiar with the types of orders that you may use and, most important of all, when to use them.

There are three broad categories of orders: market orders, price orders, and contingent orders. All three categories are described here, with comments added regarding their appropriate and inappropriate use.

Market Orders

These are the simplest orders. Market orders are understood by all traders, and are the easiest orders to understand and to place. All you need do is tell your broker to "buy" or to "sell" at the market. In effect, this is a message to the pit broker who will execute your order that you are willing to accept any price you get.

While the exchange maintains certain rules about what pit brokers may do with your market order, using a market order is often an indication of immediacy or even of desperation. Using a market order is making a significant statement of trust in your broker and the pit broker. In a fast market anything is possible in the way of a fill. Typically the order will be filled one or two ticks away from what you thought you might get.

Many traders have no idea what a "fast" market is or what it means. The given exchange will designate a market as fast when it feels that trading activity is so volatile that floor traders need to be absolved of most responsibility to get you a quick price fill on a market order.

Typically an order must be filled within 3 minutes after reaching the floor. In a fast market it could be filled at just about any time. In addition, floor traders have the right not to accept certain orders in fast markets.

Placing a market order in a fast market takes a major leap of faith. Anything can happen. When would you use a market order? Clearly, a market order is used to assure you a fill when you are in a state of urgency. In the long run, market orders, particularly those placed in fast markets, will cost you. The ticks lost in entry and exit will add up, and you won't be happy with the result. Other types of market orders are Market on Close orders and Disregard Tape (or Market Not Held) orders.

Market on Close (MOC)

The MOC order (also affectionately referred to as "murder on close") is a specialized type of market order that tells the pit broker to buy or sell for you at any price during the last minute of trading. This type of order also requires that you take a leap of faith. It basically says that you want to be filled urgently. Urgency and good price fills are often incompatible. If you use a market order of any type, particularly in a fast market, be prepared for the worst.

Disregard Tape (DRT) or Market Not Held

This is a specialized order to the pit broker. In effect, it says to the pit broker, "Here is a market order; please use your best judgment in getting me a price fill. I will not hold you liable if I get a bad fill. You are not required to fill me in the allotted 3 minutes. Disregard the ticker tape and get me the best fill you can using your best judgment." At times this type of order will get you a better fill. It is best used when entering or exiting large positions, because it gives the floor broker a chance to do a better job for you. Naturally, the skill of the floor broker is important in such cases.

Price Orders

There are many different types of price orders. Each is designed to serve a specific purpose.

Sell Stop

A sell stop order is always placed at a specific price, below the price that a market is currently trading at. It is used either to stop you out of a long position or to get you into a short position as the market declines and shows its weakness.

As an example, suppose you are long September T bonds. The market is at 110-12. You want to protect your position. You place an order as follows: "Sell 1 September T bond @ 109-12 stop." This means that when your stop price is hit, your order becomes a market order. The floor broker will get you a fill at any price he or she can. Most often you will be filled a little lower than your sell stop. If this is a new short position, the same procedure applies. The only difference is that you will be short rather than flat (i.e., no position).

Sell Stop Close Only (SCO)

This is a sell stop order that is executed in the last minute of trading. If the market is at or below the price of your sell stop close only, you will be filled at whatever price the pit broker can get for you. Some exchanges, notably the Chicago Board of Trade, do not accept SCO orders.

Buy Stop

This order is placed at a specific price above the market. It is used either to stop you out of a short position or to get you into a long position as the market rallies and shows its strength. A buy stop order is always placed above the price a market is currently trading at. A buy stop order is placed at a given price.

As an example, suppose you are short September T bonds. The market is at 110-12. You want to protect your position. You place an order as follows: "Buy 1 September T bond @ 111-02 stop." This means that when your stop price is hit, your order becomes a market order. The floor broker will get you a fill at any price he or she can.

Most often you will be filled a little higher than your buy stop. If this is a new long position, the same procedure applies. The only difference is that you will be long rather than flat (i.e., no position).

Buy Stop Close Only (SCO)

This is a buy stop order that is executed in the last minute of trading. If the market is at or above the price of your buy stop close only, you will be filled at whatever price the pit broker can get for you.

To place a close only order you would say, for example, "Sell 1 July Belly @ 7020 stop close only." Some exchanges, notably the Chicago Board of Trade, do not accept SCO orders.

Buy or Sell Stop Limit

This is a stop order that specifies to the broker that you will only accept a fill at the limit of your price order. In other words, if your sell stop limit is 49.55, then you will get a 49.55 (or better) fill unless the market shoots through your price, thereby not allowing the pit broker to fill you. The risk in using a stop limit order is that it will not get filled. To place a stop limit order, you say, "Sell 1 December Gold 39850 stop limit."

Another way to place a stop limit order is to state the size of the limit. In other words, you specify a range of prices for the limit order. As an example, "Buy 1 December Hog @ 4750 stop with a limit of 65" means you will accept a fill between 4750 and 4765 inclusive. This type of order gives the pit broker a little more leeway.

I prefer to use stop limit orders wherever and whenever possible. Note, however, that not all exchanges accept such orders.

Market if Touched (MIT)

An MIT order to buy is placed below the current price. When the market hits the buy price, the floor broker will buy the given commodity at the market for you. The MIT sell is placed above the market. When the market rallies to the indicated price, the floor broker will sell at the market for you. MIT buy orders are used for the purpose of buying into a price decline, such as in the case of a drop to support. MIT sell orders are used to sell into a rally to resistance.

Because an MIT order becomes a market order as soon as the indicated price is touched, your price fill can, on occasion, occur well beyond the price you wanted, particularly in a fast market. An MIT order is used as a method of making certain you are filled on your order. Assume that July cocoa is trading at 1478, and you want to go long when the market declines to a support level you've calculated. An example of an MIT order you might use in this case is: "Buy 1 July Cocoa @ 1440 MIT." This means that if the market drops to 1440, the floor broker will try to buy your cocoa at any price possible or, in order words, at the market.

Fill or Kill (FOK)

This is an order type that few traders know about, and even fewer traders use. It is a way of getting information back promptly as to whether your order has been filled or not. An FOK order is entered at a specific price.

As an example, consider the following order: "Sell 1 September S&P @ 67050 FOK (fill or kill)." The pit broker will attempt to fill your order three times. In other words, the pit broker will bid or try to buy three times. If it is not filled then, your order will be "killed," that is, canceled, and you will be told that your order has been "killed." Using this type of order, you don't need to wait hours and hours to find out whether you've been filled.

Although FOK orders can be advantageous, keep in mind a few guidelines. Don't enter an FOK order that is far from the market. An FOK should be within a few ticks of the current price. You broker will be annoyed with you for wasting time on FOKs that are far from the market. Also, don't put in too many FOKs that aren't filled or your broker will also get angry, particularly if your broker is a discounter. Remember that it costs time, energy, and effort every time an order ticket is written.

FOK orders are also good to use when you have a large order to fill either on the buy or the sell side. Sophisticated traders can often use FOK orders to test the strength or weakness of a market. Finally, remember that a floor broker has the right to refuse such an order at his or her discretion.

Contingent Orders or Dual Orders

This is the third broad category of orders. A contingent order typically involves two sides of an order, or the cancellation of one order and the placement of another order.

Spreads

As you know, a spread involves two markets traded at the same time. When a spread order is placed, there are two sides to the order, unless the spread sides (or "legs") are placed separately. Placing orders separately is referred to as legging in or legging out. I do not recommend this procedure. Rather, I advise placing both sides of a spread at once. Spread orders are placed as a difference between the two markets.

Hence, if the spread is July versus December corn, and July corn is at 450 while December corn is at 400, the spread is designated as +50 July. To enter this spread at the current difference, you would place the following order: "Buy July corn, sell December corn @ +50 July."

If the same spread was at 350 July corn and 400 December corn, the order would read: "Buy July corn, sell December corn at –50 July." In the second case, July is at a discount to December. In the first case, it is at a premium.

One Cancels the Other (OCO)

At times you may wish to place a contingency order. If, for example, you go long and want a stop loss but you also want to get out on the close, you could use a contingency order known as an OCO, which stands for "one cancels the other." Let's say you're long Swiss francs from 8640 and want to place a stop at 8612 to sell out, but you also want to be out by the close of trading if your stop is not executed.

To do this, you enter an OCO order as follows: "Sell June Swiss franc @ 8612 stop (or stop limit) OCO MOC." This means that if you are stopped out, your MOC sell will be canceled. If you are not stopped out, then you will be out MOC and the sell stop will be canceled.

Cancel Replace

This is a simple procedure. When you have an existing order that needs to be canceled and replaced with a new order in the same market, you simply advise your broker that you have a "cancel replace" order.

Your order might read as follows: "I have a cancel replace order in June Swiss franc; cancel a buy @ 8620 MIT; buy @ 8634 MIT."

Tips for Order Placement

- *Use stop limit orders instead of stop orders.* In many cases you will be filled. If you are concerned about not being filled, put a one- or two-tick limit on your order.
- *Fill or Kill orders can be used to your advantage in several ways.* If you need to exit or enter a trade and you don't want to wait to find out if you've been filled, then use the FOK order. You'll get quick feedback and you'll probably save money. If you've never used such orders before, get your feet wet before using them extensively.
- *Use FOK orders to test a market.* One good way to find out how strong or weak a market may be is to use an FOK order. For example, suppose June S&P futures are trading between 1106.50 and 1106.90. You have a buy signal at 1106.50. Trading volume is light. Following the buy signal, prices move quickly to 1106.90 and you don't want to chase the market. You are concerned that the signal might not work this time, because the market fell back quickly to the original breakout price of 1106.50. You are hesitant to buy. You can test the market by placing your FOK order to go long at 1106.45 or 1106.40, knowing that this is below the recent range of trades.

  You enter your order and watch the tape. It reads 1106.55 when you enter your order. The ticks then go as follows:

  1106.65 ... 1106.55 ... 1106.55 ... 1106.55 ... 1106.60 ... 1106.65 ... 1106.65 ... 1106.60 ... 1106.65 ... 1106.60 ... 1106.70 ... 1106.65 ... 1106.70 ... 1106.75 ...

  The market comes close to your bid but never hits it. The order is returned killed. What does this mean? It most likely indicates a market with a good demand. It suggests that you had better get on board quickly. You may even want to use a market order to do so.

- *MIT orders are acceptable but not always efficient.* They are good for trading within a support and resistance channel; however, they will cost you ticks.

- *OCO orders, where accepted, are very helpful.* They will help you bracket the market with different strategies and should be used whenever needed.

- *Use First Open Only orders when appropriate.* Some New York markets have staggered openings (e.g., sugar). In these markets, each contract month is opened individually in chronological order, traded for a few minutes, and then closed so that another month may be opened. Once the process has been completed, all months are opened again at the same time. The same procedure is used for closing. Should you need to buy one of these markets on the open, you are advised to specify that you want your order good for the first open only. All too often the second opening price is distinctly different from the first opening price, which can cost you money.

- *Insist on prompt reporting back of order fills.* It is absolutely necessary for you to know when you've been filled and when you've not been filled. You must be strict with your broker in demanding fills back as soon as possible. Do not accept excuses, particularly in currencies, T bonds, S&P, and petroleum futures, where flash fills are easily given. A flash fill is one for which you may remain on hold as your order is hand-signaled to the pit. While there are some conditions in which delays are understandable, delays are anathema, particularly to the day trader, and must be avoided whenever and wherever possible.

- *Know which exchanges will accept certain orders.* The rules change from time to time and from one market condition to another. If you don't know the rules, find them out. The Chicago Mercantile and IMM will accept almost all orders almost all the time. The Chicago Board of Trade is a stickler for accepting only certain types of orders. (For example, CBOT does not accept MITs.) Some New York markets have restrictions as well. Check with your broker if you have questions.

- *Find out how your broker places your orders.* Does he or she call the floor? Are your orders put on a wire for execution? Does your broker need to call someone who will call someone else who will then call someone else? This all takes time. Day traders can't afford for their orders to take that much time. Ask your broker for his or her procedures and deal only with those who can get you the fastest fills. Doing anything else will cost you money, no matter how low the commission rate. Don't be penny-wise and pound-foolish.
- *GLOBEX (24-hour) trading requires that you use even more discretion in order placement.* Be very careful. Learn the rules so you can deal effectively with the lack of liquidity.

As you can see from this discussion, the types of orders you use and the way in which you use them are very important in charting a course toward successful futures trading. If you're a new trader, please spend a few hours, or more if necessary, learning the basics of effective order placement. If you have questions, ask your broker. I cannot overemphasize the importance of order placement. Unfortunately, most trading courses don't teach this skill, as well as a number of other very important basics of trading.

Finally, a word to traders who use discount brokers: Be particularly careful when placing orders with a discount broker. They're not paid to watch over your shoulder for correct use of orders. You pay them for their order execution, so don't expect them to educate you or correct you unless your order is totally senseless. Their job is to provide order execution, not to hold a client's hand.

There's probably enough to learn about orders to fill an entire book. For our purposes, suffice it to say that it's in your very best interest to learn about orders, order placement, and when to use the many different types of orders that are available to you. Learn how to place orders effectively and you'll come out ahead in the short run as well as in the long run.

DAY TRADING, SHORT-TERM TRADING, AND POSITION TRADING

A position commodity trader initiates a position in the market with the intention of holding that position for more than a short time period. There is no specific amount of time that defines a position trade. Suffice it to say that a position trade is longer than one day and likely longer than ten days. Some traders define a position trade as one lasting many months. For the purposes of this book, however, we can consider any trade longer than ten days to be a position trade. Position trading is designed to profit from longer-term price trends by getting in at a price and waiting for the market to move far enough to provide substantial profits.

By default, then, a short-term trade is one that is ten days or less in duration but longer than one day. Just as with a position trade, there is no hard-and-fast rule here. Different traders have their own ideas as to what constitutes a short-term trade.

All traders can agree on the definition of a day trade. Clearly, a day trade is a trade that you are into and out of the same day. A trader can make numerous day trades within the time frame of a day. A trade that is held beyond the time frame of one day is no longer a day trade; it is a short-term trade and could eventually become a position trade.

There was a time when virtually all futures traders were position traders, except those actually trading on the floor of the exchange. Prior to the availability of sophisticated real-time electronic quote equipment, a trader had to rely on either the newspaper or a broker for price information. The newspaper, of course, provides only the daily price range and the closing price, and brokers could not provide up-to-the-minute price information quickly enough to allow short-term trades to be made with confidence.

By purchasing a personal computer, some software, and the necessary equipment for data reception, as well as paying the required exchange fees, an individual can receive tick-by-tick price information as trading is being conducted. Tick-by-tick data is also available via the Internet. This makes it possible to day trade from home with confidence in the price information being used. As a consequence, day trading has become popular with a large group of traders who attempt to extract profits from the price moves that occur during the course of a trading day.

Most of the techniques for day trading are very similar to position trading—developing charts, trend lines, moving averages, and so forth—with the exception that the time periods used are much shorter, 30-minute or 60-minute periods versus daily charts. With the software currently available, the day trader need never keep a chart by hand again. There are systems that will run any of dozens of technical analyses on historical data as well as on current price data. There are also professionally developed trading systems that will provide real-time buy or sell signals to the day trader.

Anyone wishing to day trade in today's highly volatile futures markets, however, should do so with caution. Intraday trading requires a major commitment of time and concentration. A halfhearted attempt will almost certainly result in failure. Day trading can get expensive, with the investment in equipment and exchange subscription fees for price quotes, as well as commission fees on a large number of trades. In spite of the expense and the risk, however, a growing number of futures traders are choosing to day trade rather than to trade longer-term positions.

Among the factors that have made day trading popular among traders are:

- Price volatility has increased substantially and, with it, daily price ranges have become extremely large in some cases.

- The speed of information dissemination has made the financial world a very small place in comparison to what it was even ten years ago.

- The affordability and availability of high powered computers, data, and programs has allowed all traders access to information and analysis that puts them on the same level as most floor brokers.

- Speed of order execution has reduced the possibility of poor price fills.

- Discount commissions have substantially reduced the cost of doing business.

In highly volatile markets that make large moves up and down within a single day, day trading can be very profitable. But it can also lead to many losses, particularly if attempted by the novice trader who approaches the markets with limited capital and no definitive trading system or method.

The Pros of Day Trading

- Day trading, if done correctly, will force you to take your losses quickly.
- A good day trader can maximize results with very little initial margin.
- Feedback as to whether you are right or wrong comes quickly, often within minutes.
- Overnight news won't affect your positions, since you won't be carrying any positions beyond the day session close.
- It is easier to accurately predict very short-term price swings than it is to predict longer-term moves.
- Certain indicators, such as daily market sentiment, lend themselves readily to use by day traders and are prone to be more accurate for such short-term use than they are for position trading.
- Due to the volatile nature of markets, there are more day trading opportunities than there are position trading opportunities.

The Cons of Day Trading

- For the most part, day trading requires full attention.
- Some traders claim that day trading profits tend to be smaller on a per-trade basis than position trading profits.
- Day traders trade more frequently and therefore generate higher overall cost for a smaller return.
- Intraday moves are too much a function of traders' responses to news and, therefore, unpredictable.
- Floor traders have an advantage over the public in filling trades quickly.

The key point to keep in mind is that day trading can be very profitable, provided you have the emotional makeup, discipline, and methodology to do it consistently.

FUTURES OPTIONS TRADING

The newcomer to the world of futures trading is the futures option, which adds an entirely new dimension to the industry. Although the concept of trading futures options may initially seem confusing, it is really quite easy to understand if an individual already has a basic understanding of what a futures contract is.

Forget for a moment that an option on a futures contract is twice removed from the underlying commodity. Think instead of what an option really is: An option simply offers the buyer the choice of whether to take a futures position or not. In other words, a futures option gives the buyer of the option the right to buy or sell the underlying futures contract at a given price at some time in the future, regardless of what the actual price may be at that time.

The beauty of such an instrument is readily apparent. Once a speculator owns an option to buy or sell at an established price, he or she may then exercise that option if it becomes profitable to do so or not exercise it if it does not become profitable to do so. The decision as to whether to exercise the option provides a clear-cut choice: enter if there is a profit, stay out if there is not.

Historically, futures options have not enjoyed a particularly virtuous reputation. In the 1860s, the Chicago Board of Trade established a prohibition on options trading as a result of various abuses of the practice, a ruling that was reversed a few years later when a new board of governors assumed control. Futures options trading has since occurred intermittently, as supporters of options trading have often squared off against opponents of the practice. The long-running battle has spawned both lawsuits and legislation, as partisans on both sides have waged an intense war around the issue. Only recently has futures options trading become sufficiently regulated and standardized to hold a recognized position next to futures trading as a legitimate and respected economic activity.

Unfortunately, much of the tarnished reputation of futures options has been well earned. In 1936, options traders were implicated in a successful attempt to manipulate the markets at the CBOT. Throughout the 1930s, unregulated options trading was occurring both at the exchanges and off the floor of the exchanges. These option "privileges" generally had expiration dates that were only one to seven days removed, lending them the image of gambling and making them virtually useless to commercial interests that wished to shift longer-term risk. These options were subsequently banned by the Commodity Exchange Act. Then, during the early 1970s, several unscrupulous firms began selling London commodity options to unwary American speculators at extremely high markups while charging huge commissions. As a result, Congress considered banning the trading of all commodity options during its 1974 hearings, but changed its mind after hearing testimony from many sources in support of the economic benefits of commodity options trading. Since 1982, futures options trading has been allowed on organized U.S. exchanges under the watchful eye of the Commodity Futures Trading Commission.

One of the difficulties in trading in futures options is that an entirely new vocabulary is required if a trader is to get involved. The most important thing to remember is that there are two kinds of options: a put option and a call option. As the names suggest, a put option conveys the right to sell the underlying option, whereas a call option conveys the right to buy the underlying option. Either a put or a call option can be bought or sold, but buying one does not offset the purchase of the other. That is, the only way to offset an options position is to complete the opposite transaction with the same option: If a put option is bought, that same put option must be sold before the trader is out of the market.

Every option has a limited lifetime and is scheduled to expire at some specified time just prior to the scheduled delivery month of the underlying futures contract. This expiration date is set by the exchange.

The strike price, or exercise price, of the option is the price at which the buyer of the option may buy (with a call) or sell (with a put) the underlying commodity. The options trader does not have an unlimited choice of strike prices. Usually, the available strike prices for a particular option are listed by the exchange in standardized increments. The buyer must choose one of those standardized strike prices when buying the option.

To review the vocabulary so far, a put provides the right to sell the underlying commodity and a call provides the right to buy. The expiration date is the last day on which the option may be exercised. It is standardized and established by the exchange. The strike price, or exercise price, is the price at which the underlying commodity may be bought (call) or sold (put).

In trading commodity futures options, there are always both a buyer and a seller of the option. The buyer, as we have seen, buys the right (but not an obligation) to buy or sell the underlying commodity at a preestablished price (the strike price). The seller of the option (also known as the option writer) sells the option to the buyer. If the option buyer chooses to exercise the option, the seller of the option is obligated to take the opposite side of the underlying futures contract.

For example, if an options trader buys a put (the right to sell) for November soybeans at a strike price of $7 per bushel and three weeks later chooses to exercise the option when the price of soybeans goes to $6.50 per bushel, the seller of the option must then take the long position in the futures contract. In this situation, the option buyer, by going short at $7 (the option strike price), can offset that position by buying soybeans at $6.50 (the present market price), thus showing a profit of $0.50 per bushel, minus the cost of the option and the broker's commission. The seller of the option, however, has lost money on the futures transaction. Because he or she is a buyer of soybeans at $7 (the option strike price) and a seller at $6.50 (the market price), the loss is $0.50 per bushel. To offset part of that loss, however, the option seller has received payment for the option from the option buyer in the form of a premium.

Most options, however, are not exercised. Rather, they are traded as if they were commodities themselves. Therefore, instead of exercising the option when soybeans went to $6.50, as in the previous example, the option buyer would likely sell the option at that point, at a price that would reflect the additional value of the option. Who would buy the put option? Someone who thought the price of soybeans would go even lower.

In this example, it can readily be seen that the buyer of an option incurs a very limited risk—the cost of the option plus the broker's commission—while the option seller incurs unlimited risk—the same risk as a futures trader. Why would anyone become an option writer if the risk is so great? Certainly, the novice options trader should stay away from writing options. However, many experienced traders include option writing as part of an overall trading strategy.

Sometimes a trader will write an option while holding the opposite position in the futures market. This is called covered option writing. For example, a trader might buy one live cattle futures contract while selling one live cattle call. If the buyer of the call exercises the option, the option seller will be obligated to sell a live cattle future at the strike price. This futures position, however, is covered by the long position previously taken, thus limiting the risk associated with writing the call. An option not covered in this manner is called a naked option and obviously is a very risky maneuver.

When a trader buys an option, the price paid is called the premium. Supply and demand and the market forces in the pit determine the amount of the premium. There are, however, several factors that contribute to the value of the option.

The most obvious factor is the price of the underlying future. This is called the intrinsic value of the option. If, as in our previous example, soybeans are trading at $6.50, a $7 put has an intrinsic value of $0.50 times 5,000 bushels, equaling $2,500. If, however, soybeans are trading at $7.50, a $7 put has no intrinsic value. It is said to be out of the money. At $6.50, a $7 put is in the money. An in-the-money option, therefore, has intrinsic value equal to the difference between the strike price and the current market price of the future. An out-of-the-money option has no intrinsic value.

A second factor that adds value to an option is time. The further an option is from its expiration date, the greater the possibility that the market might move in the right direction and thus increase the intrinsic value of the option. Therefore, an out-of-the-money option with 60 days to expiration is worth more than an out-of-the money option with only 15 days to expiration.

A third factor contributing to the value of an option is the volatility of the market. The more volatile the market, the more an option buyer is willing to pay for an option in order to alleviate some of that risk. Conversely, an option writer must charge a higher premium to offset the greater risk taken by writing an option in a volatile market.

Computer programs are available that will help a trader figure the value of an option. In addition, many options traders use their own rule-of-thumb formulas to arrive at an approximate value of a given option. Anyone seriously interested in trading options would be well advised to read one or more of the many excellent books on options trading now on the market.

Margin in Options Trading

For an option buyer, there is no margin cost per se; there is only the cost of the premium plus commission costs. To many novice traders, this characteristic of options trading is very attractive. They can go to sleep at night without worrying whether they might receive a margin call in the morning.

An option seller, however, must post margin exactly as if he or she were trading a futures contract. The reason is clear: If the option buyer elects to exercise the option, the option writer immediately has a futures position and probably at a loss, since the buyer would not likely exercise unless there was a profit to be made.

Exit Alternatives

The option seller, or writer, has no discretionary choices available once the option is sold and the premium has been received. From that point on, all of the decision-making power lies with the buyer, who has three choices. First, the buyer of an option can simply allow the option to expire worthless. This alternative would be chosen if the option remained out-of-the-money and therefore never attained any intrinsic value.

A second alternative is to offset the option by selling an identical option, just as one would do in a futures contract. Remember, however, that to offset an option, the identical option must be sold. A put does not offset a call or vice versa. Likewise, selling an option at a different strike price does not offset the original option. The only way to offset an option that has been purchased is to sell an identical option at the same strike price.

The third alternative available to an option buyer is to exercise the option. This alternative would be chosen if, as in the soybean example, the option is far enough in the money that its intrinsic value exceeds the original cost of the premium and commission. The strategy would be to exercise the option, then offset the futures position, and take the profits.

Advantages of Options Trading

Trading in options offers several advantages to trading in the underlying futures. The most popular and popularized advantage, of course, is that an option has limited and known risk. The option buyer risks only the cost of premium plus commission. The worst that can happen is that the option expires worthless and the entire original investment is lost; but there is never a margin call.

A second advantage that options trading offers is leverage. It is possible to buy an out-of-the-money option with 60 days to expiration for $300 to $800. If the market makes a fairly good move during that 60 days, the option can provide profits of several thousand dollars.

A third advantage of options trading is staying power. If a trader is convinced that a certain market is due for a major bull market move, he or she might buy a call rather than taking a long futures position, with the idea that if, in the short term, the market goes lower before embarking on its run up, there will not be the risk of excessive margin calls or, worse yet, the necessity to get out of the market at a loss because of dwindling capital.

For hedgers, options are particularly attractive because, especially in a volatile market, they can preserve needed capital if prices move too far in the wrong direction. If a futures position is held as a hedge, an adverse move can result in substantial margin calls, thereby tying up additional capital. With an option, however, only the original cost of the premium is invested.

Disadvantages of Options Trading

Naturally, any speculative venture that can be packaged and sold as attractively as options can must have a down side, and options certainly do. All of those brokers who extol options as a wonderful investment because of their limited risk factor neglect to mention that it is just as hard, if not harder, to make money in options trading as it is in futures trading. Although the loss exposure is limited and known, a loss is still a loss, and several limited losses in a row add up to a large loss.

Limited risk doesn't mean the trader can't lose money; it only means that he or she knows up front how much can be lost. Profitable options trading, as with all futures trading, requires strategy and discipline. The risk with options, however, is that a trader can be lulled into a false sense of security and therefore neglect to keep a watchful eye on the market.

Another concern with buying options is that, to show profits, prices must move far enough to first cover the cost of the premium. Thus, many small price changes that would have been profitable to a futures trader can turn out to be unprofitable to an option buyer. In soybeans, for example, if a trader buys a put option at a strike price of $6.50 and pays $460 premium plus 20 percent commission ($92) when beans are trading for $7, the price of beans would have to fall below $6.39 before any profit would be made. (A one-cent move in soybeans is $50. The cost of premium plus commission is $552.00. If beans fall 11 cents below $6.50, the strike price, the option would show sufficient intrinsic value to cover most of that cost.) Had a trader simply sold short at $7, the same move would have netted $3,050 minus commissions.

A final disadvantage to options trading is the high cost of commissions. Because options traders are usually taking a long-term position, the volume of trading in an individual account is not high, causing brokers to charge higher commission rates for option trades. Some brokers charge unwary clients as much as 40 percent of the premium as a commission. On a $2,000 premium, that amounts to $800 in commission costs. Other brokers charge only their standard commission fee. Anyone wishing to trade options would be well advised to shop around for a broker who provides the desired level of service at a reasonable commission rate. Otherwise, the only one making money might be the options broker.

Some Strategies for Trading Options

Options trading offers a plethora of trading strategies, ranging from the most elementary to some that are quite esoteric and sophisticated. The reader is cautioned to consult a more thorough text on options trading before attempting any sophisticated trades. Nevertheless, some of the more popular strategies are presented here as examples of what can be done with options alone or with options and futures together.

Strategy 1: Long Call

Buy a call option rather than going long. Although this strategy seems simple enough, even a plan this elementary requires some decision making and some knowledge of the market. If a trader expects a short-term move, he or she might buy an in-the-money option or one that is near the money. Although they cost more, such options will move at the same rate as or faster than the underlying future. Alternatively, a trader might buy an option further from the money by virtue of its nearer expiration or larger distance from the strike price. Although such options may cost less, they may move only one-third as quickly as the underlying contract.

The ratio between the price move of the futures and the price move of the option is known as the delta. A futures contract has a delta of one: Each time the price moves one cent, the value of the contract position moves one cent. An option with a delta of 0.33 moves approximately one-third as fast as the underlying contract. To make informed decisions about the best strategy to pursue, in even a plan as simple as this, it is wise to use an options evaluation program.

Strategy 2: Long Put

Buy a put option rather than selling short. As with the first strategy, several alternatives are available for an expected short-term move or a longer-term move.

Strategy 3: Synthetic Long Call

Use a put option to protect a long futures position. To an extent, this is a spread strategy. If the market shows an extended rise in price, the futures position will show significant profits, and the cost of the protection is limited to the options premium plus commission. If prices fall, however, the option will increase in value as the futures contract declines, although not necessarily on a par. Remember that time decay is also a factor in the value of an option.

Strategy 4: Synthetic Long Put

Sell short the futures while buying a call for protection. The opposite of strategy 3, this works very similarly to buying a put, and it requires the right combination of strike price and expiration to provide protection.

Strategy 5: Long Straddle

If a major move is expected, but the direction is impossible to predict, buy both a put and a call. With this plan, the only way to suffer a loss is if the market fails to make the expected move during the life span of the two options.

Strategy 6: Covered Option

Sell a call or a put, but cover the position with the opposite futures position. If a call is sold, cover with a short futures position. If a put is sold, cover with a long futures position.

Strategy 7: Butterfly Spread

Buy a nearby option, buy a deferred option, and sell two midterm options for a long butterfly. Sell the ends and buy the middle for a short butterfly. This spread strategy can combine exceptionally low risk with tremendous profit potential, if the timing is correct and the market has been conceptualized accurately. For this strategy to work, there must be a differential in long-, short-, and intermediate-term movements. This set of circumstances can occur quite easily in the interest rate market when short-term rates decline while long-term rates hold steady or when long-term rates decline while short-term rates go up.

Strategy 8: Short Straddle

Sell both a put and a call. Used when volatility is declining, this strategy allows a trader to collect both premiums. Maximum profit is earned if the options expire while the futures price and the strike price are the same.

Strategy 9: Long Strangle

Buy a put and a call that have different strike prices but a common expiration date. Similar to a straddle, which consists of buying options with the same strike price and expiration date, the purpose of a strangle is the same: to be positioned when a major breakout occurs.

Strategy 10: Short Strangle

Sell a put and a call with different strike prices and a common expiration date. Like a short straddle, this strategy is designed to profit from markets with low volatility. This position creates unlimited risk, however.

MARKET ANALYSIS

In order to determine the probable direction of a market, traders use various forms of market analysis. The idea behind market analysis is to find trades that are likely to be profitable. Of course, the key word here is "likely," because the process of selecting a trade or making a forecast involves a method of analysis that is not always correct.

In analyzing a market for the purpose of selecting trades, the trader is making an educated guess based on a system, method, or procedure that supposedly has had a successful record in the past. The process that is used in making decisions about what to buy or sell and when to buy or sell is known as market analysis. There are two types of market analysis, technical analysis and fundamental analysis; and there are combinations of both.

Methods and Systems of Market Analysis

In the pursuit of profits and high accuracy, commodity (and stock) traders often develop systems and methods of market analysis. Such methods can vary in complexity from the ultrasimple to the highly intricate. They can be run on a computer or they can be determined manually. The decision is entirely up to the trader. There are literally hundreds (if not thousands) of trading systems and methods. Some are worth pursuing, but most are worthless. Be very careful in selecting a system or method. Consult Chapters 10 and 11 for more information. The selection of a system or method is critically important.

The Advantages and Disadvantages of Systems

Systems trading has its good points as well as its liabilities. Among the major positive points is the fact that a trading system will keep you objective and focused on the markets. You will have a specific set of rules to follow, and you will have specific ideas on managing your risk, in addition to several other aspects that are important in the quest for profitable trading.

The disadvantage of a trading system is that it is rigid and often inflexible. It requires you to follow its signals. Some traders claim that a rigid approach will not work. Others disagree. You must decide for yourself, based on the information in this book, your experience, and the information you will get from other books, courses, and traders.

Categories of Systems

Trading systems fall into several categories:

- Trend following systems,
- Breakout systems,
- Market pattern systems,
- Support and resistance systems,
- Swing trading systems,
- Artificial intelligence systems, and
- Market structure systems.

Each system has its specific theory, rationale, rules, and methods. Within each of the above general categories you will find many different systems. The problem for the trader is finding systems and methods that make money. Profitable systems are few and far between. They are neither easy to develop nor easy to find. Hopefully the information presented in this book will help you find winning systems.

TECHNICAL VERSUS FUNDAMENTAL TRADING

In the futures and stock markets, the fundamentalist point of view focuses exclusively on economically based indicators, which are believed to facilitate the process of price forecasting or trade selection. The various fundamental indices are incorporated either individually or in combination to arrive at trading decisions. Such basic factors are crop size, weather conditions, supply and demand statistics, economic forecasts, and interest rate trends. Federal Reserve policy, export statistics, plantings, breeding, intentions, housing starts, cross-currency rates, government programs, and consumption are also taken into account. The essence of this approach is to determine the balance of supply and demand in order to determine how that balance will affect future prices.

The purpose of fundamental analysis is to determine what the price of a given stock or futures market may be in several days, weeks, months, or years. The accuracy of the decisions depends to a great extent on the availability and accuracy of information. It also depends to a certain degree upon the prevalence of "normal" conditions. Any exaggerated shift or aberration in conditions can distort the data and, therefore, the outcome as well.

Real estate investors are subject to the same limitations and potential problems when analyzing fundamentals. There may be new fundamentals that have not played an important role in the past, or not all of the fundamentals may be known. Furthermore, the fundamentals may be incorrect or may be incorrectly interpreted.

The technician, on the other hand, makes judgments by purely mechanical or mathematical rules. The technician is not concerned with the economy, supply, demand, crop size, earnings, or weather. Technicians study specific chart formations, mathematical indicators, moving average signals, geometric formations, cyclical events, and so forth. Even those who trade the markets according to astrology are technicians of sorts, because they follow very specific guidelines in arriving at decisions. Insofar as they are true to their principles, technicians do not consider any inputs other than their data when reaching trading decisions. The avowed chartist is a technician dedicated to following specific kinds of chart patterns. Chartists ideally refuse to waste time either reading or discussing the fundamentals. Such information can only confuse the issue.

Being a market technician has certain advantages: It permits greater objectivity, it allows for more mechanical execution of trades, and it deals with the true data and its derivatives—namely, prices, volume, and open interest—and mathematical derivations of these indicators. On the negative side, the technical approach isolates the trader from worldwide events, which can and do affect markets significantly. For the technician, this limitation is more of an asset than a liability inasmuch as it excludes from the calculations unquantifiable fundamental developments.

Ultimately, the relative success of each market orientation seems to be more a function of the trader than of the approach itself. In fact, despite the seeming objectivity of technical trading rules and of fundamental statistics, the end result is almost entirely dependent on who interprets the data.

CHAPTER 7

Hedging with Spreads

In previous chapters, I gave you a cursory explanation of hedging and risk transfer. Now that you have more knowledge of orders, position trading, the differences between a buy (long) position and a sell (short) position, and how a sell and buy balance each other, a more thorough discussion of hedging is in order. The basic purpose for the existence of futures trading is the transfer of risk from producers and users of a commodity to speculators (futures traders). When a businessperson uses the futures market to protect against adverse price movements, the process is called hedging.

Hedging involves taking a position in the futures market that is opposite to the position held in the cash or spot market. In other words, if a businessperson owns or buys a commodity in the cash market, he or she would then hedge that position by selling an equivalent quantity in the futures market. This selling hedge locks in a price for that inventory while it is being held.

If prices go down during the time the commodity is being held, the holder of the commodity loses money in the cash market.

However, an equivalent price drop in the futures market allows the businessperson, by virtue of being a seller, to realize a profit. This profit offsets the loss in the cash market and maintains the net price to the holder at a level very close to the original value of the commodity.

Likewise, if the price of the commodity rises, the holder will show a profit in the cash market and an offsetting loss in the futures market, maintaining the value of the inventory at a constant net value.

The buying hedge is used by a businessperson who anticipates buying a commodity at a future date and wants protection from a possible price increase. This person is said to be short the cash market (he or she is "short" of the commodity at the present time) and so would take a long position in the futures market (be a buyer). If prices do go up, this person will have to pay more for the commodity but at the same time will make an equivalent amount in the futures market, thus offsetting the loss in the cash market. If prices decline, the commodity can be bought more cheaply in the cash market, but this advantage is offset by a loss in the futures market.

Hedging, then, not only protects against the possible losses from adverse price movement; it also takes away the possibility of windfall profits that can accrue as the result of favorable price moves. To the cautious businessperson, however, such potential profits represent too great a risk and are best transferred to the speculator.

In theory, hedging provides ideal price protection to the businessperson, but in practice this protection may be less than ideal. A number of factors can affect the net value of the hedge, and they often do.

When we began our discussion of hedging, we assumed that cash prices and futures prices would move together at exactly the same rate. In practice, this rarely occurs. Conditions in the spot market can pressure prices up or down while not affecting the more distant futures months. Also, local conditions can affect the local cash price while the futures price, which reflects national and international conditions, is unaffected.

The difference between the futures price and the spot price is known as the basis. For a hedge to work perfectly, the basis must remain constant to the end of the hedge. Thus, if the difference between spot corn and December corn futures is 2 cents when the hedge is put on, the basis must also be 2 cents when the hedge is lifted and the corn is sold, if the hedge is to work perfectly.

In fact, the basis will likely change, and the change in the basis will result in either fewer profits or more profits for the hedger. If the local spot price of corn, for example, declines 20 cents by the time it is sold, but the futures price declines only 15 cents, then 5 cents per bushel is left unprotected, as the basis changed by 5 cents. Table 7-1 demonstrates the results.

Table 7-1: Base Example

Date	Cash	March Futures	Basis
November	$5.30/bushel	$5.47/bushel	$-0.17
February	$5.10/bushel	$5.22/bushel	$-0.12
Gain or Loss	$-0.20	$-0.15	

Various factors can cause a differential between cash and futures prices. First, there are many grades of each commodity traded on the cash market, and each grade changes price at a different rate. A futures contract, however, is limited to one specified grade. It may be that the price of the grade being hedged moves more quickly on the spot market than the grade covered by the futures contract. Second, local cash prices may reflect local market conditions that do not affect futures prices, which are indicative of national and international conditions. Third, more distant futures months are less affected by current market conditions than are spot prices. Fourth, the commodity being hedged may not be exactly the same as the commodity covered by the futures contract. A clothing manufacturer, for example, may want to hedge the price of yarn in the cotton futures market, but the price of yarn, because it reflects different manufacturing costs than the price of cotton, may not fluctuate exactly with cotton prices.

A further limitation of hedging is that the futures contract covers a specified quantity, which may be different from the size of the inventory being hedged. If a farmer expects to sell 18,000 bushels of corn, for example, he or she is only able to hedge 15,000 bushels by selling three contracts of corn. The remaining 3,000

bushels are unprotected. If the farmer decided to sell four contracts, the additional 2,000 bushels would be a speculative investment. Either way, there is some risk left untransferred.

Hedging, then, covers only major risk factors for individuals
and companies engaged in various business ventures. It does not
provide complete insurance, but it does significantly reduce the
price risks associated with doing business. Hedging is essentially
the exchange of one kind of risk, price fluctuation, for another,
basis fluctuation.

SPREADS AND STRADDLES

Just as there is often a differential between the cash price and the
futures price of a commodity, so is there often a difference in the
price fluctuations of various contract months of the same commodity or in the fluctuation of price of one commodity traded on
different exchanges. This price differential can result from any
number of circumstances.

In a normal market, the price of the spot month, or the contract month closest to delivery, is usually quite close to the cash
price of the same commodity, even though, as we have seen, there
may be some variance. This phenomenon is easy to explain and is
a logical consequence of the fact that a futures contract can be held
to delivery.

If the price differential between a futures contract at expiration and the spot price of the same commodity were significant, a
trader could easily make money by moving between the two markets. If, for example, the futures price of corn at expiration is 10
cents higher than the cash price, a speculator could simply sell
corn on the futures market, buy corn on the cash market, and make
delivery of the cash corn to fulfill the futures contract obligation.
The result would be a risk-free profit of 10 cents per bushel, less
commissions and transaction fees.

Likewise, if the futures price is 10 cents lower, a speculator
can buy on the futures market, take delivery, then resell on the cash
market for a 10-cent profit. Dealing with the cash market is not as
difficult as it sounds. Usually, it involves simply the exchange of
warehouse receipts.

In a normal market, also, the price of each succeeding contract month after the spot month is higher than the price of the contract immediately preceding it. This normal price increase, called a premium, represents the carrying charges involved in holding a commodity in inventory—charges such as storage fees, interest on the capital invested in the commodity, and insurance against loss. Thus, a normal market is also commonly referred to as a carrying-charge market.

Sometimes, however, a market becomes inverted, or backward, and the price of each successive contract month is lower rather than higher. They are said to be at a discount to the front month. This usually results from buying pressure on the cash market, which drives prices up and thereby encourages those who are holding the commodity in storage to sell rather than to hold.

This situation is also known as a short squeeze and can result either from normal market conditions (e.g., a temporary shortage) or an attempt by some individual or group of individuals to corner the market by buying all available supplies, thus driving prices up artificially and putting the squeeze on those who must purchase the commodity (the shorts). These kinds of market conditions can provide opportunities for lower-risk profits to the astute spread trader, although spread trading is not necessarily less risky than trading outright positions.

A spread is simply the simultaneous buying of one contract and selling of another. To be a true spread, however, there must be some reason to believe that the conditions that will cause price movement in one contract will also cause price movement in the other.

There are two types of spreads:

1. *Intracommodity Spread:* First, there is the intramarket spread, in which positions are taken in two contract months of the same commodity. If a trader notes, for example, that the price differential between May corn and July corn exceeds normal carrying charges (July is at a premium to May), he or she might buy a contract for May corn and sell a contract for July corn. Later, as the differential narrows to bring the July corn contract more into line with normal costs, the trader will realize a profit on the change in the difference. The intramarket spread trader is not con-

cerned with the absolute price of a commodity, only the changes that occur in the premium or discount.

2. *Intercommodity Spread:* The second type of spread is known as the intercommodity spread. As the name implies, this is a spread between two different commodities—buying one and selling the other. Again, to be a true spread, there must be some relationship between the two commodities that will tend to cause the prices to move in the same direction simultaneously. If they do not, the spread becomes a dangerously risky trade, as the two positions can easily move in opposite directions, incurring losses on both trades. Such movement, of course, defeats the purpose of spread trading. In a typical spread, one of the trades will show a loss while the other will show a profit. The profit to the trader occurs when the relative difference between the two prices (the premium or discount) changes in a favorable direction.

In certain markets, there are relationships between commodities that will allow true spread trading. Among the grains, for example, corn may become a substitute for beans as a feed if the price of beans gets too high, and vice versa. Thus, the prices tend to move together. Another common intercommodity spread is the crush spread, which is a trade involving soybeans and its two derivatives, soybean meal and soybean oil. When the beans are crushed, they produce meal and oil. In all such intercommodity spreads, there is a natural relationship that tends to limit the magnitude of the price differential between the commodities. To profit from such a relationship, however, the spread trader must know the history and the characteristics of the relationship.

Another intercommodity spread relationship exists when one commodity is traded on different exchanges, such as Kansas City wheat, CBOT wheat, and Minneapolis wheat. This is also an intermarket spread. Whenever the price difference for a commodity between two exchanges exceeds the normal cost of transporting the commodity from one delivery point to the other, there is every reason to believe that the differential will narrow at some time in the future to reflect the true delivery cost. If wheat were selling at a significantly higher price in Chicago than in Kansas City, for example, merchants would buy the wheat in Kansas City and ship the wheat to Chicago to sell it, if the price difference exceeded the transportation costs.

Also, producers would ship to Chicago rather than Kansas City to sell their wheat if the price there would pay all shipping charges and still show a higher return. This relationship tends to limit the difference in prices that can occur among the various exchanges and thus presents a potential spread opportunity any time the price differential exceeds transportation costs between two exchanges.

TRADING SPREADS

Although spreads are among the most consistent and reliable of all trading methods, few traders recognize their value. This has been the case for many years and it's not about to change. Although traders are always searching for the best trading tools and systems, they often overlook techniques that have had a history of good reliability.

Spreads are among my favorite vehicles. Some spreads have exhibited high reliability and strong seasonal tendencies for many years.

As noted in my book, *Weekly Seasonal Spread Charts* (MBH, 1999), commodity traders often ignore the spread as a speculative vehicle, considering it more the domain of professional commercial interests. Spreads, however, offer greater potential for profit and higher reliability than net positions in the futures markets, particularly when the seasonal or cyclic tendencies of spreads are studied and used advantageously.

There are those who say that spread trading also involves less risk than trading in net positions, but this is a gross misstatement of the facts. Although there are some seasonal commodity spreads that are inherently less risky than certain net market positions, there are other extremely high-risk spreads at the opposite end of the continuum. As with all futures trading, spread trading remains a high-risk, high-reward venture.

Profits in spread trading are made in one of three ways:

- The short position makes more money than the long position loses during the period of time the contracts are held; or
- The long position makes more money than the short position loses during the time the contracts are held; or
- Both positions make money.

Losses occur in just the opposite fashion:

- The short position loses more money than the long position makes; or
- The long position loses more than the short position makes; or
- Both positions lose money.

Another name for a commodity spread is straddle, which states in a more concise fashion the exact nature of a spread. With a spread, the trader is effectively straddling the market, very much like a rider straddles a horse: with one leg on each side of the saddle. In fact, a popular phrase in commodity trading is "lifting one leg" of a spread, which refers to the action of exiting one position while leaving the other position on, thereby remaining net long or net short, depending on which side of the spread or straddle was exited.

Why Trade Spreads?

There are a number of reasons for trading spreads.

1. *Spreads are often very reliable from the standpoint of seasonality.* In other words, some of the most reliable and repetitive seasonal moves have occurred in spreads. Certain spreads move in given directions a majority of the time during certain times of the year. Although spreads aren't 100 percent reliable, they do show strong seasonality.

2. *Spread margins are generally very low or even zero,* depending on the type of spread and the brokerage house you're dealing with. Hence, you can get more leverage with spreads. As a result, spreads are good vehicles for new traders who may have limited margin funds to commit to the futures markets.

3. *Some (but not all) spreads are lower in risk than either long or short positions.* But there are some spreads that are very volatile, so don't conclude that all spreads are lower in risk than flat positions.

4. *There are a number of good timing indicators* for entering and exiting spreads.

Margin Requirements on Spreads

Exchange margins for certain recognized spreads are often considerably lower than the margin required for net futures positions. Many intracommodity spreads have extremely low margins or margins that are "marked to the market." In other words, there is no specific margin on these spreads. This reflects the exchange's belief that a spread is generally less risky than a net position, because the potential losses in one position are at least partially covered by the potential gains in the other.

Certainly, in an ideal spread situation, as prices of one leg of the spread change, the prices of the other leg change at nearly the same rate and in the same direction, so that the losses incurred by one side are offset by the gains in the other while the premium or discount changes advantageously in order to provide profits to the trader.

Low margin requirements, however, can lure a trader into a false sense of security. For one thing, as with all futures trading, the trade might move disadvantageously before it makes the right move. A trader who has met only the minimum margin requirements might find that such a move necessitates a margin call or, worse yet, a forced liquidation of both positions at a loss. A good strategy for avoiding such a circumstance is to maintain at least twice the minimum margin required in the trading account in order to provide plenty of leeway for each position.

Commissions on Spreads

Spread trading is by its nature often a low-profit trade. Because profits accrue not from the magnitude of the price move in the market but from the change in the difference in prices between two positions, the potential for large profits on any one trade is minimal. Many spread trades accrue profits of only $200 to $300. If the brokerage fee is $15 to $100 per side, then the net profit from the trade can be quite small. It behooves the spread trader to trade spreads that have a sufficiently high profit potential or to pay lower commissions.

Spreads As an Index to Market Behavior

Spreads can often be helpful in determining the validity of net market trends, even when the spreads are not traded themselves. Most spreads tend to divide themselves into bull or bear categories quite readily. Thus, in a typical bull market, the nearby contract month is likely to gain over the deferred contract month. Conversely, a bear spread and a bear market go hand in hand, wherein the nearby contract month tends to lose to the distant contract month, a situation that tends to continue throughout the span of the bear trend.

Thus, market technicians and fundamentalists alike use spread behavior as an index to the present and future direction of the markets. The assumption is that the majority of traders interested in spreads are professionals, and when these professionals, for example, begin accumulating nearby months while selling the distant months, their behavior is based on extensive fundamental knowledge of the markets and is reflected in the changing spread relationship.

Market Research and Study

The fact is that, with some quality assistance from one or more good sources, spread trading is probably a better strategy for the part-time trader who has little time to watch the markets than is net position trading. Conducting the research necessary to locate good potential spread trades is somewhat easier than doing the technical or fundamental analysis necessary to trade net positions successfully. This does not mean that profits are any easier to come by—they're not. The education and preparation necessary for effective spread trading is just as critical as with all futures trading. But with the market information available to the average part-time trader, who depends on the newspaper and a broker for price information, spread trading may be easier to do profitably.

Still, maintaining current information on all the potential spreads is probably unrealistic for most part-time traders, or full-time traders for that matter, unless they have a computer system that can regularly update charts.

THE SEASONAL SPREAD

One way of analyzing spreads is the seasonal method. This is not a technical method, but rather a method based on the history of spreads. By looking at the behavior of a given spread over a period of many years, we can construct a chart that shows us how a spread has acted during the year and how often, in terms of percentage of time, it has moved in a given direction.

The Seasonal Spread Chart is the tool I use to isolate seasonal patterns in spreads. The patterns we look at are those that have shown a tendency to repeat more often than not.

Weekly Seasonal Spread Composite Charts

The spreads I'll be discussing are shown in weekly composite chart form. These charts show all years of the spread in our historical database collapsed into one chart.

Take a few minutes to examine the chart shown in Figure 7-1. It illustrates the information that's available from the Seasonal Spread Composite Chart. Refer to this guide when you look at the other charts in this chapter. The most important thing is to compare the composite chart with the current spread trend of the market. See how closely the current spread is behaving to its composite; then make a decision as to what you ought to do.

Reading the Charts

The following explanations can save you considerable time and frustration as you study and learn how to use these charts. Refer to the sample composite chart in Figure 7-1 as you read these instructions.

1. *Name of the Spread Shown:* This line lists the contract month and spread that is plotted.

Figure 7-1: Weekly Seasonal Spread Composite Chart

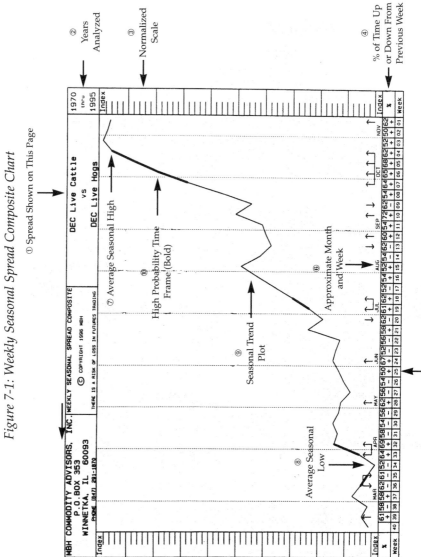

① Spread Shown on This Page

② Years Analyzed

③ Normalized Scale

④ % of Time Up or Down From Previous Week

⑤ Week Number

⑥ Approximate Month and Week

⑦ Average Seasonal High

⑧ Average Seasonal Low

⑨ Seasonal Trend Plot

⑩ High Probability Time Frame (Bold)

2. *Years Covered:* For example, "1967 through 1996" means that these years were used in preparing this chart. When a market has not been actively traded for very many years, there is less of a database and therefore less reliability.

3. *Scale:* This is the normalized rate of change index, which is used as a reference point. The scale values are not shown; they would be essentially meaningless inasmuch as they are of no specific value in using the seasonal trends other than to indicate the average magnitude of change.

4. *Percentage of Years Up or Down and Arrows:* These figures show the weekly percentage of time up or down, for the specific week number listed under the percentage reading. If the data plot (see #9) for a given week is up from the previous plot, and the reading is, say, +75 percent, then this is an indication of upward seasonality for the indicated spread.

   Percentage readings from +59 percent to +100 percent indicate reliable bullish seasonals, and percentage readings from −59 percent to −100 percent indicate reliable bearish seasonals. Arrows up mark strong periods of bullish seasonality and arrows down mark periods of bearish seasonality

   Note also the following conditions:

   a. *Plot Is Down and Percentage Reading Is +59 Percent or Higher:* This means that the spread tends to move up during this approximate week more years than it moves down; however, the usual down move is much larger than the net up move, thereby accounting for the down plot. Upside potential during such weeks may be small in terms of magnitude, although upside moves can be large.

   b. *Plot Is Down and Percentage Reading Is −59 Percent or More Negative:* This means that the spread has moved down 60 percent or more of the time for this approximate week during the years examined, and that the size of the decline during down years is generally larger than the size of the rally during up years.

   c. *Plot Is Up and Percentage Reading Is −59 Percent or More Negative:* This is an indication that even though most years are down, for those years that were up, the moves were relatively large. If you sell short on this type of combination you can expect a potentially small but reliable profit.

d. *Plot Is Unchanged (Sideways) from Previous Week:* This is
an indication that the magnitude or size of the move for
this appropriate week is in equal balance between up
and down. This does not necessarily mean a sideways
trend for the week. Trend can only be determined by the
accompanying percentage reading. If it is +59 percent or
higher, then you can expect generally higher prices. If it
is –59 percent or more negative, you can expect a down
move. The sideways plot means only that the up and
down moves are about equal in size.

5. *Week Number* is indicated under the percentage probability
reading. The week number tells us how many weeks are
left to contract expiration. These are full weeks. The last full
week of trading would read '1' since it is the final full week
in the life of the contract. A reading of 34, for example,
means that this is approximately the 34th week prior to
contract expiration.

These figures are important in calculating the week number
according to exchange expiration dates for any given year.
Note that these week numbers will allow you to determine
relative time for any year. Remember that the month listings
and number of weeks per month are approximate and that
the actual weeks will change somewhat each year.

6. *Month and Week* are indicated by the listings shown. Please
note that the number of weeks in any given month, using
Friday as the last day of a week, will vary from year to year.
Sometimes November has five Fridays, and in other years
it has four. The weeks listed are only reference points. If
you wish to adapt your chart for other trading years, simply determine when the given contract is due to expire and
work backward, using the trading week as a guide.

Once you have learned to use these charts you will find
that it is not necessary to pinpoint the exact week. If a given
market is conforming well to its seasonal trend, you can
superimpose actual weekly prices onto the seasonal chart
to see whether there is a timing lead or lag. A clear acetate
sheet can be used for this purpose.

7. *Average Seasonal Spread High* is indicated by the highest plot
on the chart. This means that during the years under study,

there has been a tendency for prices to hit their contract high around this week or month. If a high is made during the last few weeks of a contract, then prices may move even higher several months thereafter, and the next contract month should be checked for this possibility. If a seasonal high is associated with high readings in the percentage column, and if a subsequent move to the downside occurs with equally reliable readings, then this is most likely a highly reliable seasonal top.

8. *Average Seasonal Spread Low:* The explanation given for season high holds true for seasonal low, only in reverse.

9. *Plot:* This line shows the weekly composite seasonal tendency for the indicated spread.

10. *Bold Line:* The bold or thick part of the line plot shows reliable seasonal moves that correspond to the arrows in item 4 (percentage of years up or down).

SAMPLE SPREAD CHARTS

The charts in Figures 7-2 to 7-5 offer good examples of spread relationships. Figure 7-2 shows a situation in which the long leg made more profit than the short leg lost; in other words, the chart shows the spread differential as it moves higher. The scale at left is not a price scale per se but rather a price difference scale. As long as the scale remains in positive territory, it is an indication that the long contract month is gaining over the short contract month.

Figure 7-3 shows the opposite situation. The scale at left indicates that the spread is trading in minus territory, which means that the short contract month is trading at a higher price than the long contract month in this period. In other words, the deferred contract month is at a premium to the nearby contract month, whereas in the situation in Figure 7-2 the nearby contract month was trading at a premium to the deferred contract month. In the case of Figure 7-3, money will be made on the spread if one is short the nearby contract month and long the distant contract month.

Figures 7-4 and 7-5 show the same basic relationship in commodity spreads but in different markets—December Treasury Bills vs. December EuroDollar and June Swiss Franc vs. June British Pound.

Figure 7-2: August Live Cattle vs. August Live Hogs

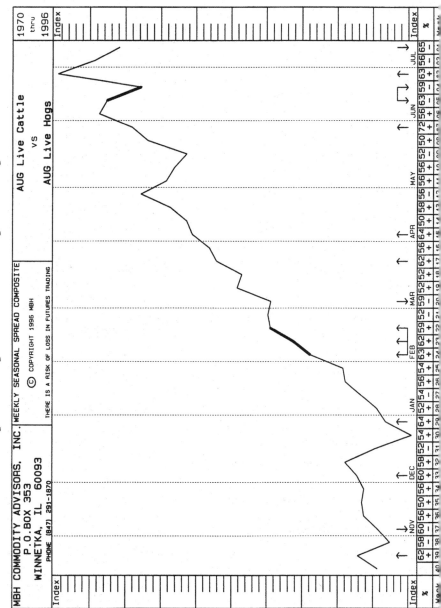

Figure 7-3: December Corn vs. May Corn

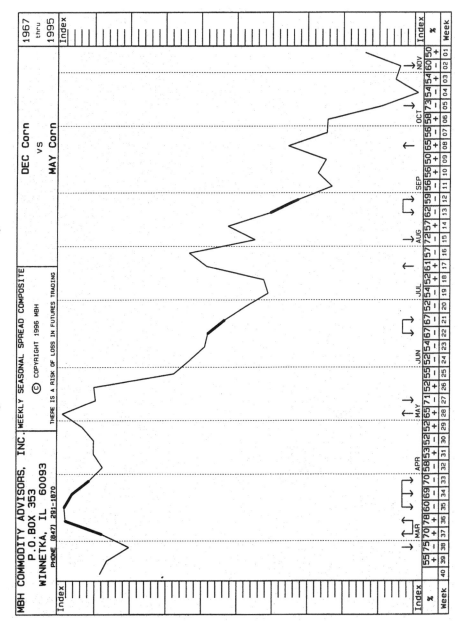

Figure 7-4: December Treasury Bills vs. December EuroDollar

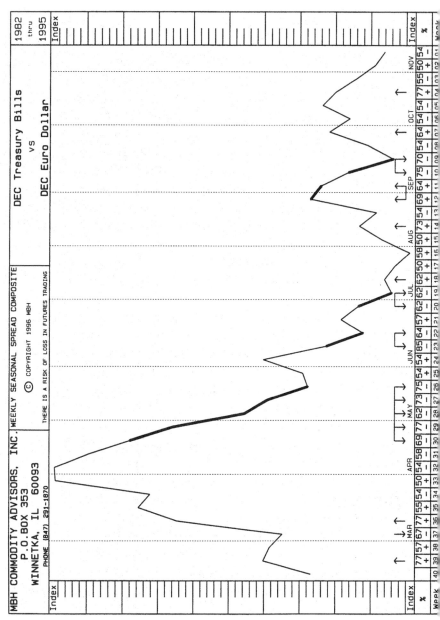

142

Figure 7-5: June Swiss Franc vs. June British Pound

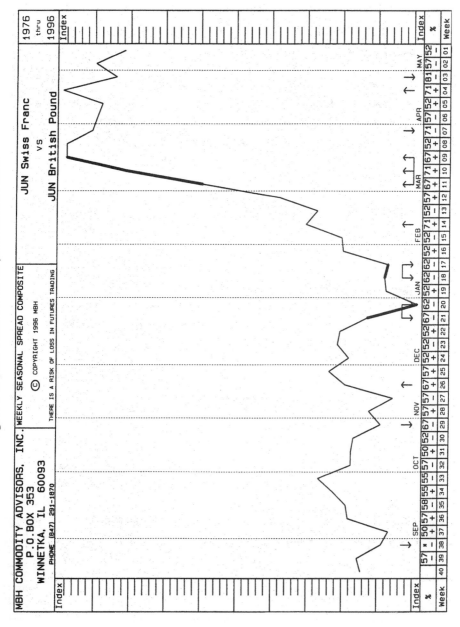

143

SPREAD ENTRY AND EXIT

The most difficult part of any trading, whether spread or net position, is actual market entry. Charts and calculations may indicate substantial profits to be made by various spread strategies, but unless the spread is entered at the right price, it might turn out to be a low-profit or even a losing trade, no matter how good it looks on paper. Market entry, however, is a move that requires both skill and a touch of artistry.

For many reasons, both psychological and technical, order placement is perhaps the greatest obstacle standing in the way of successful trading. The time that elapses from identifying a signal to actual market entry can be critical. Thus, a successful spread trader must know the various entry and exit orders available for spreads and the advantages and disadvantages of each.

Entry at the Market

The most certain way to establish a spread (or net position) is to enter at the market. Although this procedure may not cause problems in most net positions, it can account for especially poor price fills in spreads. In order to appreciate why spread price fills can be especially poor when done at the market, it is important to understand how the floor trader executing a spread order fulfills that obligation. Because most pit brokers (floor traders) are extremely busy and because they cannot be in two places in the pit at once, it is not incumbent upon them to shop around for the best possible spread price. If an order is given to them at the market and market volume is especially thin (low), they will simply execute at the going price. When the market is thinly traded, the going price on the long side will be higher than expected, and the going price on the short side will be lower than expected. Hence, a trader can come out behind in two ways. Instead of getting just one poor price fill, as in a net position, the trader will end up with two poor price fills at a spread differential that is usually not close to what was expected. The thinner the market, the more likely you are to get a poor fill. Whether entering or exiting a market, a trader should use market orders only as a last choice.

The only advantage of a market order is that it guarantees a position unless a market is locked at limit. There are a few conditions, however, under which a market order is advisable. For example, if an ideal opportunity to enter or to exit a given spread has been missed; if a stop point has been penetrated and it is important to exit the market immediately; or if a spread position has been carried into the delivery period and it is absolutely necessary to liquidate in order to avoid delivery, a market order is justified. In any event, the rule of thumb is that entry at the market or exit at the market almost always guarantees a poor price fill.

Legging In and Legging Out

A common but not necessarily wise procedure for spread entry and exit is the legging in and legging out procedure. As the term implies, this technique involves entering a spread one side, or leg, at a time or exiting a spread one side, or leg, at a time. Typically, a spread is legged in or out by traders who have been carrying a net position that went against them and who then spread the position up in order to avoid further loss. Hence, they have legged into a spread many times with good reason, and when it comes time to close out one side of a spread, they leg out. This is a technique that can not only complicate matters but also increase the risk of losses.

Spread Entry on Price Orders

The method of entering spreads that makes the most sense is entering on a price order. In other words, an order is placed with the broker to establish a spread at a specific premium or discount. The advantage of this technique is, of course, that a spread will not be entered at a price different from the one expected.

The single great disadvantage of this method is that the order may not get filled. If the order is placed at too ambitious an entry price (the trader is trying to save money) while the trader is expecting the market to come to that price, the entire move can be missed. On the other hand, entering the market may cause the trader to lose a good percentage of the potential profit simply in poor order fills. Order placement at specific prices is as much an art as it is a science.

CHAPTER 8

Fundamental Analysis

At a commodities seminar many years ago, I was approached by an individual who had a keen interest in the soybean market. As he sat down, newspaper in hand, he said, "It rained in Illinois and Indiana last night. The price of beans was probably down yesterday."

He then turned to the business section, ran his finger down the futures prices until he came to soybeans, and exclaimed, "Yep! Down three cents." With a self-satisfied air, he closed the newspaper and laid it on the floor next to his chair, content with his very simple but correct fundamental analysis of the soybean market. I wish that all analysis of futures markets could be so simple and accurate!

His basic reasoning, of course, was correct. The weather had been dry up until that time, leading to predictions of lowered production and higher prices. The higher prices would be caused by lowered supply in the face of steady or increased demand. The recent rain would cause increased production, leading to greater supply and hence to lower prices. To the layperson, the logic seems faultless. But if fundamental analysis of the futures markets were that simple and easy, there would be many more wealthy commodity traders in the world.

To be a successful fundamental analyst requires careful consideration of a massive amount of information. Fundamental analysis has its roots in economics. Economic theory is not just one theory; rather, there are many economic theories. Similarly, there are many different approaches to fundamental analysis. The common element in all approaches to fundamental analysis is the study of the purported causes of price increases and price decreases in the hope of ascertaining changes prior to their occurrence. The success of all the approaches rests upon the availability of accurate assessments of the variables analyzed, as well as knowledge of variables that may not be known to other fundamental analysts.

The plethora of statistics available to the fundamentalist at any given point in time can be overwhelming. The fundamentalist must be selective and be prepared to evaluate a massive amount of data. As a consequence, there is no one typical fundamentalist. Rather, there are many different types who evaluate different kinds of data at different times. There are those who, by virtue of their skill and expertise, can provide accurate forecasts, and there are those who, working with the same tools, make worthless forecasts.

SUPPLY AND DEMAND

The basis of fundamental analysis is supply and demand. But even a concept so simple as that is not without its complications. Basically, a fundamental analyst assumes that anything that decreases supply will tend to raise prices, and anything that increases supply will tend to lower prices. Conversely, increased demand will raise prices, and decreased demand will lower prices.

Now we get into the hard part of supply and demand: To an economist, demand for an item means simply how much of a commodity or service buyers are willing and able to buy at a particular price, at a certain time, in a given place. Normally, there is a close correlation between price and consumption. As price goes up, consumption drops, and vice versa.

However, other factors must be considered when measuring demand. For instance, what is the general state of the economy? Steak will likely sell more poorly during a depression than during prosperity, regardless of lowered prices. Also, what about consumer tastes? In recent years, the American public has become keenly aware of the potentially unhealthful consequences of eating too much red meat. This has resulted in a decline in the demand for beef, independent of price.

A third factor to consider when measuring demand for a product is the availability of alternative products. Consumers may eat steak at lower prices but switch to chicken when the price of steak rises. In the case of wheat, however, there is no readily available substitute for the making of flour for bread, so a switch to another product is less likely during a price increase. Economists measure this tendency to switch by using an index they call elasticity of demand. It simply rates a product according to the estimated percentage of consumers who will switch to another product as the price rises.

Just as demand for a product is difficult to measure, supply of that product is not always simple to calculate either. As a rule, supply consists of the carryover stocks from the previous marketing year plus the amount being produced this marketing year plus the amount being imported. But, like demand, there is an elasticity of supply regarding the price factor. As the price of a commodity rises, more sellers are willing to sell the product, and vice versa. As the price of an agricultural product goes up, for example, more farmers switch to growing that crop. As a consequence, available supply is closely related to price.

Supply is also determined in part by the ability to store the product. The more perishable the commodity, the less likely it can be held off the market in anticipation of better prices. Even with storable commodities, the cost and availability of adequate storage space are important factors in the determination of supply.

As you can readily see, even the seemingly simple concept of supply and demand becomes very complicated in the process of fundamental analysis of the commodity markets. Fortunately, there are some sources of information that can be helpful.

MARKET REPORTS

The U.S. Department of Agriculture (USDA) provides a number of very thorough and generally accurate reports on daily, weekly, and monthly price movements. The USDA also produces periodic reports estimating ending stocks. These, of course, change during the year as other factors come into play. In addition to government reports, there are private market-reporting services for many commodities, as well as detailed reports published by the exchanges that provide important statistics on the cash markets.

The analysts who use all this information to make forecasts for the major producers and the large brokerage houses develop an economic model into which they insert the various statistics as they become available. Often, this model is computerized so that voluminous quantities of data can be handled quickly and easily, and the forecasts can be readily updated as new data become available.

SEASONALITY

If we study cash commodity prices over an extended period of time on a month-to-month basis, we find that during certain months of the year price tends to top, whereas during other months price tends to bottom. Furthermore, during certain times of the year uptrends are common, while during other times of the year downtrends are common.

Each cash commodity market has its own seasonal price tendencies, but virtually all commodities follow a definite seasonal pattern. Because perishable commodities must be brought to market quickly, prices of those commodities tend to rise and fall as the product becomes more or less available. Anyone in the northern states who has had a taste for strawberry shortcake in February knows that fresh strawberries are very expensive at that time of the year, if any can be found at all. In May and June, however, fresh strawberry shortcake with whipped cream is a readily available and usually temptingly priced dessert.

Less perishable, storable commodities like the grains generally are priced lowest at harvest time, as the available supply is relatively large in relationship to demand; but seasonal price moves of these commodities tend to be less volatile during the rest of the year than those of perishable commodities. Usually, with the grains, the price at times other than harvest reflects the price of the grains plus storage costs.

Monthly seasonal price tendencies can be charted for each commodity when the price history of that commodity is known. By comparing monthly average prices for a commodity over the history of that commodity, a chart can be developed like the one in Figure 8-1. The chart tells us the monthly seasonal price tendency for wheat. If the plotted line in any of the charts is up in one of the months, we know that prices have a tendency to rise during that month. If the line moves down, prices have a downward tendency. The row of numbers along the bottom reveals the percentage of time that tendency has held true. The chart in Figure 8-1 indicates that wheat prices tend to fall from May through August and then rise through December.

Weather and Prices

Weather patterns cause prices to vary during a growing season. A dry spring establishes expectations for a crop shortfall. A late freeze creates the probability of reduced production. A freeze in South America during their summer season can cause futures prices to shoot up, particularly in soybeans, coffee, and orange juice.

Weather affects commodity prices primarily during the growing season. However, because of what amounts to a worldwide market, it seems that the growing season now stretches year-round, and weather conditions anywhere on the planet can have an effect on the price of one commodity or another.

Seasonal Tendencies in Futures Prices

A market analyst wishing to use the concept of seasonality for trading in the futures market, particularly a speculator who trades on a short-term basis, will find that charting seasonal tendencies of futures prices on a week-to-week or day-to-day basis is more suited to the needs of the short-term trader than is the monthly cash seasonal. In this case, seasonal futures tendencies are specific to the futures contract month.

Figure 8-1: Wheat Cash Monthly Seasonal Chart

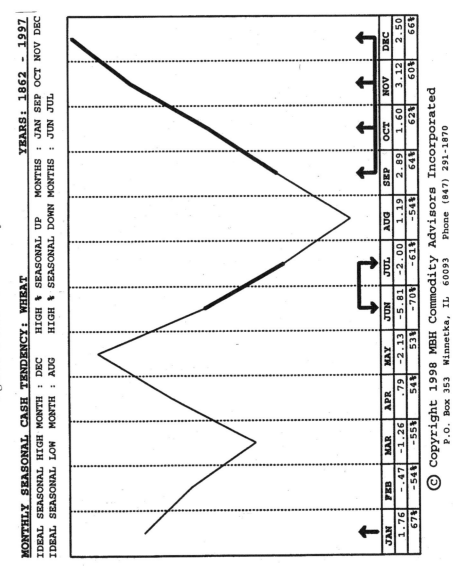

MONTHLY SEASONAL CASH TENDENCY: WHEAT   **YEARS: 1862 - 1997**

IDEAL SEASONAL HIGH MONTH : DEC   HIGH % SEASONAL UP   MONTHS : JAN SEP OCT NOV DEC

IDEAL SEASONAL LOW MONTH : AUG   HIGH % SEASONAL DOWN MONTHS : JUN JUL

	JAN	FEB	MAR	APR	MAY	JUN	JUL	AUG	SEP	OCT	NOV	DEC
	1.76	-.47	-1.26	.79	-2.13	-5.81	-2.00	1.19	2.89	1.60	3.12	2.50
	67%	-54%	-55%	54%	53%	-70%	-61%	-54%	64%	62%	60%	66%

© Copyright 1998 MBH Commodity Advisors Incorporated

P.O. Box 353   Winnetka, IL 60093   Phone (847) 291-1870

152

Figure 8-2: Sugar Weekly Seasonal Composite Futures Chart

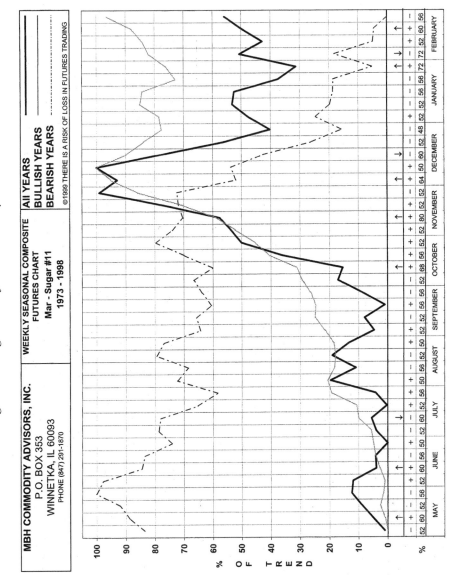

When we analyze the statistics for each futures month, we arrive at a chart that looks like the one in Figure 8-2. Again, the direction of the plotted line reveals the seasonal tendency, up or down; but this time the figures along the bottom indicate the percentage of times prices closed up for the week.

Thus, a high number would indicate a high probability of prices closing up for a given week, whereas a low number would represent a high probability of prices closing down. By noting very high or very low numbers on the chart, the analyst can identify weeks that have had a very consistent seasonal tendency.

Because of the research that has gone into the development of these seasonal charts, I have been asked whether this kind of seasonal study is fundamental analysis or technical analysis. My reply is that seasonality is the most basic kind of fundamental analysis, but I have studied it and used it in a very technical way. That is, I don't pay attention to what causes seasonal movement. I simply record the historical patterns of seasonality and use simple probability to predict future patterns.

CYCLIC PRICE CHANGES

Prices of all commodities tend to repeat up-and-down trends in a relatively predictable fashion over a prescribed period of time. The cyclic method of analysis and forecasting has its roots in the work of Edward R. Dewey, founder of the Foundation for the Study of Cycles. With the advent of computer technology and the ease of access to data, the use of price cycles has been popularized in recent years. Yet cyclic analysis does not have many followers today.

For one thing, the application of cycles to the marketplace is not nearly as simple a matter as is the demonstration of their existence. Although the process of identifying price cycles from price data is fairly easy, the intricacies of cyclic analysis are such that a commitment must be made in order for a trader to achieve lasting success in trading with this system. Even when a trader decides to use cyclic analysis as a method for trading in the markets, other timing devices and filters are necessary in order to determine when to get in and out of the market.

Much has been written about business cycles, price cycles, and the like. Suffice it to say that a proper understanding of price fundamentals requires a thorough knowledge of price cycles. It would be essential to know, for instance, that corn has a price cycle of approximately 5.7 years and that the low of that cycle occurred in early 1988, before making any predictions about corn prices based on estimates of supply and demand. There is also a 30- to 34-month price cycle in corn that must be considered.

Futures and cash prices demonstrate many different cyclic lengths, ranging from the ultra-long term to the ultra-short term. On the short-term end of the spectrum, we have the approximately four- to five-day cycle in silver prices. On the long-term end of the continuum, we find the approximate 54-year cycle in most commodity prices; this represents about the longest cycle that commodity traders study.

Figure 8-3 illustrates the various price cycles of live cattle. Cycles are measured low to low, high to high, or low to high, and various types of measurements are possible. Price cycles can vary considerably in length, thereby making it difficult, if not impossible, to make precise predictions about the future behavior of the cycle. At times, there is even an inversion of cyclic highs and lows, with tops being made when lows should be made. This tends to occur when the market is at a major turning point.

Using cyclic analysis as a trading method requires: 1) projecting the cycles, 2) forecasting the next high or low, and 3) timing your entry into the market. Computer programs can help you find cycles by matching dates and cycle lengths and testing them in the past, as well as projecting them into the future. Once the cycle has been identified, simply counting into the future establishes a time frame or time window during which the cycle should ideally top or bottom. A suitable timing indicator then provides the signal to enter the market. Figures 8-4 to 8-6 illustrate a few of the timing indicators that can be effective when the cyclic top or bottom is imminent. Technical indicators are discussed in Chapter 10.

Although cyclic analysis is fascinating, using it as a specific trading system is not recommended for the novice trader.

Figure 8-3: Live Cattle Monthly Futures

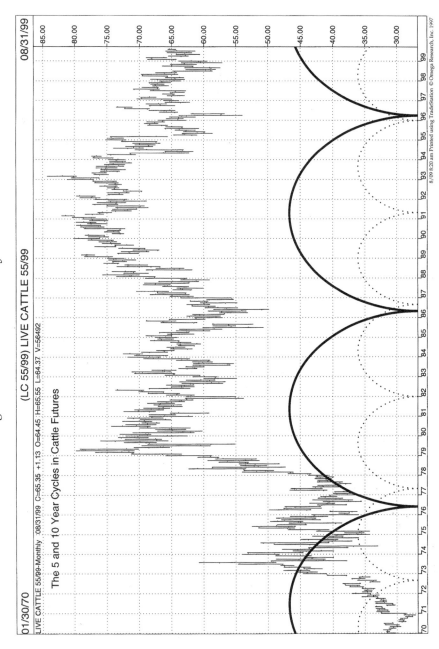

| 01/30/70 | (LC 55/99) LIVE CATTLE 55/99 | 08/31/99 |

LIVE CATTLE 55/99-Monthly 08/31/99 C=65.35 +1.13 O=64.45 H=65.55 L=64.37 V=56492

The 5 and 10 Year Cycles in Cattle Futures

8/09 8:20 am Printed using TradeStation © Omega Research, Inc. 1997

Figure 8-4: Timing Signals, Upside and Downside Reversals

Upside Reversal

Downside Reversal

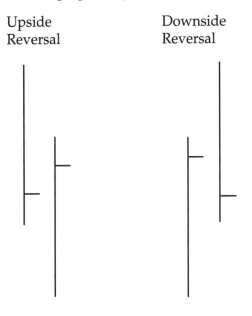

Figure 8-5: Timing Signals

Low–High Close

High–Low Close

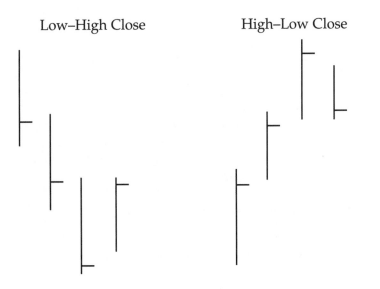

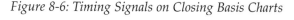

Figure 8-6: Timing Signals on Closing Basis Charts

SECULAR TRENDS

Less predictable than seasonals and cycles but significant never-theless as an influence on prices are price trends resulting from long-term changes in supply and demand. Such changes as demo-graphic movements, long-term weather changes, changes in cus-toms and tastes, government policies, the discovery of new uses for a commodity, and large-scale changes in consumer purchasing power may move prices of a commodity into a different range than it previously traded in.

Other secular trends can be created by crop substitution, reval-uation of the dollar, new technology, and increasing or decreasing the available crop acreage. Secular trends must be taken into account in any long-range prediction of price movement.

Government Price Support Programs

The government is an ever-present but often fickle influence on commodity prices. Because of its tendency to react much too slowly and to respond all too often to political issues, the government can often exacerbate rather than solve market problems. Nevertheless, government programs have a significant influence—in some cases the most significant influence—on the prices of commodities. Through loans to farmers, acreage allotments, direct cash incentive plans, programs to dispose of surplus crops, and programs to take land out of production altogether, the government intervenes in myriad ways with the market economy.

Government Reports

I mentioned earlier the market and price reports published periodically by the USDA. The government also publishes many other reports about the economy that may have a strong effect on commodity prices. For example, the monthly balance of trade report in October 1987 seemed to be a catalyst for the stock market crash that month. The various reports on wholesale prices, consumer prices, trade deficits, unemployment, money supply, stockpiles of goods—the list goes on—all have a more or less direct and significant effect on prices.

Political Influences

Political decisions anywhere in the world may affect commodity prices significantly. In many developing countries, the government may elect to support the price of a particular commodity in order to enhance its value on the world market. Other countries may adopt protectionist attitudes, which result in tariffs and other trade barriers, to protect local producers from outside competition. As Figure 8-7 demonstrates, prices of crude oil were affected dramatically by the news of Saddam Hussein's invasion of Kuwait in 1990.

OTHER FORCES AND FACTORS
AFFECTING COMMODITY PRICES

In addition to weather, there are other forces and factors that affect commodity prices.

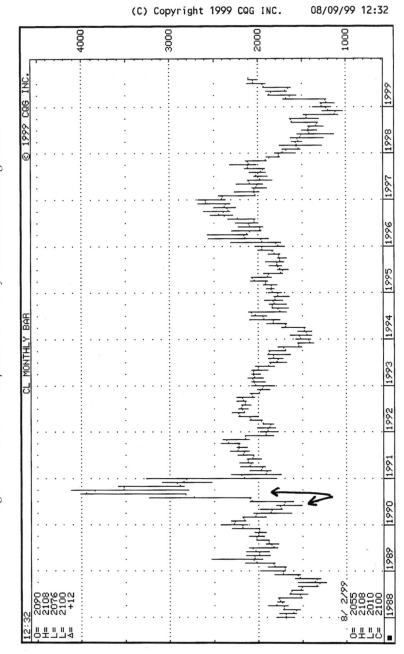

Figure 8-7: Crude Oil Explodes on News of Hussein's Annexing Kuwait

International News

Many commodities, particularly those that have an international source—sugar, petroleum, copper, platinum, coffee, and cocoa, for example—are especially vulnerable to news of war or international tensions. News of war can lead to hoarding as well as to a greater demand for raw materials for defense and stockpiling. Moreover, there is the possibility of imports being cut off. On the other hand, the prospect of losing major export markets can significantly depress the prices of domestically produced commodities.

Currency Fluctuations

Now more than ever before, a critical factor in the profitability of business operations is the exchange rate between currencies. When the dollar is strong against foreign currencies, exports from the United States are more expensive and therefore less desirable. As the dollar declines, American goods become more competitive on the world market, and exports tend to increase. As foreign markets open up, however, demand for some commodity might increase, leading to a rise in prices domestically. It is possible to envision the unlikely scenario of commodity prices rising domestically while actually becoming more competitive internationally.

General Business Conditions

People are more willing to spend their money during optimistic times. When the economy is healthy, unemployment is low, the experts are predicting prosperous times ahead, and business is expanding, demand tends to be high for commodities. But when the threat of recession arises, unemployment creeps up, business slows, and people become nervous about the future, demand falls. Consumers become less willing to spend.

PRICE ANALYSIS

The individual who is serious about analyzing price by the fundamentals faces quite a job. He or she must first determine the general business climate, whether it is inflationary or recessionary, whether unemployment is rising or falling. Next, check the trend of commodity prices by looking at one or more of the following: the Consumer Price Index, the Farm Price Index, the Dow Jones Averages, the Futures Price Indexes, the Reuters Spot Index, or the Commodity Research Bureau Futures Price Index.

After checking the general situation, the specific circumstances regarding individual commodities must be checked: What is the seasonal price pattern? What is the long-term price trend? What about government price supports? Expert subsidies? What are the figures on current production and carryover stocks? What are the prospects for demand domestically? What about foreign production? Currency exchange rates? Foreign political situations? Are there weather circumstances that may be significant?

Fortunately for many fundamental analysts, there are computer programs that factor in much of the above information and develop price forecasts. Even with computer help, however, anyone who has the desire to be a fundamental analyst must feel overwhelmed at times by the scope of the information that must be processed and the number of variables that must be considered.

Large brokerage houses and large producers and users generally have the resources to maintain the staff and equipment to carry out adequate analysis of all the fundamental forces that move the market. The average futures trader will find it more difficult, if not impossible, to develop a viable and thorough program of effective fundamental analysis. Even the most sophisticated of systems will not be perfect. There will always be unexpected variables that the analysis failed to consider. I have always maintained that the markets work perfectly as they respond to the multiplicity of forces that act upon them. It is our inability to find, parse, and correctly weight the impact of these factors that limits our results and the success of our fundamentally based forecasts.

CHAPTER 9

Technical Analysis: Chart Patterns

The futures market is in many respects an international laboratory for the study of group psychology. In Chapter 8, we made the point that price is determined by the balance between supply and demand, and by elasticity of demand and elasticity of supply. What creates elasticity in supply and demand? Human nature does.

Consumers are quite varied in their perceptions of what constitutes a good price, or when an item is a bargain, or, for that matter, when they can afford a particular item. Two individuals making an identical salary may be totally at odds when it comes to a decision regarding whether they can afford a new car, for instance. Obviously, when purchasing decisions are being made, much more enters into the decision than simple supply and demand. For example, an individual who just received a 15 percent increase in salary might be inclined to shop for a new car, but if the same person encounters a rumor that the company is having problems and

163

might be laying off 20 percent of the work force, the decision to buy the new car may well be deferred.

Similarly, in the futures market, two individuals can perceive the same fundamental information and arrive at opposite conclusions regarding the impact of that information on prices. In fact, this is the key phenomenon underlying price fluctuations that result from trading. Because the activity of speculating in futures contracts requires a buyer and a seller, there must always exist opposing forecasts of price moves for there to be a "liquid" market (i.e., one in which transactions can occur quickly and easily).

Many traders in the futures market believe that the patterns of group behavior in the futures market can be recorded and studied and that predictions regarding futures behavior can be made based on recurring patterns. In other words, it might be possible to overlook fundamental information and focus entirely on the patterns of price movement because these patterns reflect the behavior of the participants, and people's behavior tends to repeat itself.

THE WAVE THEORIES

Anyone with more than a casual knowledge of stocks or commodities has likely heard of the Elliott wave. Developed by R. N. Elliott in the late 1920s and early 1930s, the Elliott wave is related to the theories of stock market behavior that were first published by Charles H. Dow.

In a series of editorials in the *Wall Street Journal* in the early 1900s, Dow proposed several basic principles regarding the stock market averages that he had established and that still bear his name. These theoretical rules are precursors of much of the technical analysis that is discussed in this chapter. Dow's theory first established the concept that all fundamental supply and demand factors that affect the market are assimilated into the price action. He went on to draw an analogy between the behavior of market prices and the ocean. He described the primary price trend in terms of the tide, while secondary trends are like the waves that follow the tide successfully higher onto the beach. Minor trends are the ripples in the waves.

Dow noted that secondary trends, which are retracements of the primary trend, usually recede approximately one-third to two-thirds of the distance covered by the primary trend. These corrections are often close to 50 percent. Dow further postulated that each major trend has three distinct phases: an accumulation period, a period of rapidly enhancing prices and improving business news, and the final period during which economic news is rosy and volume increases markedly as the public begins to participate actively in the market.

Elliott adopted Dow's comparison between the ocean and the stock market in his scholarly extension of this pioneering work. In Elliott's original theoretical treatises, and in the work that has expanded and refined Elliott's principles, we find five waves within major bull markets ("tidal wave" bull markets). Each of these five waves can be divided into five subwaves. In the correction phase, each move involves three waves, which can also be divided into three subwaves. (See Figure 9-1.)

Although based on elegantly simple precepts, Elliott's wave theory is quite complex and difficult to utilize in market trading. Anyone wishing to apply wave theory to a trading program would be well advised to study thoroughly the original material by Elliott, as well as the expansion of that work done by A. H. Bolton. Robert Prechter has some more recent work on the Elliott wave and is highly recommended as a good resource for the Elliott wave theory.

Because price charts register human behavior as it is communicated through price changes of commodities, certain patterns of price movement recur often enough and are associated with certain outcomes with sufficient frequency to be considered significant predictors of price movement. People who chart prices in the futures market generally use one of two kinds of charts: the bar chart or the point-and-figure chart. Each has advantages and disadvantages.

THE BAR CHART

If you have ever seen a price chart of the futures market or, for that matter, the stock market, you probably have seen a bar chart. This particular chart is designed to illustrate three specific characteristics of price during a particular trading period: the opening price, the closing price and the range of prices from high to low through which trading occurred during the trading period. A price bar might represent a period as short as five minutes or as long as a month. The most common is the daily bar chart.

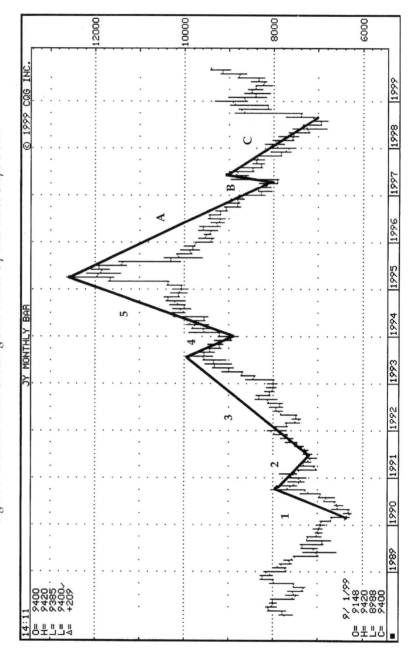

Figure 9-1: Elliott Wave Showing Five Waves Up and Three Steps Down

Figure 9-2: Bar Chart of Comex Gold

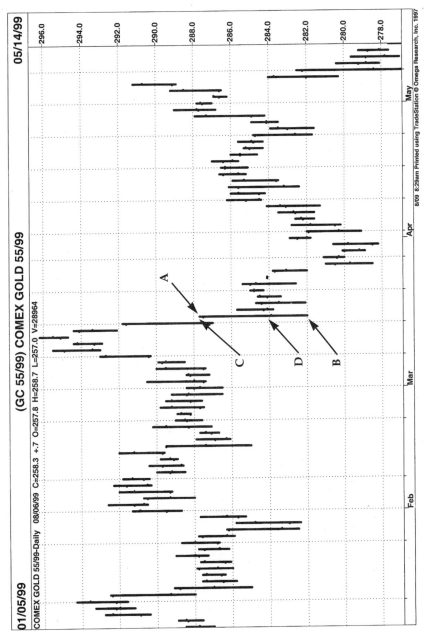

Figure 9-3: Bar Chart of December Hogs

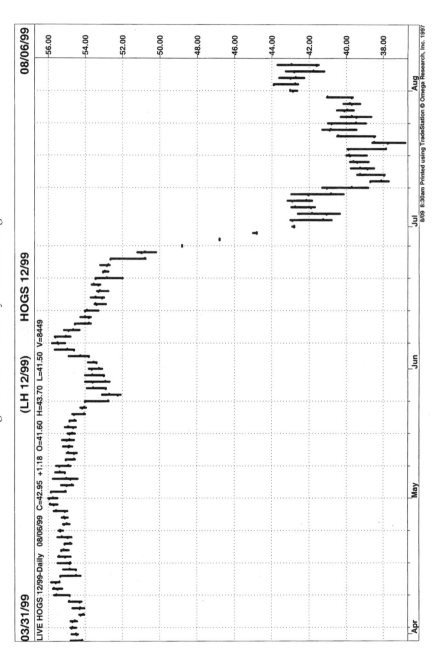

168

Figure 9-2 presents a typical price bar. The vertical bar represents the range of trading for that particular day. The highest price of the day is at point A, and the lowest price of the day is at point B. The horizontal line intersecting the price bar from the left is the opening price. On this day, the opening price is shown by C. Conversely, the horizontal line intersecting the price bar from the right is the closing price. On this day, the closing price is shown at point D.

Figure 9-3 shows a bar chart of December Hogs.

THE POINT-AND-FIGURE CHART

A point-and-figure chart resembles a game of tic-tac-toe, with all its boxes filled with either an X or an O (or an X and a box). The purpose of this chart is to provide information not included in a bar chart. Whereas the bar chart records price range during a specified time period, a point-and-figure chart doesn't record time; rather, this kind of chart records reversals in prices of a commodity.

As price moves up, it is recorded as an X in the price box. As price moves down, it is recorded in the price box as an O. As the person who builds the point-and-figure chart, you can decide the value of each box in the chart. If you want a very sensitive chart that records most of the price action, each box can be worth one tic on the price of the commodity. A less sensitive chart can be developed using other increments, such as one cent versus one-quarter cent.

As the chart builder, you can also decide when prices will be recorded: every time they occur or only when certain larger moves have occurred. For example, a point-and-figure chart in lumber might register a price change of one dollar per board foot, with each box being worth one-quarter cent. Then an X would be entered only when price advanced one cent, but four boxes would be filled in when a one-cent move occurred (Figure 9-4).

However, the primary function of the point-and-figure chart is to record price reversals. The procedure is to continue marking an X (if the price is rising) or an O (if the price is falling) until a significant price reversal occurs. Again, you decide what is a significant price reversal. Obviously, you would not consider a one-tic reversal significant. If it were, the chart would be filled with meaningless X's and O's.

Figure 9-4: Lumber Point-and-Figure Chart

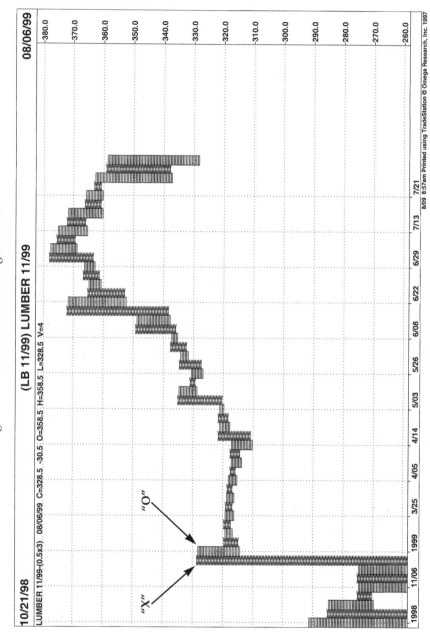

To avoid too many reversals, you might decide that three tics, or three boxes on the chart, is a significant reversal. When the price moved at least three tics in the opposite direction from the last entry, that reversal would be registered by filling in O's next to the appropriate prices if the reversal was down or X's if the reversal was up. For normal use, a three-box reversal chart, as described, is probably unrealistic to keep unless you are on the floor or right next to a quote machine. Unless there is a need for such close monitoring of a market, boxes of higher value should be used, so that fewer entries will be made.

CANDLESTICK CHARTS

Sokyu Homma first developed the method of predicting price movements by looking at the previous day's movement. The method was later termed the "Sakata Constitution." In the 1700s, Homma lived near the *shonai* (rice) distribution center, where he began trading at his local rice exchange. He was far more successful than others, but he kept his ideas secret. He was eventually promoted to the *bushi* (samurai) level and moved to Edo, where he began to trade at the Edo (Tokyo) Regional Exchange. He used his secret methods to amass a huge fortune.

Homma probably charted as a matter of expedience, inasmuch as he found it necessary to see the highest and lowest price movements at a glance. If someone asked him how the rice market was doing, he didn't need all the information gathered from various rice paddies. He used a line called the "anchor line." It consists of an arrow pointing up when the closing price is high and an arrow pointing down when the closing price is low. After much trial and error, the candlestick line was created to show the highs and lows of the day, as well as the open and close, with the color of the candle indicating the move or direction—white for bullish movement and black for bearish movement.

This method is useful for several reasons:

1. Candlesticks give you much more information each day than do traditional bar charts. While traditional bar charts show you the open, high, low, and close of each day, they do not readily make the relationship between these four

important variables apparent. Candlesticks give you this information immediately upon visual inspection.

2. While traditional bar charts can also be used analytically to give you specific patterns and formations, there are many more candle patterns than there are bar chart patterns, and each candle pattern is based upon many years of study and analysis.

3. Candlesticks identify support and resistance that may be used once a trend has been established. This allows short-term traders to use candle formations.

4. Candlestick patterns can also be used for day trading provided you have learned how to effectively recognize the necessary candle formations.

The most important thing to remember about candlesticks is that they are not a mechanical method of trading. Candlestick charts allow you, the trader, to use your skill and insight in order to achieve profitable results. While no system, method, or indicator can guarantee success in futures trading, using candlesticks can improve your odds of success. Remember that the effective use of candlesticks requires work and education. Figure 9-5 shows a candlestick chart for Live Hogs.

GANN CHARTS

W. D. Gann is best known for his work with market patterns. Gann used a system of angles and projections to determine specific price targets (see Figure 9-6).

Although the method is popular today, many years after its original introduction, there is a lack of strong statistical evidence to support its accuracy. The method is more subjective than many traders would like to see, yet this does not undermine the validity of the theoretical basis.

Figure 9-5: Candlestick Chart of Live Hogs

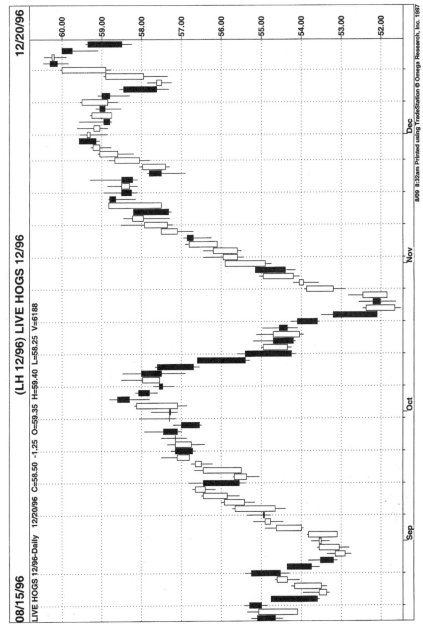

Figure 9-6: Gann Angle Chart of Live Hogs

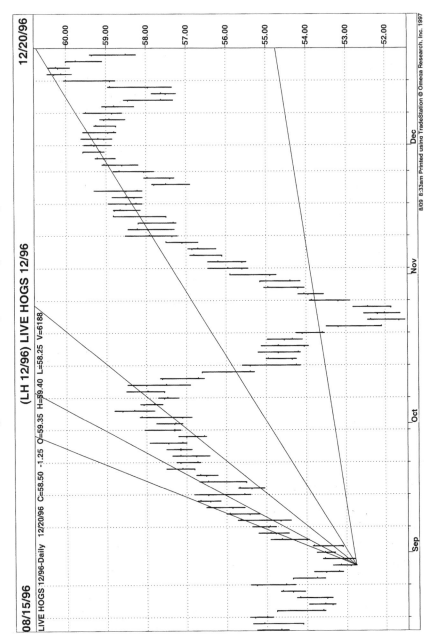

174

TRENDS

The elementary information that every technical analyst wants to know first is the price trend: the long-term trend, the intermediate trend, and the short-term trend. Perhaps the most frequent mistake made in the futures market is following a trade signal of one kind or another without considering the current trend. "Bucking the trend" can be deadly. Establishing an accurate trend line, however, is not necessarily an easy task. Different chart analysts use different materials or choose different points on the chart by which to draw a trend line.

Figure 9-7 demonstrates a clear trend line, showing a definite bull trend in the hog futures market. Notice that for many weeks prices remained above their "support" trend line. When prices topped and turned lower, they remained below their "resistance" trend line for many weeks.

How to Find and Use Trends

Traders know that markets move in trends. Some argue that markets only move in strong trends about 20 percent of the time. While I disagree, it's a moot point. If a trader can determine the existence of a trend as either up, down, or sideways, then the first major obstacle to successful trading has been overcome. As you know, there are many ways in which a trend can be determined. Some ways are clearly better than others. The greatest enemy of the trend trader is time lag. The longer it takes to spot the start of a new trend, the less money can be made, and the greater the odds of getting into a trend when it is about to change again.

This result is euphemistically called "bad trade location" or "getting whipsawed." The fact is that any delay in knowing when the trend has changed is deleterious to traders. This is why trading systems fail and why moving average systems are often the worst culprits when it comes to whipsaws. Are there methods for finding trends that avoid or minimize some of the pitfalls inherent in the process? Yes, but you must be very selective in making your choices. Also, remember that determining a trend is only half of the process. Once we know the trend, we need to know what to do with the knowledge.

Figure 9-7: Trend Line of Live Hog Futures

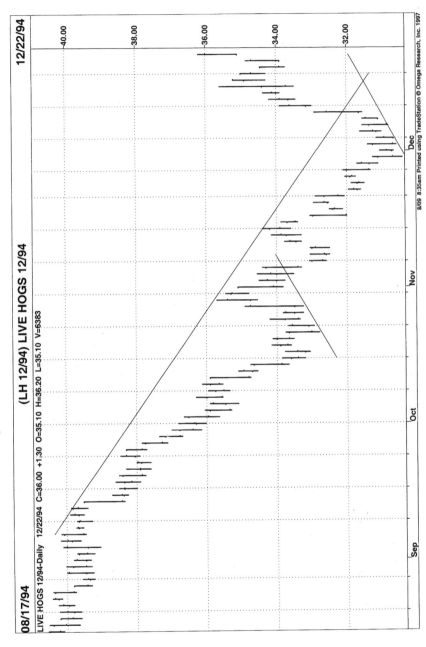

Sixteen-Day Highs or Lows

This method is a variation on the theme of work originally done in the 1960s by C. W. Keltner. The concept is simple and very effective. At the end of the trading day, compare the closing price with the highest high and the lowest low (intraday highs and lows) for the previous 16 days.

- If the closing price today is higher than the highest intraday high of the previous 16 days, then the trend is up and a buy signal has been generated.
- If the closing price today is lower than the lowest intraday low of the previous 16 days, then the trend is down and a sell signal has been generated.

In an uptrend, you buy declines to support, whereas you sell rallies to resistance in a downtrend. When using the 10/8 channel all you need to do is buy the bottom of the channel in uptrends. This is the support level. In a downtrend you sell the top of the channel.

When using the 16-day high or low method, you can use traditional trendline support and resistance methods, or you can use the channel support and resistance levels as your entry points.

Rules for Profitable Trend Trading

To trade effectively with the trend, follow these rules:

1. Determine the trend. If you're going to trade with the trend then the most important step is to find the trend. It's not sufficient to simply intuit that the trend is up or down.

2. Once the trend has turned in a given direction, as determined by a reasonably objective measure or measures, the next step is to buy at what has been determined to be support or to sell at what you have determined to be resistance.

3. In uptrends you must buy at support. In downtrends you must sell at resistance.

4 If you are a seller in an uptrend, you're probably losing money. If you are a buyer in a downtrend, you're probably losing money.

5. If you buy at support, don't be too quick to sell out your position. Use a stop loss and ride the position as long as possible. Do the same if you sell at resistance.

6. It is far better to get stopped out than to close out a winning trade that is moving with the trend. What you gain in potential breakaway moves is far greater than what you gain in taking a quick profit.

The Trend Is Your Friend

I don't know who coined the expression "The trend is your friend," but I do know that it's one of the most useful reminders I've ever heard when it comes to futures and stock trading. In my younger years, I wasn't aware of how important it was to know and follow the trend, but I have come to recognize the great value of doing that.

Knowing the trend and following the trend are two distinctly different things. Many of us are able to know the current trend of a market either by simple observation or by the application of a particular methodology. But the vast distance between knowing the trend and using the trend to your advantage is the space that separates winners from losers.

The topic of trends is vast and cannot be fully discussed or analyzed within the short space of several pages. There are literally hundreds of ways to look at trends and possibly thousands of ways to use trends in futures trading. Some key points to remember about trends are:

- The major trend affects most minor trends.
- The major trend is the path of least resistance.
- Prices are most apt to move along the path of least resistance.
- Losses taken on trades within the major trend tend to be smaller.
- Knowing the major trend can improve your timing.
- Timing signals consistent with the trend are more accurate than signals that oppose the trend.
- The biggest price moves occur with the major trend.

- Seasonal moves tend to be more accurate when they are consistent with the major trend.

Essential Timing Model (ETM)

The Essential Timing Model (ETM) in Figure 9-8 is the basic timing model that I believe facilitates profitable futures trading. The steps and procedures are self-explanatory; however, a little clarification might help. You will notice that I place the determination of trend as the first task. Once this has been done, the road becomes clearer. The next step is to go with the trend.

If the trend is up, then the only rational choice is to go long. There are two ways to go long. The first is to buy an upside breakout. This means that you buy on strength as prices make a new high for a given time frame (e.g., a new 10-week high, etc.) or as prices penetrate a resistance level. Trades in a downtrend work the same way, but in reverse. There are many different technical methods for accomplishing this end, but the key is to go with the existing trend once it has been established.

The Bottom Line

Attempting to pick bottoms and tops is like trying to be the first to climb a mountain—it's risky and dangerous and you could take a serious tumble. On the other hand, if you succeed, then you're often in for a great move. The problem with attempting to "top

Figure 9-8: Essential Timing Model

- Determine the trend.
- Up or down or no obvious trend
- *If trend is up, then buy only.*
    a. Buy strength (breakouts up)
    b. Buy weakness (support)
- *If trend is down, then sell.*
    a. Sell weakness (breakouts down)
    b. Sell strength (resistance)

pick" or "bottom fish" is that you're wrong much more often than you're right. What's the answer to this trader's dilemma? The best method I've found is to avoid being bold, to avoid being a hero, and above all to trade with the trend.

Most trading success is facilitated by knowing the existing trend (within whatever time frame you are trading) and by trading with the trend. That is, of course, the path of least resistance, and therefore the path that facilitates success. The final part of this methodology is, in many ways, the most crucial. Many good traders have said that 90 percent of their profits are made on 10 percent of their trades. What does this mean? Simply stated, it means that 90 percent of what happens will be neutralized. The real money will be made in only a few big trades. The way to get those few big trades is to identify trends and ride them until they end.

REVERSAL PATTERNS

Several chart patterns are indicators of trend reversals (changes) and signal a price top or bottom. In a price top, the number of available buyers declines and sellers begin to dominate the market, causing prices, which had been rising, to begin falling. In a price bottom, conversely, buyers begin to dominate the market, reversing the recent downtrend in prices.

One of the most reliable reversal patterns is the head-and-shoulders formation, which looks much like a W with an extended center leg (Figure 9-9). In a typical head-and-shoulders top, prices rally and decline at S, forming the left shoulder. They then rally again at H as buyers try once again to maintain the bull market trend. This second rally sends prices higher than the shoulder, forming the head. As prices fall back again, the third rally at S is not able to reach the price level at H, forming the right shoulder. At this point, sellers have assumed the stronger position in the market, and as prices penetrate the "neckline," a bear market ensues.

Another reversal pattern is the triangle formation (Figure 9-10). A triangle, as shown, following an extended decline, is a signal that prices may have bottomed. Although rising prices encounter resistance at A, buying pressure increases on each rally until a breakout finally occurs at B. Similarly, a descending triangle following an extended uptrend often signals a market top.

Figure 9-9: Head-and-Shoulders Top Formation

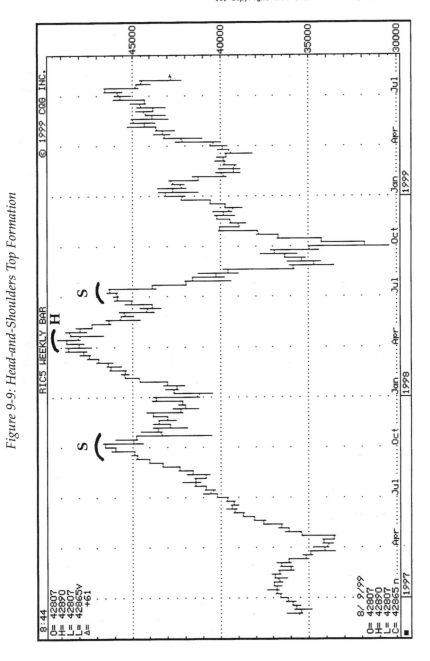

181

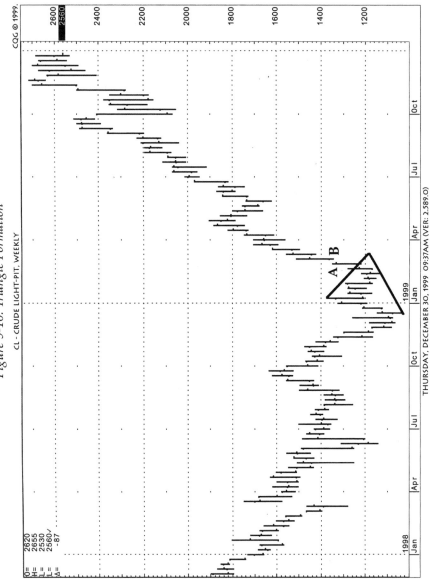

Figure 9-10: Triangle Formation

Price gaps, as shown in Figure 9-11, can be useful in chart analysis. A common assumption is that gaps will be filled; that is, sooner or later prices will trade in the range left open by the price gap. Chartists designate common gaps, breakaway gaps, measuring gaps, runaway gaps, and exhaustion gaps.

Other chart formations include key reversals (Figure 9-12), island reversals (Figure 9-13), double tops (Figure 9-14) and bottoms, flags and pennants (Figure 9-15), saucer bottoms, and triangles (Figure 9-16). To the trained eye, these formations can provide significant information. Often, however, as the patterns are forming, one can only speculate as to what is actually occurring. The formations are much easier to define after they are completed, which, of course, is often too late to be of significant value. Thus, the reading of chart formations is often akin to Monday-morning quarterbacking.

Figure 9-11: Price Gaps

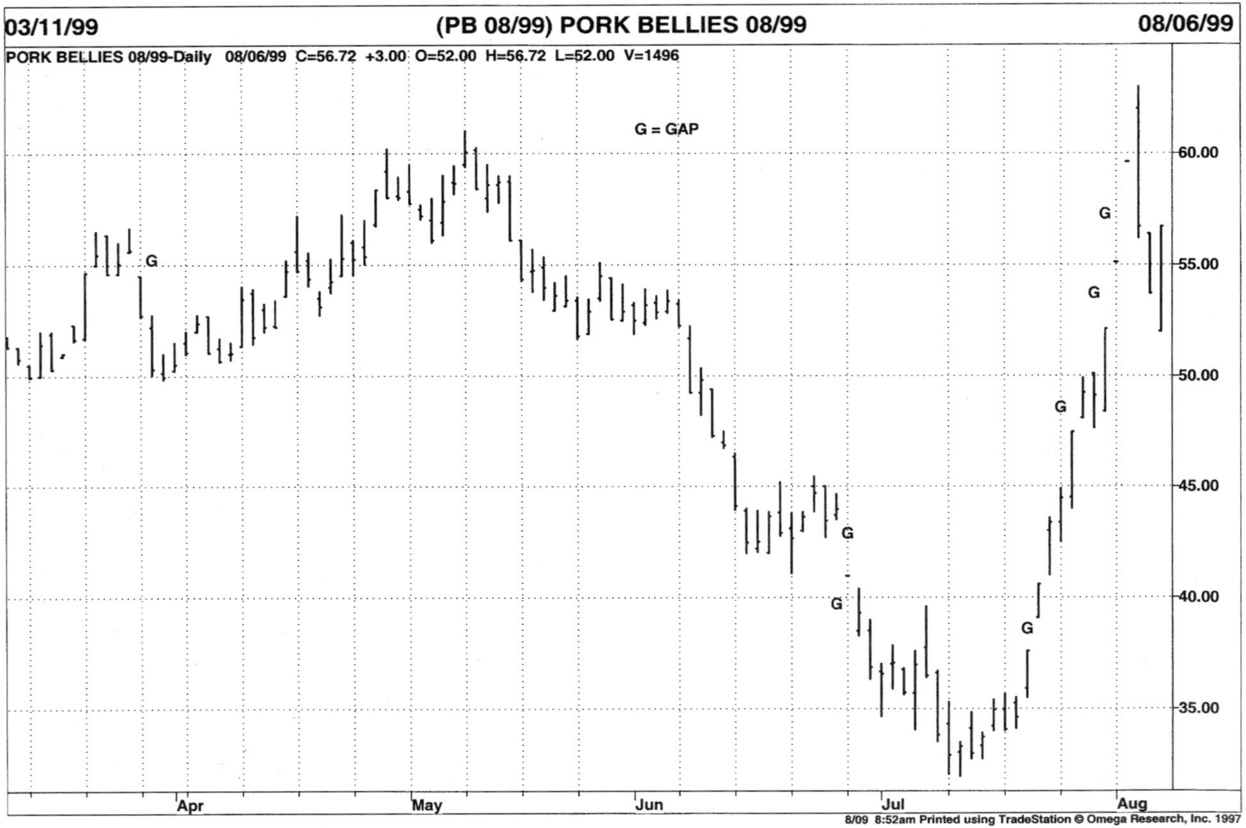
03/11/99
(PB 08/99) PORK BELLIES 08/99
08/06/99
PORK BELLIES 08/99-Daily 08/06/99 C=56.72 +3.00 O=52.00 H=56.72 L=52.00 V=1496
G = GAP
G
60.00
55.00
50.00
45.00
40.00
35.00
Apr
May
Jun
Jul
Aug
8/09 8:52am Printed using TradeStation © Omega Research, Inc. 1997

Figure 9-12: Key Reversal

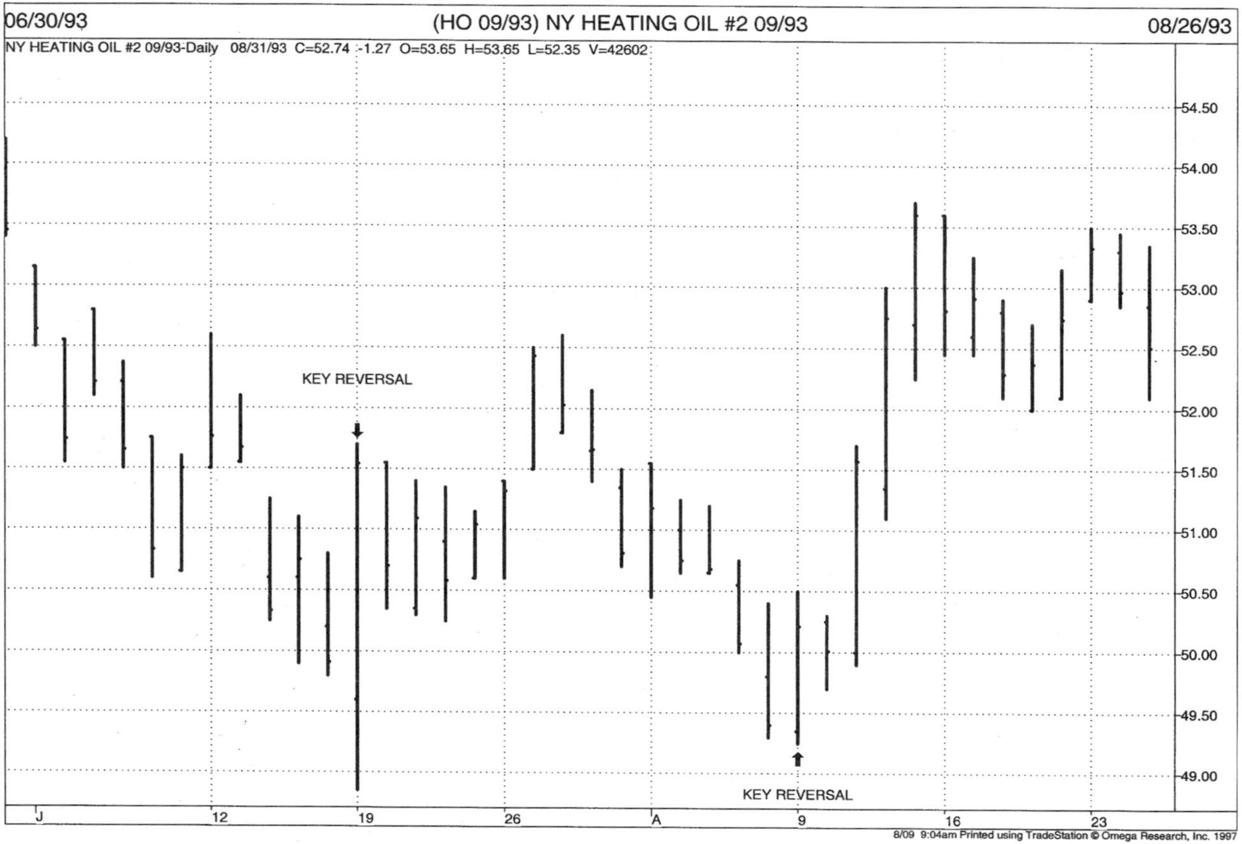

185

Figure 9-13: Island Reversal

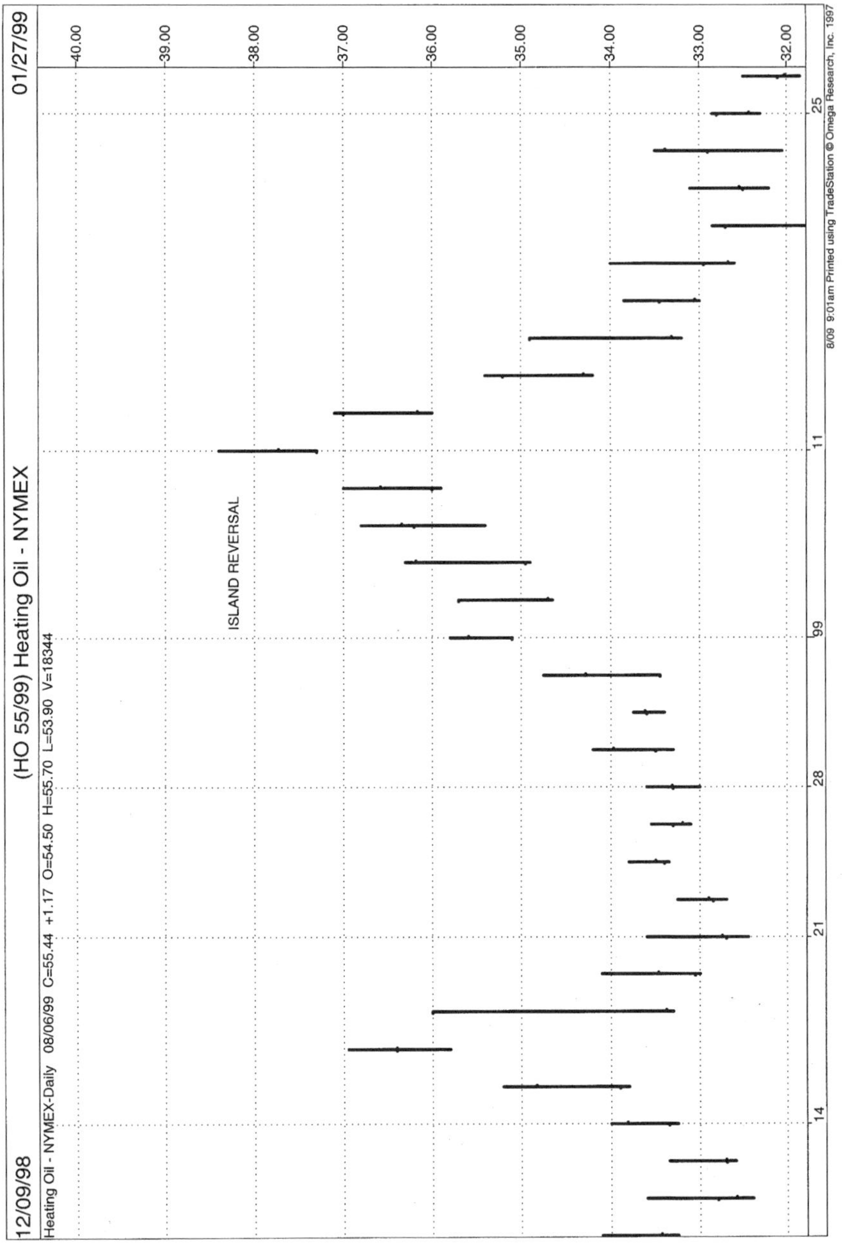

Figure 9-14: Double Top

187

Figure 9-15: Flag and Pennant

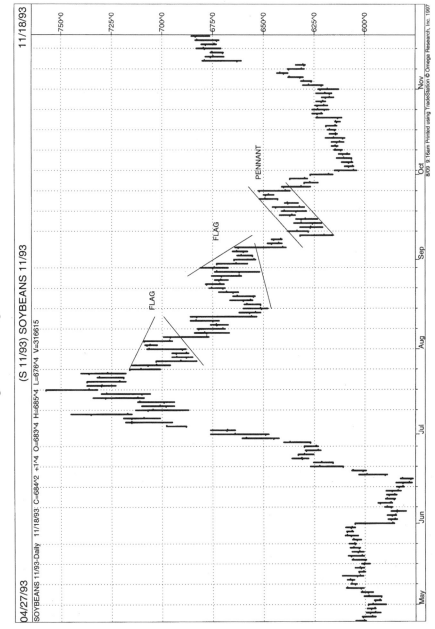

04/27/93   (S 11/93) SOYBEANS 11/93   11/18/93

SOYBEANS 11/93-Daily 11/18/93: C=684^2 +1^4 O=683^4 H=685^4 L=676^4 V=316615

Figure 9-16: Saucer Bottom and Triangles

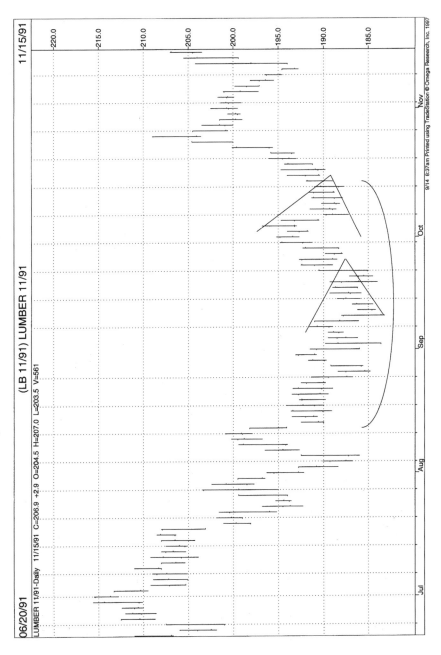

CHAPTER 10

Technical Analysis: Timing Indicators

The focus on forms of technical analysis continues in this chapter with a discussion of various timing patterns. As stated previously, it might be possible to overlook fundamental information and focus entirely on the patterns of price movement, because these patterns reflect the behavior of the participants, and people's behavior tends to repeat itself. Read about the various timing indicators and study the chart examples to learn the importance of these indicators and how to make them work best for you.

Good chart reading can provide a great deal of valuable information about a price trend and significant price trend reversals. This information, however, is not sufficient to make good trades. A successful trader must know how to time the trades in order to get into the market at the right time and catch the desired move.

A number of techniques are available to assist in the timing of trades. Among the better-known and more frequently used techniques are moving averages, stochastics, relative strength indicators (RSI), and oscillators. They are all systems for using past price information to generate buying and selling signals.

MOVING AVERAGES

Trend lines and chart patterns provide obvious assistance to the technical analyst. Both are useful for predicting future market moves. Unfortunately, both chart patterns and trend lines are subjective in nature. Two analysts can view the same chart and find two different patterns and two different trend lines. What is needed is a more objective system for defining trends and for providing more precise entry and exit signals.

In the 1950s, Richard Donchain advanced the notion that a different type of trend line could be used to establish buy-and-sell signals, as well as indications of support and resistance. Rather than the familiar straight-line trend method, Donchain advanced the notion that a moving average of prices could be constructed in order to provide market timing indicators.

A moving average is a simple mathematical manipulation of raw data that provides up-to-date or moving indications of market activity. Instead of examining price highs and lows for the entire history of the current contract, a moving average constantly progresses and examines only a defined segment of time, particularly in the recent past.

A 10-day moving average, for example, includes only prices for the last 10 days, ignoring what has transpired before. In so doing, it provides a more sensitive measure. On the 11th day, the oldest day in the data is dropped and the average is recalculated with the current daily data. At any given point in time, only 10 days of data are used.

The calculations for a moving average are very simple and straightforward. For a 10-day moving average, simply add the 10 most recent closing prices and divide that sum by 10. The following day, drop the earliest price in the series and add the current price. Again, divide the sum by 10. On each succeeding day, repeat the calculation. Before long, if each day's moving average is plotted and connected, you will have a fluctuating trend line that follows the price line (Figure 10-1).

Figure 10-1: Moving Average Line and Price Bars

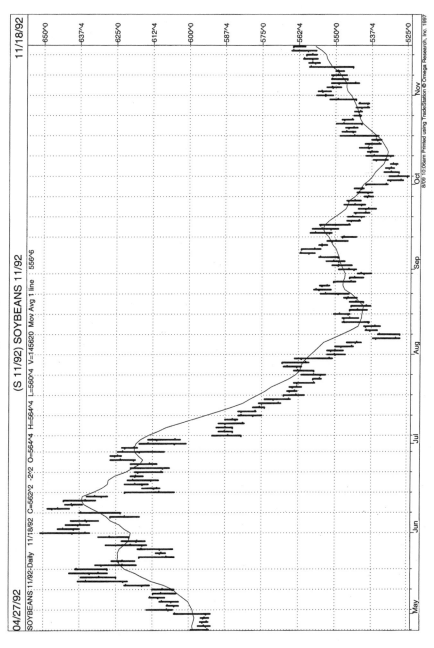

04/27/92	(S 11/92) SOYBEANS 11/92	11/18/92

SOYBEANS:11/92-Daily 11/18/92 C=562^2 -2^2 O=564^4 H=564^4 L=560^4 V=145620 Mov Avg 1 line 556^6

8/09 10:06am Printed using TradeStation © Omega Research, Inc. 1997

A moving average of prices may be calculated using any number of periods (e.g., 2-day, 3-day, 10-day, 14-day) or any period length (e.g., 5-minute, 10-minute, hourly, daily, weekly, monthly). Theoretically, if the daily price is consistently higher than the moving average of prices, it means prices are trending upward (bullish). Conversely, if the daily price is consistently lower than the moving average, the trend is downward (bearish). When the daily price line crosses the moving average line, however, it might indicate a change in the price trend (Figure 10-2), which might be a signal to take action in the market.

As you can see in Figure 10-3, the moving average makes its direction changes after the daily price has already changed direction. The greater the number of periods included in the moving average, the more it lags behind the daily price movement (compare Figure 10-2, a 3-day moving average, with Figure 10-4, a 14-day moving average).

Notice that as the number of periods in the moving average increases, the fluctuations in price action become smoother. The moving average tends to reduce the effect of price variations. Notice also that daily prices may go one way while the moving average is going the other: Prices may go lower while the moving average continues higher, and vice versa.

Multiple Moving Averages

Many analysts have found that a single moving average is not accurate enough to use as a timing device, particularly in choppy markets (Figure 10-5). In such markets, a trader can get whipsawed back and forth by false signals and lose a great deal of money in the process. To help solve that problem, analysts often use more than one moving average. When two moving averages are used together (Figure 10-6), the longer moving average—in this case, a 10-day average—can define the trend while the shorter moving average (a 3-day average, in this case) provides timing signals.

A further refinement is to use three moving averages. Specifically, the 4-day, 9-day, and 18-day averages seem to work best together. Figure 10-7 shows this combination, and the signals that can be generated from its application. With this system, a signal is theoretically given when the 9-day average crosses the 18-

Figure 10-2: Three-Day Moving Average (Price Line Crosses Moving Average)

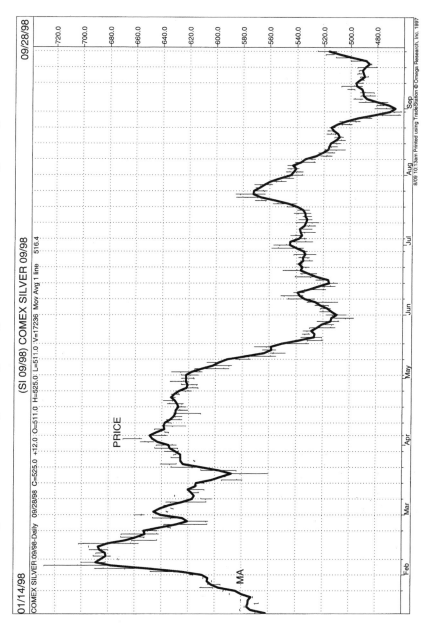

Figure 10-3: Moving Average Making Direction Change

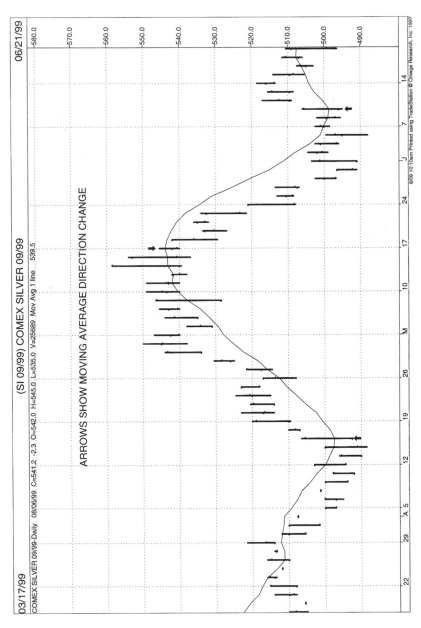

196

Figure 10-4: Fourteen-Day Moving Average

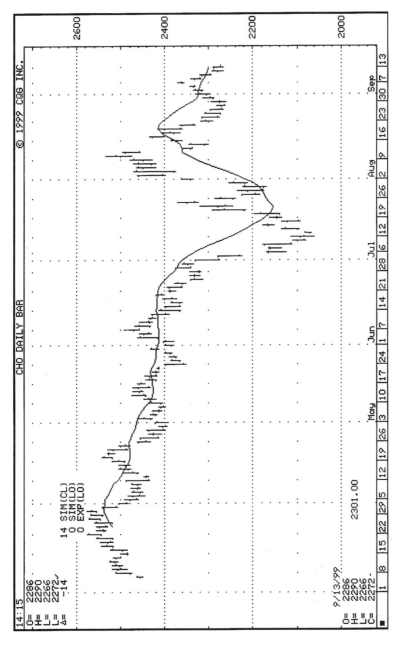

Figure 10-5: Moving Average in Narrow Trading Range

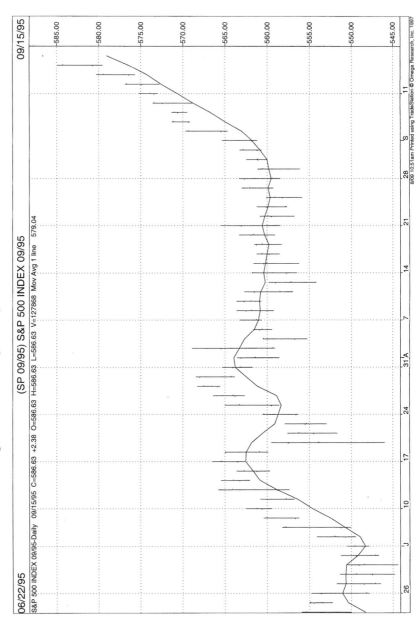

198

Figure 10-6: Three- and Ten-Day Moving Averages with Timing Signals

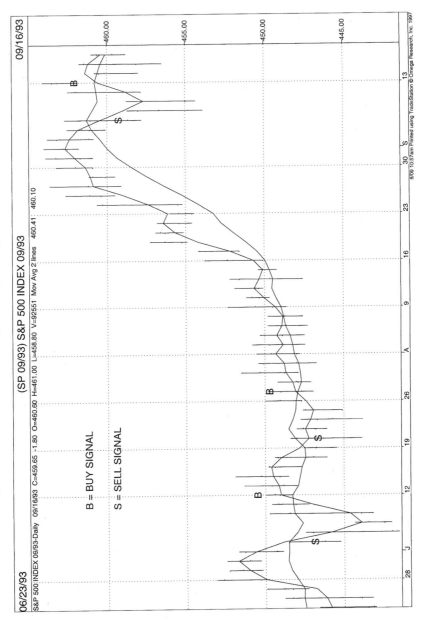

06/23/93   (SP 09/93) S&P 500 INDEX 09/93   09/16/93

S&P 500 INDEX 09/93-Daily   09/16/93   C=459.65 -1.80   O=460.60   H=461.00   L=458.80   V=92551   Mov Avg 2 lines   460.41   460.10

B = BUY SIGNAL

S = SELL SIGNAL

8/09 10:57am Printed using TradeStation © Omega Research, Inc. 1997

Figure 10-7: 4-Day, 9-Day, and 18-Day Moving Averages with Buy-Sell Signals

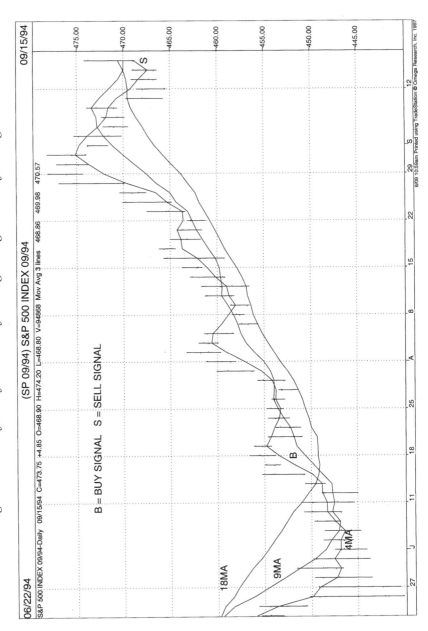

B = BUY SIGNAL   S = SELL SIGNAL

day average. To avoid false signals, the 4-day moving average should be higher than the 9-day average for a legitimate buy signal and below the 9-day average for a legitimate sell signal.

Traditional Moving Average Indicators

Whether you use one, two, or three moving averages, the concept is generally the same. Either the market price must close above or below its MA to signal a buy or a sell, or the MAs themselves must change their relationship to one another in order to signal a trade.

Traditional MA indicators tend to do extremely well in major trends, and can make you a lot of money by signaling when a major trend begins. But they will give many false (i.e., losing) signals, they will often get you into a move well after it has started, and when a change in trend occurs they will often not get you out until after you have given back a considerable amount of your profit. Hence, some moving averages tend to be very inaccurate and often have considerable drawdown as well as causing many consecutive losing trades.

Types of Moving Averages

There are several different types of moving averages. Here is a brief description of each along with comments about their assets or liabilities:

Simple Moving Average (SMA)

This is the most basic of all moving averages. It is computed by adding up all the numbers in the series and dividing the sum by the total number of entries. The good news about the SMA is that it's easy to calculate manually. The bad news is that it tends to give many false signals.

Smoothed Moving Average (SMO)

This is a more complex MA, which, by mathematical manipulation, slows the MA so that it is less responsive to small changes. The main positive feature of this MA is that it gives fewer false signals. The liability is that it tends to make its turn somewhat later than other MAs.

Exponential Moving Average (EMA)

By using exponential conversions, the EMA creates a moving average that is supposedly more responsive to prices. I find the EMA to be of little value in basic MA system development.

In using oscillator variations of the MA theme, the EMA is very useful. In this category I include such indicators as the MACD (moving average convergence divergence).

Weighted Moving Average (WMA)

This is my favorite MA. It applies more weight to recent prices or to whatever portion of the data one wishes. The weighting can also be a function of other variables, such as daily price range, volume, or other user-determined factors.

I've found this to be one of the most useful types of MAs. Unfortunately, not many of the standard computer quote and analysis systems include the WMA as part of their built-in software.

Variations on the Theme of Moving Averages

There are many variations on the theme of moving averages. These include MA-based oscillators such as the moving average convergence divergence (MACD), the MA Channel, MAC, and various high-low MA combinations. These variations on the MA tend to be more accurate and more sensitive than simple MA combinations of the closing price.

The MACD was specifically designed for S&P trading by Gerald Appel, while the MAC is my brainchild. The MAC can also be used to determine concise support and resistance levels.

Using the Moving Average

Technical analysts use the moving average in various ways. The moving average alone is used like a flexible trend line: While the moving average is increasing, the trader maintains a long position; when the moving average reverses direction, the trader liquidates the position. Though useful, this technique unfortunately misses most of a market move because of the time delay before the moving average changes direction.

To reduce the delay, a moving average can be used in conjunction with the daily price. As Figure 10-8 clearly shows, the daily price line will often cross the moving average line, and the number of crossings increases as the number of periods in the moving average decreases. These crossings can provide market signals. When the moving average changes direction, a new position may be taken. When the price line crosses the moving average, the position is liquidated. Used this way, the signal occurs much earlier and a position may be taken that will catch more of a market move.

An even more sensitive use of the moving average is to combine it with a bar chart. Used this way, a moving average of the highs and a moving average of the lows will create a channel called a volatility band (Figure 10-9). When prices move out of this channel, a new trend may be developing. When prices are outside the channel for two consecutive days, this may constitute a signal to take market action.

Improving on Moving Averages

Of all the popular timing indicators available to traders, moving averages still attract the most attention. But when I look at the history of traditional moving averages, I have to ask myself why traders are so enamored with these indicators when their accuracy is so low.

Moving average–based systems are most attractive when they're making money (as are all systems). Traders often begin using these systems just prior to major periods of drawdown and then get caught in the decline. In spite of the serious drawbacks inherent in the use of moving average–based systems, there are a number of things we can do to improve their results and accuracy.

1. *Begin using a Moving Average (MA) based system after it's had a drawdown.* The drawdowns in MA systems are characteristically very large. The best time to begin using an MA system is after a period of severe drawdown. This is, of course, true for any system that has had a good track record, but this is the time when most traders avoid systems. The simple fact is that if you want to use an MA system, you ought to find one that has performed well and then begin using it when it has virtually "collapsed."

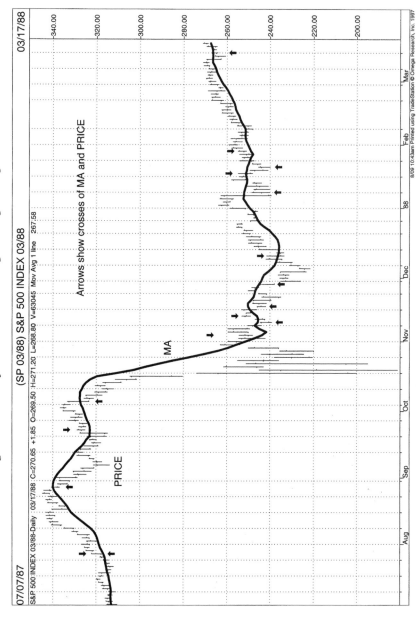

Figure 10-8: Daily Price Lines Crossing Moving Average

Figure 10-9: Volatility Band Channel of Moving Averages of Highs and Lows

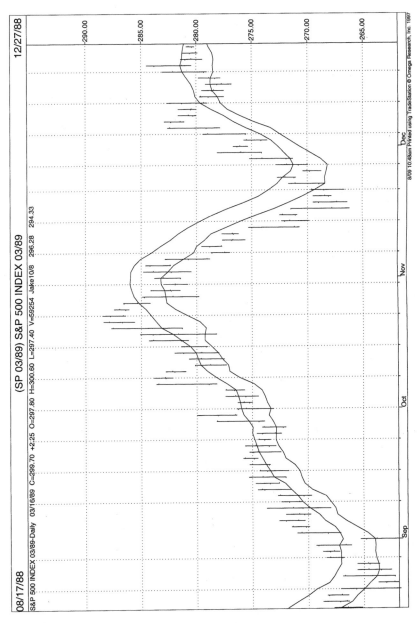

2. *Monitor consecutive losses.* One of the most overlooked aspects of any system is the number of consecutive losers. MA systems are notorious for having very low accuracy and, hence, a large number of consecutive losers. While the norm for most systems is from seven to twelve consecutive losers, MA systems can show many more consecutive losers than that! What's the best way to take advantage of this information?

   The answer is simple: Find an MA system that's done well in the past and go with it after it has had a large number of consecutive losers. The best way to do this is to monitor an existing system or to develop one on your own using system development software. There are a number of excellent programs available for testing and developing systems. Developing a system that backtests with great results is a very simple process.

3. *Test other types of MAs.* Many MA-based systems use simple moving averages of closing prices. My work with other types of MAs suggests that performance can be improved dramatically by using weighted or exponential MAs.

4. *Use variations on the theme of MAs.* The vast majority of MA-based systems use closing prices in calculating their timing signals. Consider using a different approach, such as the midpoint price of the day, the highs and lows of the day, or even the daily price range. There are many variations on the theme of MAs. Consider using some of them. The versatility of system-testing programs is such that the variations can be tested quickly.

5. *Use confirming indicators.* One excellent way to filter out false signals is to use a confirming indicator that is not moving average–based. Moving averages and seasonals, for example, make a good combination. Another useful combination is cycles and moving averages.

6. *Use different MAs for entry and exit.* This is one of the most important suggestions I can give you with regard to moving averages. Markets are not linear. In other words, what may work for entry on the long side doesn't necessarily work for entry on the short side. Markets decline faster

than they rally. Hence, timing signals should be adjusted accordingly to compensate for this difference.

7. *Use different entry and exit methods.* This approach is essentially similar to point 6, except that it uses a different timing method for selling short than it does for going long. A good system-testing program will give you an analysis of how the buy and sell signals fared as a group. You can then judge which indicators work better for buy signals and which work better for sell signals, allowing you to set up a hybrid MA system.

Conclusions about Moving Averages

Moving average signals are popular among many money managers and speculators. Their popularity derives from the fact that moving average signals meet many of the specific criteria of effective systems, specifically:

1. Moving average signals are specific and objective and almost force traders to follow the rules.
2. Moving average signals can keep the trader in the market at all times, closing out a long when going short and covering a short when going long. This is valuable, because the trader will thus be in a position when a major move begins.
3. Moving averages are trend-following systems. In other words, when a good trend is in effect, the likelihood of the moving average having a position consistent with the trend is very high.

Additionally, moving averages are quite easy to use in this age of computers. In fact, a computer can quite easily be programmed to generate specific buy-and-sell signals with various moving averages. The variations are endless. Moving averages are not predictors of market action, however. A moving average is a follower, not a leader. It never anticipates; it only reacts.

The best moving average for a hedger is probably not the best one for a speculator. A hedger would probably prefer a longer-range moving average, while a speculator would choose a shorter-range, more sensitive one. A portfolio manager might prefer a longer-range moving average than any professional trader would.

STOCHASTICS

A curious phenomenon often occurs in the futures market. As prices increase, the closing price is usually closer to the upper end of the price bar, and as prices decrease, the closing price is usually closer to the lower end of the price bar. This phenomenon is curious only because of its consistency, not because it is unexpected.

As I have said so often, the chart of a market is really a diagram of the behavior of the players in the market. Therefore, in a bull market, the buyers are stronger than the sellers and tend to push prices up toward the end of the day, while in a bear market the converse is true. Toward the end of a trend, however, as the pressure that has supported the trend weakens, a new pattern develops. In a bull market, buying pressure weakens as a reversal approaches. The result is that prices continue to hit new highs, but the closing price moves closer to the low end of the price bar, or the low price of the day. A bear market reversal will see a similar pattern in reverse.

Stochastics is simply an oscillator that measures the relative position of the closing price within the price bar, or the daily price range, and uses that information to forecast a market turn. Most quote systems offer stochastics, and many chart services carry the stochastic graph at the bottom of the chart.

The mathematical calculations involved in stochastics are too complex for the scope of this book, but the pattern looks like a double oscillator. The slow line, which is called %D, is a three-day moving average of the faster line, which is called %K. As the %K line crosses %D, market signals are given. With stochastics, significant signals result from left and right crossovers (Figure 10-10), extreme turns, and reduction of speed.

The stochastic indicator (SI) was popularized by Dr. George Lane. The relative strength indicator (RSI) is essentially similar to the SI. The difference is that SI has two values while RSI has only one. The second SI value is derived by computing a moving average of the first SI value.

Both indicators are often used to indicate theoretically "overbought" or "oversold" conditions. They may both be used as timing indicators as well. However, the concepts of overbought and oversold are not useful and they can get traders into trouble. Both

Figure 10-10: Stochastic Indicator

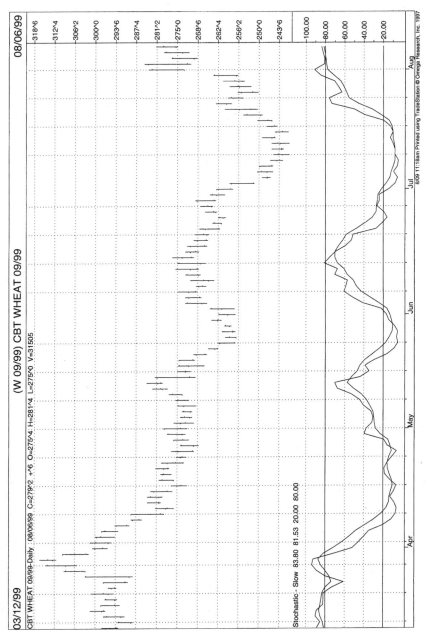

209

indicators tend to continue in what is called overbought or oversold territory for a long time. As prices move higher and higher,
the indicator remains overbought, and vice versa. The problem is
that traders often equate the term "overbought" with a market top
and "oversold" with a market bottom. This is not always the case.
Many times a market will push higher and higher while traders
continue to fight the trend based on an "overbought" RSI or SI
reading. The same can hold true in downtrends. Don't use the SI
and RSI for determining overbought or oversold conditions. Use
these indicators as timing methods when the readings cross above
or below certain values.

CYCLES

Cyclical methods are based on the fact that price history repeats.
The Foundation for the Study of Cycles has documented a considerable body of evidence to support the cyclical approach to trading. Jay W. Forrester at MIT has developed a highly intricate and
statistically valid method of evaluating long-term economic cycles.
A significant body of academic theory and research supports the
existence of economic cycles and market cycles.

    Cycle trends and cyclical patterns are relatively easy to find
and can be subjected to mathematical testing and evaluation. Price
cycles exist in virtually every market and in many different time
frames. But remember, cycles are not always accurate. At times cycle
lows and highs are skipped, and at times cycles can bottom late or
early, and at times they can top late or early. Hence, timing is an
issue of major importance. Use timing indicators with cycles. Do not
make the mistake of thinking that cycle lengths are written in stone.

MOMENTUM AND RATE OF CHANGE

Although these indicators are derived using different mathematical operations, their output is the same in terms of highs, lows, and
trends. I believe that both momentum and rate of change (ROC)
have been ignored and underrated as trading indicators and as
valid inputs for trading systems.

    These indicators are very adaptable. Beyond their use as indi-
cators, they can be developed into specific trading systems with

risk management. They can also be used for the purpose of timing spread entry and exit. They are lagging indicators to a given extent. As a result, they tend to be a little late at tops and bottoms.

Momentum and rate of change indicators can be plotted against their own moving averages in order to reduce the time lag of signals. They can also be used with seasonals and cycles as confirming indicators.

KEY-DATE SEASONALS

Key-date seasonals are very specific. A very special approach to seasonal trading and timing, they provide exact entry, exit, and stop loss criteria. But we have only a limited data history in some futures markets, so high-percentage historical accuracy is suspect in some cases. Use key-date seasonals with trends and timing to filter years that will not work.

MARKET SENTIMENT INDICATORS

These indicators are based on the concept of contrary opinion. The idea is that the majority will be wrong most of the time. There are several indicators or sources from which contrary opinion can be evaluated. These include Market Vane, the USDA Commitment of Traders Report, Odd Lot Short Sales (for the stock market), and my own Daily Sentiment Index. The theory is simply that when bullish sentiment is too high, prices tend to top and when bullish sentiment is too low, markets tend to bottom.

Market sentiment and contrary opinion have a lengthy history of validity and reliability. They can be used in an objective way, preferably with timing and other technical tools. They can also be used with fundamentals and as inputs in neural network systems. Market sentiment indicators tend to be leading indicators. They can also be used for short-term and intermediate-term swings. But these indicators are sometimes too early in picking tops and bottoms. In some cases the data is not timely, since there is a lag between the time it is collected and the time it is made available to traders. Some measures of market sentiment are not objective (e.g., examining newspaper headlines and stories for their bullish or bearish content). Use these indicators in conjunction with market trends and timing. Use moving averages of market sentiment data to develop a timing approach.

WILDER'S RELATIVE STRENGTH INDEX

In the early 1980s, Welles Wilder and I, along with a group of other traders, toured the Far East for several weeks presenting seminars on our various methods of market analysis. During our tour, I learned a great deal about Wilder's methods and gathered from my discussions with him that he considered his Relative Strength Index (RSI) to be his best work.

RSI uses a mathematical formula to determine market strength, weakness, probable low or probable high. Over the years traders have used the RSI in many ways. Some swear by it while others swear at it. Yet swearing at the RSI merely reveals that the trader has not correctly understood how the RSI is best used.

Divergence

One excellent application of the RSI is to use it as a method of finding markets that are divergent. In other words, the RSI can be used to help you find markets that are in uptrends, but weak and in danger of topping; or in downtrends, but growing stronger and likely to bottom. Divergence can be either bullish or bearish.

> *Bullish Divergence*: When an indicator is moving higher but price is moving lower, bullish divergence exists, suggesting that a top is likely very soon.

> *Bearish Divergence*: When an indicator is moving lower but price is moving higher, bearish divergence exists, suggesting that a bottom is likely very soon.

Figures 10-11 and 10-12 illustrate divergence using RSI. Figure 10-11 shows RSI moving lower as price moves higher. This condition is termed bearish divergence, as noted above, and usually precedes a price decline. Figure 10-12 illustrates a similar situation. Bullish divergence occurs when price moves lower while RSI moves higher.

Figure 10-11: RSI Divergence (Bearish)

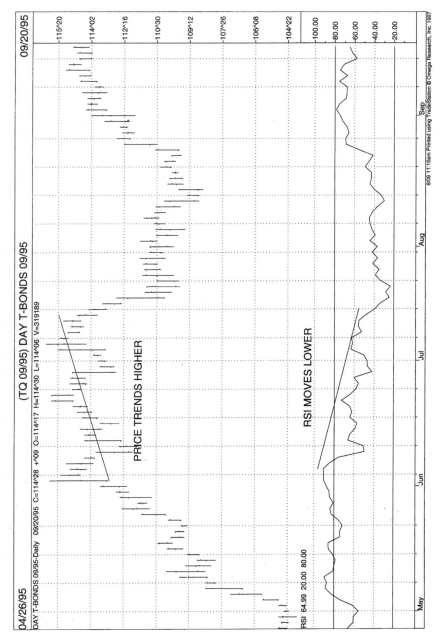

Figure 10-12: RSI Divergence (Bullish)

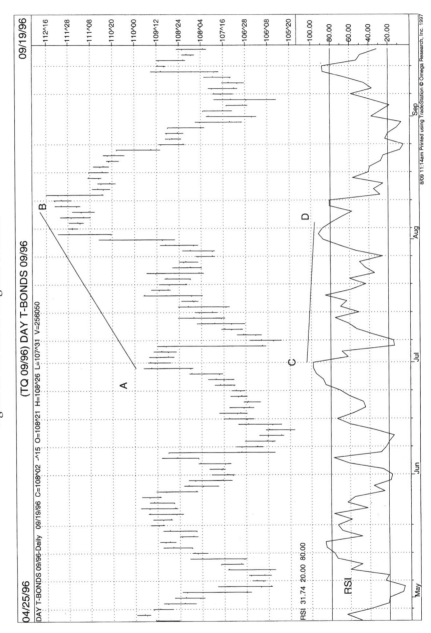

214

OSCILLATORS

If a trader can know when prices are losing their momentum, you might have a good idea that the present trend is about to reverse itself. If the price X days ago is greater than the current price, the value will be negative; if the price X days ago is less than the current price, the value will be positive. When these values are plotted, they form a curving line that moves around a zero line, as in Figure 10-13.

When the difference between the prices is the same for several days, the line will be straight. As the difference increases, the line moves up. As the difference decreases, the line moves down. This is the measure of momentum, or the rate of change in prices. This measure of the momentum of change can be normalized. At that point, we have a momentum oscillator.

This is the most fundamental of the various kinds of oscillators that are used by market analysts. All oscillators tend to look alike on a chart. They consist of a band across the bottom of the chart, with a line that fluctuates, or oscillates, above and below a midpoint. Some oscillators use a zero midpoint, with +1 and -1 representing the boundaries. Others use a scale from zero to 100. Whatever form they take, oscillators are designed to measure the underlying strength of a price move in the market.

Oscillators are normally used in conjunction with other trend-following analysis tools and are subordinated to them. They are rarely used alone. Although valuable in trending markets, oscillators are particularly useful in nontrending markets, where prices are fluctuating within a price bond, commonly called a trading range.

A momentum oscillator is helpful in alerting the trader to an overbought or oversold market condition. When the oscillator reaches the extremes of the chart, it may indicate that the price move has gone too far, too fast, and is due to change direction. A momentum oscillator is useful in three ways. First, it provides overbought and oversold signals, as just mentioned. Second, as the oscillator crosses the zero line, it gives buy or sell signals. Third, a momentum oscillator measures divergence: When the direction of price is different from the direction of the oscillator, this can be a particularly strong signal.

Figure 10-13: Daily Oscillator

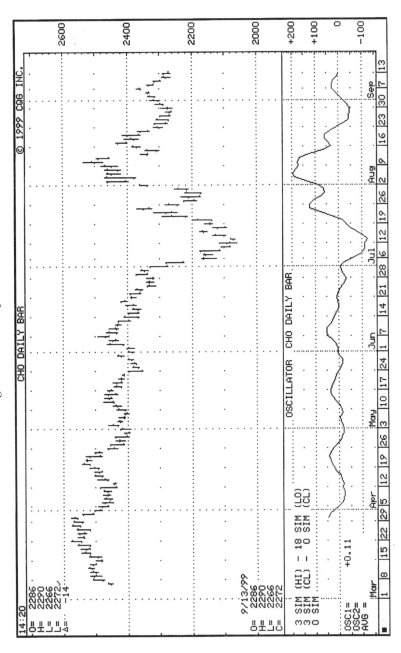

Momentum oscillators can be very helpful tools for a trader to use. However, they suffer from two significant shortcomings. First, momentum oscillators tend to be very erratic because they are subject to extreme price moves on either side of the calculation. Second, momentum oscillators lack a standardized upper and lower boundary applicable to all markets. These weaknesses have made the momentum oscillator difficult to work with and have led to the development of more sophisticated and useful oscillators.

Larry Williams has become well known among futures traders in recent years for his performance in the Robbins Trading Company World Cup Championship of Futures Trading. His trading in that competition was based on oscillator systems he has been developing and refining for many years. In 1972 he published a description of his A/D oscillator. This was followed by the %R oscillator, which is really a 10-day stochastic. Most recently, he has developed what he calls the ultimate oscillator, which seems to combine the original A/D oscillator with Wilder's RSI.

Another variation of the use of oscillators is the Cambridge Hook, developed by Dr. James Kneafsey. This system combines an outside reversal day (a higher high followed by a lower close) with both Wilder's RSI and a measure of volume and open interest. When all three conditions are met, the signal is very accurate in predicting trend reversals.

VOLUME AND OPEN INTEREST

I have frequently been asked whether volume and open interest are useful indicators, either separately or in combination. The simple answer is that traders can extract some meaningful information from both volume and open interest, for a few very specific applications.

Before giving you some ideas of how volume (Vol) and open interest (OI) can be used as market indicators, I present the traditional interpretation of the relationship between Vol and OI. Understanding that will help you to have a sense of their accuracy (or lack thereof), so you will be immune to the many opinions that analysts form regarding the direction of a market based on the Vol and OI relationship to price. Most often the relationship will not prove valuable to you.

Most technical analysts do not make decisions based on only one or two pieces of information. Some market information is of a primary nature; that is, distinct market signals are communicated. For example, price is a primary market indicator. Other information is of a secondary nature. It is used to substantiate or confirm the primary signals. Volume and open interest are secondary indicators, but they are significant to many traders. Many persons new to futures trading are confused by the concepts of volume and open interest. Once you understand the distinction, however, you will also understand the significance of each.

Volume is the total number of contracts traded on a given day. To find the volume, add the total of the short positions taken that day, or add the total of the long positions taken that day. Do not add the two together. (Remember, a contract requires both a buyer and a seller.)

Open interest is the total number of contracts still outstanding at the end of a given day. To find the open interest in a market, add the number of short positions still being held at the close of the trading day, or add the total number of long positions being held at the end of the day. Do not add the two together.

Even though there is a dearth of research regarding the relationship of volume and open interest to the market, most market analysts watch both statistics closely, along with price. Newspaper price charts carry the volume and open interest figures on a daily basis, which makes it relatively easy to use the data even without sophisticated market quote systems.

The common wisdom among traders and analysts is that, generally, rising prices combined with declining volume and open interest are seen as a signal for a price reversal. When volume and open interest are both increasing, the common thinking is that the present trend will continue because open interest tends to increase during a trending period. These relationships are shown in Table 10-1.

Two valuable rules on the application of volume and open interest come from Larry Williams, in his classic book, *How I Made $1 Million Trading Commodities Last Year*:

1. A sideways market that over a brief period of time shows a large drop in OI is an indication that commercials are covering shorts and that the market is likely to move higher.
2. A sideways market that over a brief period of time shows a large rise in OI is an indication that commercials are establishing new shorts and that the market is likely to move lower.

Such situations tend to precede large moves; however, they occur very rarely. Such extremes should be viewed with interest, inasmuch as they can prove valuable when used in conjunction with other timing work.

Table 10-1: Volume and Open Interest Interpretation

Price	Volume	Open Interest	Market
Increasing	Increasing	Increasing	Technically strong
Increasing	Decreasing	Decreasing	Technically weak
Decreasing	Increasing	Increasing	Technically weak
Decreasing	Decreasing	Decreasing	Technically strong

FIBONACCI NUMBER SERIES

Charles H. Dow first noted that retracements of price waves were often 50 percent of the original wave, with the range extending from one-third to two-thirds. R. N. Elliott, in carrying Dow's work further, based his own wave theories on a series of similar percentage relationships or ratios that have their roots in ancient Egyptian and Greek civilizations. The Egyptians used a ratio of 0.618 or 1.618 in their construction of the Great Pyramid of Giza. The ratio of the elevation to the base is 0.618, a ratio that the Egyptians called the golden ratio. The Greeks applied this same ratio, which they called the golden mean, to the construction of the Parthenon.

It was left to a relatively unknown thirteenth-century Italian mathematician named Leonardo Fibonacci, however, to discover these mathematical ratios and, by so doing, give his name to a number series that seems to be elemental to much of the physical world in which we live. Having observed and studied the Great Pyramid, Fibonacci carried the numerical relationships further when he studied the mathematical problem of the reproduction of rabbits.

Having established the basic conditions that every month a pair of rabbits produces a new pair of rabbits, which then become reproductive from the second month on, producing new pairs at the same rate, without any deaths occurring, Fibonacci developed his "summation series":

$$1, 1, 2, 3, 5, 8, 13, 21, 34, 55, 89, 144 \ldots$$

At first glance, this number series seems to be only a random grouping of numbers. The relationship becomes clear, however, when you discover that each number in the series is the sum of the previous two numbers. Moreover, the ratio of each consecutive pair of numbers approaches 0.618 or 1.618 after the first four numbers: $1/2 = 0.50$; $2/3 = 0.667$; $8/13 = 0.615$; $21/34 = 1.618$. These numbers and ratios seem to occur throughout the natural world: in the sunflower, in the chambered nautilus, in a musical octave (8 white keys and 5 black, totaling 13) and in the artistic works of Leonardo da Vinci.

By applying Fibonacci ratios to the stock market, Elliott discovered that these mathematical relationships could be observed there as well. It is fascinating to think that market prices—which, as we have said, reflect human behavior and psychology—would follow patterns of activity so closely related to seemingly elemental relationships that exist throughout nature. Yet as Elliott has demonstrated, the ratios of the various waves and retracement waves often fall very closely within the Fibonacci ratios of 0.50, 0.618, and 1.618.

Traders use Fibonacci ratios and numbers to project support and resistance levels and specific dates or targets that are Fibonacci numbers.

CHAPTER 11

Managing Risk

Most professional futures traders advocate a strict approach to risk management in order to facilitate success. In this chapter I touch on some money management issues and tell you about stop losses and how they can help keep your risks lower.

Speculators often learn early in the futures trading game that risk management is the key element to success or failure. I rank risk management even higher in importance than your trading system or trader experience, although I hasten to add that the success of any trading system or risk management method is, to a certain extent, a function of trader expertise.

Notwithstanding the importance of experience, risk management is an issue that all traders must deal with. Seemingly outstanding trading systems have been rendered less than worthless for lack of solid risk management, and mediocre trading systems have shown excellent profits as a result of effective risk management.

PRESERVATION OF CAPITAL

To put it succinctly, you must preserve your capital by cutting your losses if you want to survive in the futures game. This may seem obvious enough, but I assure you that it is easier said than done. Many traders find it virtually impossible to manage their money.

Proponents of capital preservation have advanced the concepts of maximization of return on each profitable trade and minimization of loss on each losing trade. Having a maximum amount you are willing to risk when you enter a trade or setting a risk limit based on technical indicators will help you achieve your goals. Although this is simple, sound reasoning, it may well be found to be incorrect and even presumptuous. The practice of using stop loss placement as a function of predetermined dollar risk is misguided. It is not necessarily consistent with the objectives of a technical system. It is a requirement imposed by psychological and financial needs as opposed to technical indicators. Even if one optimizes stop loss procedures by basing them on market history, the logic may not necessarily be any more solid. A reasonable alternative is to let each trade take its natural course and allow the indicators to get you in and out, but with a fail-safe level established for each trade that will get you out if the indicators fail. Each speculator must find his or her particular solution to this dilemma.

MAXIMIZATION OF CAPITAL

The second function of successful money management is the maximization of capital. Some traders feel that they must be in the market at all times or that they must trade every day if they are to maximize their capital. I suspect that operating on this basis alone is a good way to minimize capital. Capital maximization is achieved by:

- Preserving trading capital for only the most promising situations.
- Allotting capital on the basis of performance and potential.
- Trading only the required amount of capital, with the excess employed in other areas of speculation or investment.

PROFIT DISPERSAL

Although it is hard to believe, this is a frequent problem. Traders often make profits quickly and give them back even more quickly because they don't have a well-prepared plan for distributing their profits. I view the marketplace as a treasure chest: When it is open, one must grab all one can get before the heavy lid slams shut. The idea is to take it quickly and to keep it out of the treasure chest.

At times, you may have to force the lid open and this will take time, energy, and money (for the proper tools). Yet, the goal is always the same—to take out more than you put in. Therefore, I urge all traders to regularly remove some profits from the market, placing them in investments that guarantee a slow but steady rate of return. Routinely removing profits from the market will help you in two ways:

- First, you'll have funds to put back into the market in the event that you need to refinance your account.
- Second, you'll have funds for other purposes.

LOSS MANAGEMENT

There are two basic approaches to loss management. One method limits losses by setting a predetermined dollar amount per trade. Using this approach, a trader decides to risk only a certain amount on each trade or on each market. This approach, however, imposes an artificial limit on the market and on your trading, and therefore seems impractical to me.

It makes more sense to manage losses by market behavior. After all, isn't it ultimately the market that must be followed? Before you decide to go with a strict maximum dollar-per-trade approach, consider loss management by market behavior as an alternative.

Before deciding which approach best suits you, consider the following:

1. Loss management by market behavior (that is, using timing signals and trading objectives only) may require you to take more risk per trade.

2. A maximum dollar-per-trade approach may limit your loss on each trade, but it may also remove you from situations that could ultimately turn out to be profitable.

3. A maximum dollar-per-trade approach may allow you to trade more markets at once, thereby allowing you to diversify your trading.

Double Up or Cut Back?

It is not uncommon for traders to double up after one or two losing trades. This practice was, perhaps, originally adapted from the blackjack card game. The mere fact that this practice may be derived from gambling puts it in a bad light among traders. However, I suggest that under the right circumstances it might not be bad to double up.

For example, if you have a system that rarely takes more than three successive losses, you can double your position after the third successive loss. But if you do so you must remember that you are taking more risk and you will not necessarily be guaranteed a profit. Ultimately, a trading system with a high number of winning trades will benefit from such a procedure, though it takes stamina and fortitude to implement.

On the other side of the coin, there is the practice of cutting back when things are not going well. There's nothing wrong with this approach. In fact, it's not a bad way to preserve capital while you try to figure out what's going wrong.

Diversification

I won't spend a great deal of time on this aspect of money management for limiting loss. The fact is that many traders fail to diversify. Your success or failure should not depend entirely upon the performance of your trading approach in only one or two markets. I suggest that you monitor and trade in a variety of markets. Avoid the thin markets, but monitor at least 14 to 18 markets regularly and diversify your trading accordingly.

Consider Multiple Positions

I find that a particularly useful strategy is to trade in multiple contracts (if you can afford to do so) but in a manner distinctly different from the old pyramiding approach. In the typical pyramiding approach, the initial entry consists of the smallest number of contracts. As the market moves in your direction, more and more contracts are added, leading eventually to an upside-down pyramid with the largest number of contracts at the highest price.

This leaves the trader vulnerable; a small reversal can bring the house down. This is not, to my way of thinking, the way to trade. I advocate building a real pyramid instead. Begin with your largest position and add successively smaller units along the way.

Another procedure particularly suitable for the day trader is to begin with multiple contracts. As the market moves in your favor you can take a profit quickly on half of your contracts, keeping the remaining contracts for a more optimistic target. I prefer this approach because it allows one to take some profits and let some profits ride.

Be Sure to Be Well-Capitalized

Avoid any type of trading until you are well-capitalized. Though this should be an obvious caveat to all traders, it's one that tends to be ignored by the overly zealous. By today's standards, any account of less than $10,000 has little chance of success. Increase your initial trading capital and you'll have more staying power. Don't begin trading with an amount so small that you are beaten before you start.

STOP LOSSES: A DOUBLE-EDGED SWORD

Risk management, simply defined, is the act of limiting losses. A number of time-tested and highly reliable techniques are part and parcel of effective risk management. Among these are the use of stop losses, futures options, spreads, position size, and asset allocation.

To a certain extent all of the above are inseparable. For example, if you are a trader carrying a position that is way too large considering your available risk capital, you may attempt to compensate for the risk exposure by using a very small stop loss. This is a counterproductive methodology and a sure invitation to losses. Similarly, if you spread a position to avoid taking a loss, you may think you are limiting your loss, but in reality you are actually doubling your risk exposure. Risk management is like all other things in life. There are hundreds of things you can do wrong and only a handful that are right. The key is to find those that are right and to do them consistently.

What makes stop losses difficult, if not impossible, to use is the fact that they're a double-edged sword. You know that their use is necessary if losses are to be minimized, yet you also know that you've been stopped out of positions many times, only to see the market go your way after you've been stopped out. What should you do? There's no doubt that stops are necessary, but using stops effectively and placing them carefully are keys to success.

Smaller Stops = Smaller Profits = More Losses

Perhaps one of the best lessons I learned about stop losses is that they have to be large enough to permit the market reasonable movement. Stop losses that are too close to the market are not recommended other than under very special circumstances. Many day traders, for example, are fascinated with the idea of using extremely small stop losses in order to limit risk. The end result of this approach may be that the accuracy of their trading may be very low, because stops will be hit very frequently.

A stop loss must be large enough to allow the market its reasonable movement. If, for example, S&P futures have shown an average daily range of 350 points, then a stop loss of 100 points may be much too small to use, inasmuch as the random behavior of the market will stop you out more often than not. Regardless of how exact or precise your trading system may be in picking concise price points, no trading system is immune to random market behavior.

A friend and business associate of many years, Larry Williams, said it best when he told me "I use very large stop losses when day trading S&P futures because I have to give the market enough breathing room . . . when I take a loss I want to really feel it."

At first, Larry's penchant for large stop losses didn't seem sensible to me. I learned to respect it after watching Larry profit handsomely from his short-term and day trades, time and time again, while I would have been stopped out using what I thought were low-risk stops. After trading side-by-side with Larry during more than 25 Real Time trading seminars we've done together, I've come to respect the value of wide stops. I've seen the sense of using large stops, although the idea of using them may be unpalatable to many traders.

Side-by-Side Comparison

Figure 11-1 illustrates my point about stop loss levels. It displays the historical performance of a trading system I developed quickly using Omega TradeStation™. The tabular presentation shows historical backtesting of the same market entry and exit rules with 11 different stop loss levels. Here are my conclusions:

1. As stop loss increases, so do net profits per trade.
2. As stop loss increases, so does system accuracy until it peaks and can no longer increase.
3. As stop loss increases, drawdown remains fairly stable. Hence more risk per trade does not increase drawdown.

Figure 11-1: System Backtest Using 11 Different Initial Stop Loss Levels

Initial Stop $	Total Profit	Average Trade	% Correct	Draw-down	Largest Loss $	Largest Win $	Consec. Losers
500	34,715.00	257.15	39%	−7,155.00	−875.00	+15,775.00	7
750	46,910.00	350.07	44%	−5,965.00	−1,645.00	+15,775.00	7
1000	48,730.00	363.66	49%	−6,650.00	−1,825.00	+15,775.00	6
1200	52,940.00	395.07	51%	−5,955.00	−1,825.00	+15,775.00	5
1400	57,395.00	431.54	52%	−2,175.00	−2,175.00	+15,775.00	5
1600	57,815.00	434.70	53%	−5,655.00	−2,175.00	+15,775.00	4
1800	56,475.00	424.62	53%	−5,635.00	−2,175.00	+15,775.00	4
2200	58,470.00	442.95	53%	−5,145.00	−2,175.00	+15,775.00	4
2800	57,480.00	435.45	53%	−5,480.00	−2,775.00	+15,775.00	4
3500	57,590.00	436.29	53%	−6,180.00	−2,875.00	+15,775.00	4
4500	60,720.00	460.00	54%	−6,165.00	−2,765.00	+15,775.00	4

4. As stop loss increases, the largest losing trade increases minimally.

5. As stop loss increases, overall profits for the system nearly double.

6 Stop loss increases to a point of diminishing returns and system performance peaks.

7. The smallest stop losses produce the worst results.

8. The largest stop losses produce the best results.

9. As stop losses increase, the number of successive losing trades decreases considerably.

As you can see, small stop losses do not do what you'd expect them to do. Big stop losses work better.

The Law of Diminishing Returns

In economic theory the law of diminishing returns states that the amount of return one derives from additional inputs of effort or resources peaks at a point and then levels off. Very similar to the law of diminishing returns in economics (which states that beyond a certain point, increased investment will not result in increased returns), the protective value of a stop loss decreases as the stop loss amount is increased. The protective value of a stop loss decreases when the stop loss gets too high. Hence, stop losses must somehow be optimized. This is a relatively simple procedure to perform with mechanical trading systems. These systems can be backtested with different stop losses and stop loss scenarios.

Naturally, critics will argue that history does not always repeat itself exactly and that using such a procedure to optimize stops is subject to the problems that are always associated with system optimization. To a certain extent these criticisms are valid, but such testing for stop losses is a viable methodology that can tell you a great deal about the optimum size of a stop loss for certain patterns or systems.

In some cases a larger stop is worse than a smaller stop, but the idea of testing for stop loss size is important. If you find that the ideal stop loss is too rich for your account, then you can either avoid the trade or research another method of risk limitation.

Remember that systems won't always work this way. The point is that sometimes less in terms of a stop loss is not more when it comes to the bottom line.

Risk Management through Margin Control

Another way to manage risk is to redefine the rules of margin. Instead of putting up the exchange minimum margins, it is often preferable to give yourself a large cushion, particularly if you're going after longer-term moves.

Some will argue that this destroys the attraction of the futures game inasmuch it removes the leverage. While there may be some truth to that, leverage is a double-edged sword—it can help you and it can hurt you. Unfortunately it hurts most people in the futures market. If you use leverage wisely, then you can use it to your advantage.

Trailing Stop Losses

The trailing stop loss has been a favorite among traders for many years. Simply explained, the trailing stop loss "trails" market moves. As your profit continues to mount, the stop loss is continuously changed to reflect the increased profit. The goal is to protect the profit from a reversal in trend.

While this sounds like a reasonable and rational methodology, it is also a flawed approach as most often used by traders. The reason it is flawed is that, once again, traders do not allow the market sufficient space for random movements. Most often, traders are stopped out of their positions with trailing stops because the trailing stops are too close to the market.

When the market responds emotionally to news, even news that is unrelated to the underlying trend, many traders with trailing stops are stopped out. It is not the trailing stop concept that's at fault; rather it's the size of the trailing stop that's the culprit.

Figure 11-2 displays the results of another experiment based on trailing stops. It was developed on the same system as Figure 11-1, but for ten different levels of trailing stop losses using a fixed initial stop loss.

Figure 11-2: Trailing Stop Losses

% Stop Trail	Total Profit	Average Trade $	% Correct	Draw-down $	Largest Loss $	Largest Win $	Consec. Losers
10	35,760.00	262.94	54%	−5,860.00	−2,775.00	+5,735.00	3
20	32,190.00	236.69	54%	−6,195.00	−2,775.00	+5,735.00	3
30	31,420.00	231.03	54%	−6,195.00	−2,775.00	+5,735.00	3
40	32,255.00	238.93	55%	−5,975.00	-2,775.00	+5,735.00	3
50	28,930.00	215.90	55%	−5,750.00	−2,775.00	+5,735.00	3
60	35,645.00	268.01	55%	−5,910.00	−2,775.00	+5,735.00	3
70	44,815.00	336.95	54%	−5,780.00	−2,775.00	+5,735.00	3
80	54,420.00	412.27	55%	−5,780.00	−2,775.00	+5,735.00	3
90	57,560.00	436.06	53%	−5,780.00	−2,775.00	+5,735.00	4
100	56,610.00	428.86	51%	−5,780.00	−2,775.00	+5,735.00	7

CHAPTER 12

Computers
and Electronic Trading

E-trading is the abbreviation given to electronic trading. The E-trader conducts his or her trading entirely by computer, entering orders to buy and sell via a modem and obtaining price order fills the same way. In addition, the E-trader usually makes trading decisions based on computerized trading software. There are many programs that are tailor-made for this purpose. As in the case of day trading, I recommend that the novice stay away from this approach until he or she has gained more experience in entering orders, analyzing markets, and risk management.

TRADING HARDWARE—HOW MUCH COMPUTER POWER WILL YOU NEED?

There are many different programs for market analysis and there will be many more developed in the future. Each has its own memory and hard drive space requirements. Hardware should, therefore, be your first consideration in preparing for E-trading. There are other considerations above and beyond the minimum memory requirements stated by the trading program developers. While the basics may meet your program needs, they may not necessarily be sufficient for the speedy operation of E-trading. If you trade actively and want to monitor many different stocks or futures contracts, you will need substantial memory and disk space in order to do so. If you're tracking markets in small time frames (e.g., one-minute charts), you will need even more memory in order to handle all the graphics and ongoing calculations. Add to this the incoming Internet data as well as your outgoing electronic orders, and you have a system that will need considerable memory and disk space.

Given these needs, I urge you to make your choice of a system based on how actively you want to trade, how much data you want to store and retrieve, and how many different systems or timing indicators you plan to have running at the same time. To some extent these considerations are academic if you decide to buy the biggest, the fastest, and the best computer that's available. In today's highly competitive market, $5,000 will buy you such a system, and with a little shopping around you can get what you want for as little as $3,000 (or even less).

I suggest that you begin with a computer system with expandable memory, in case you need additional power. Furthermore, select a high-speed, state-of-the-art machine with a large amount of storage space. I strongly recommend a built in CD/ROM drive so that you can store historical data on CD once your hard drive has reached more than 75 percent of its capacity. In fact, you may wish to have several hard drives in your machine. Finally, I recommend that your machine have high-end graphics capability as well as a video board with sufficient memory. Much of your work as an E-trader will depends on visuals in the form of charts and graphs. Having fast, high-quality graphics as well as high-resolution video will help you considerably.

How Requirements Will Change Over Time

Technology moves very quickly in the computer field. What is state-of-the-art today will be outdated in several months and will be archaic in a few years. The system you buy today will likely outlive its usefulness in several years, so do your best to buy a system capable of being upgraded. Some manufacturers now offer computer systems on a monthly charge basis that are continually upgradable as major advances are introduced. Remember that in developing your trading methods, you will likely create many files, charts, systems, methods, and indicators. These should be stored in an organized fashion and backed up regularly so that when you upgrade to a more advanced computer hardware configuration, the job of transferring your data will not be difficult or even impossible.

Coming Advances in Computer Hardware

Computer hardware is becoming more advanced and sophisticated daily, and progress is so rapid that it can often be frustrating. Prices are coming down as quality and processing speeds are going up. A computer system bought today may be cheaper in several months and may no longer be state-of-the-art. There are even more changes coming; by the year 2005, the progress is likely to be astounding, making the most advanced machines today totally archaic by then. Computing speeds will increase well beyond today's fastest machines and data storage may no longer be maintained on a hard drive. Rather, I suspect that data will be stored on chips rather than on mechanical media such as CD/ROM, disk drives, or hard drives. This will markedly increase data access and processing speeds and will allow the E-trader to trade many more markets and to enter orders more quickly, have them filled more quickly, and trade more often.

Clearly there's a limit to how fast data can be processed and orders entered and executed. We may soon reach the point of diminishing returns, until a new level of technological sophistication takes us over the next barrier. What all this means for the E-trader is simple enough to figure out: It means that E-trading is here to stay; that over the next few years, E-trading will become more efficient, sophisticated, and pervasive; and that there will be many more opportunities for those who know how to play the game.

SOFTWARE DECISIONS

When planning to E-trade, the second major decision that a trader must make is the choice of software. There are many different kinds of trading software, some cheap and some very expensive. Some software delivers excellent value for the money while other software is overpriced and not worth the money. Naturally, beauty will be in the eye of the buyer.

What you plan to do with your trading software and the type of trading you plan to do will, of course, dictate your choice. This section presents an overview of the various categories of trading software and explains what's available so that you can determine what's right for you. It should be noted that many E-trading Web sites provide clients with their own custom trading software. For some traders this may be sufficient if you do not have a specific system or method you have developed using other programs. I highly recommend that you get your own analytical and testing software.

Categories of Trading Software

There are generally four categories of trading software. They are:

- *Market Tracking Software:* This software tracks prices, has some charting capabilities, and can help you display prices in a quote board format. But it has limited ability to display market indicators and cannot backtest systems or methods.

- *Market Tracking and Indicator Software:* This type of software is more advanced than market tracking software in that it can keep track of many different markets in different time frames and it allows you to display numerous timing indicators on your charts. It may also contain position-tracking features to update your portfolio in real time with each change in price. Both end-of-day and real-time versions are often available.

- *Market Tracking and Analysis Software:* This software will perform all functions of the first two categories and also allow you to write system codes for custom indicators and systems. These programs often contain options evaluation modules and will also allow you to backtest systems that you have developed. Some contain optimizing programs to allow you to determine the best combination of timing indicator lengths, variables, stop loss points, and other risk management features. There are many different levels of sophistication and prices. Some are available via monthly lease only and others are available for a one-time charge with an additional cost for monthly data.

- *Specialized and Add-On Programs:* Hundreds of add-on programs that work with market tracking and analysis software are also available. These programs are designed to enhance the operation of other software packages. Their functions vary from accounting to artificial intelligence. The majority of these programs offer specific trading systems, some of which reveal their logic and indicators while others are "black box" systems that do not reveal to their buyers what they do or exactly how they work.

Black Box Systems

You may see advertising for computerized trading systems that promise fantastic trading results. The price is usually very high and, in most cases, the results never match the claims made by the promoters. Frequently these systems are "black box" systems, meaning that the logic, rules, and system codes are not revealed to the buyer. What you buy is a black box whose insides you will never see.

The major problem with the black box system is that you will not learn anything about improving performance of the system when it fails, because you won't know how and where it went wrong. If you know how a system works, you can at least study your losses and perhaps determine what went wrong so that you can learn from your losses.

Caveat Emptor

It is always best to fully evaluate any program, system, method, piece of trading software, data, order entry system, analysis program, or otherwise before you spend. Follow the dictum of Occam's Razor, which says that given the choice between a simple effective solution and a complicated effective solution, the simple solution is best. You will most likely encounter all types of products, the majority of which are unnecessary or overrated. Although

I am certainly in favor of any tool that will help you succeed as a trader, via electronic means or otherwise, bear in mind that more expensive and sophisticated tools do not necessarily make for bigger profits.

Given the plethora of programs available, it can be difficult to decide which is best for you. While a given program may make fantastic claims, you may not have the capital, experience, time, or financial ability to follow it. You must know how much the trading system requires you to invest, how bad the drawdowns have been, and what will be required from you in time. Systems can seem very attractive at first; however, after close examination, they may not be right for you. Be sure to consider your available capital, time, and ability to ride losses before you buy a system.

The explosive growth in Internet communications and Web sites in the mid-to-late 1990s has opened a vast new area of information and electronic trading. Charts, news, market updates, and recommendations are now available via the Internet. With so much information available you'll need to be very selective in your choices. Many advisory services are unsuitable for the new trader since they risk too much money on their recommendations. Be very careful about the advice you follow, making certain it meets the necessary requirements discussed in this book.

LIVE MARKET DATA

The electronic trader must have sufficient trading capital, effective systems or methods, and a reliable stream of live data in order to effectively compete in the game. A variety of considerations must be taken into account in selecting a data vendor. While cost may be an important factor to some traders, the fact is that the most reliable data feeds tend to be the more expensive ones. Before going into the details of cost, let's examine the major categories that should be evaluated in making your decision.

End-of-Day Data, Delayed Data, or Live Data

Some people believe that the E-trader can only conduct trading on live or tick-by-tick data, but I do not agree. It is entirely possible to enter orders electronically using end-of-day data. Your trading capital will be limited, so you need to be frugal and highly selective. There are a number of worthwhile programs that will cost less than $500, provided you are satisfied with analyzing end-of-day data. This does not mean that you cannot enter orders electronically via the Internet through your on-line broker. Nor does it necessarily mean that you cannot trade certain methods within a one-day time frame. It means that your graphs, charts, and trading systems will not be updated tick-by-tick, but this is not a limitation and may prove to be an asset.

Some methods are not as time-sensitive as others and can do their work well enough with data that is slightly delayed. Delayed data is often available at no charge or at significantly reduced cost at various Internet sites or through brokerage firms who provide it as a service to their more active trader clients. Some data delays are 10 minutes, whereas others run as much as 20 minutes delayed.

Active E-traders will want to use live data, or data that comes into the trader's computer on a trade-by-trade basis during the time the markets are open. Live data feeds allow you to execute orders promptly so that you can enter and exit markets quickly when a trade has been signaled. Live data is considerably more costly than end-of-day data, depending on the type of live data feed you use—sometimes as much as 20 times the cost of end-of-day data. But those who trade using real-time data often feel that they would not be able to do their trading without it.

I make no value judgment as to which type of data feed is best for the individual trader. Traders vary not only in their personalities but also in the types of systems they trade, so the type of data used must be suited to your application. If you plan to trade numerous times daily, then your best choice will be an efficient and accurate data feed that is not delayed.

Delivery Mode

Stock or market data can be delivered in several ways. Some traders obtain their data free of charge, either via television business news or in delayed form via the Internet. Tick-by-tick data is also available via the Internet, and as the speed of this data transmission mode improves over time, it will be the preferred method of delivery and will be the most cost-efficient method. Data can also be delivered via dish antenna by satellite, which is highly reliable as well as fast and reasonably priced. For those who cannot receive live data in this form, a telephone line can be used for modem delivery, although the delivery of data via the Internet will gradually replace telephone delivery. The delivery of price data via cable television lines is rapidly becoming a viable choice inasmuch as it is cost-efficient and high-speed.

Because active E-traders are highly dependent on reliable and fast data delivery, the method of delivery must be relatively free of errors and service interruptions. If a trader has taken a position in the market and then suffers a disruption in data delivery, the result could be an unnecessary loss; if there is no position when the data is disrupted, a trade could be missed. In either case the result is not good. Therefore you should always consider the reliability of the data service before you invest in it.

To find out which data service meets your requirements, talk to other E-traders. Find out what they're using and how they like it. Before you sign up with a data service, ask questions. Find out if they'll let you have a trial period before you sign on. Above all, be careful of long-term contracts. Many data providers no longer require long-term contracts. Some data vendors do require a lengthy commitment; avoid this type of arrangement.

Error Correction

Many E-traders do not realize that errors in data transmission can prove very costly. A data transmission error can be either obvious or subtle. As an example, consider the following string of prices as they come across the data line:

22.50...22.51...22.50...22.51...22.52A...22.52....29.70...

(Note that the "A" indicates an asked or offered price.)

Clearly, the last number in the series is incorrect. It shows a price that is considerably different from the price at which the given market is trading. In such a case, the error is obvious to the trader and will show on a chart as obviously outside the current range of trading. Recognizing such an error, the trader can repair it manually (as is required in most cases), or the computer program may find the error and correct it automatically (the preferred method). The correct price could be obtained from your broker.

More often than not, such errors are obvious and can be corrected promptly. However, some errors are not obvious to the trader and can, therefore, affect the timing methods, indicators, or trading systems that are being used. A subtle error might appear in a stream of data like this:

22.50...22.51...22.50...22.51...22.52A...22.52....22.53...22.59...
22.53...22.52...

The 22.59 price is an incorrect price that may later be changed, but the trader will not know for certain whether this price is correct or not. In most cases a trader would not notice this error at all. Depending on the trader's system, this one incorrect price could generate a signal to buy or to sell. In the event that several incorrect prices appear, the trader could very well enter a position that would not otherwise have been indicated by the system.

As you can see, receiving correct data is vital to the effective functioning of the E-trader. Some data sources are notorious for numerous errors, while others are relatively free of errors. There is at least one data source that corrects its errors automatically once it has found them. If your trading approach is dependent upon the availability of correct data, then you are advised to ask your prospective or current data vendor how often errors occur and whether they are corrected automatically.

Costs

The more data you get, the more expensive the price will be, so I urge you not to get more data than you can use. Futures traders can sign on to get live data on virtually all major exchanges in the world, but unless you are a professional money manager who trades an international portfolio of commodities or stocks, that much data is not necessary. While it's a good idea to trade a diversified group of stocks or commodities, a trader can realistically handle only so many markets effectively. There is no need to clutter your computer with vast amounts of unnecessary data. You are better off trading fewer markets well than many markets poorly.

Costs for data range from free of charge to as much as $1,000 monthly, depending on the amount of data needed and the form in which it is delivered. Active traders who wish to trade from their brokers' offices can, in many cases, have free access to live data and to data analysis software, as long as they conduct their activities from the brokerage office. This is much more common in stock trading than it is in futures trading. Be sure to evaluate all of your choices.

The Cost of Privacy

While the cost of data, a computer, software, and telephones is significant, the value of privacy is also important. Some traders are lured into trading from their brokerage firms' offices in order to take advantage of the many perks offered to clients who actively day trade or short-term trade. Yet many traders are either unduly influenced by the activity in such trading rooms, or simply prefer to trade from the peace and quiet of their own homes or offices. My preference is for solitude and quiet. Regardless of what you decide, know your personal needs before you sacrifice your privacy and solitude for the din of a trading room.

HISTORICAL DATA: ACCESS, STORAGE, AND RETRIEVAL

Historical market analysis is built upon research, which depends on the availability of data. With so many markets and so much data to evaluate, traders can find themselves inundated with huge data files that cannot all be handled at one time on even the largest of disk drives. Therefore, I urge you to prepare in advance for data storage, preferably on CD/ROM. This will not only free up space on your computer, but it will also allow your computer to run faster. When you need the data for research, you can retrieve it and use it as needed.

Historical research also depends on accurate data. In the same way that live E-trading can be thrown off course by incorrect data, so can historical market research. Hence, you would do well to check your historical data for errors and to fix them as soon as possible. This brings me to the point of historical data as a means of beginning your research. Just as there are numerous live data vendors, there are also vendors who sell historical data on stocks and futures. You can buy both end-of-day data and tick-by-tick data dating back many years. Costs can vary considerably. In some cases it is free, whereas in other cases it can be quite costly; evaluate your many options here as well.

Unless you plan to trade or need to trade all of the markets, you won't have to buy data on everything. Remember, however, that in order to develop your own trading style you will need to do some studying and research that will require historical data. The amount of data you'll need is a function of how far back you plan to carry out your research.

CHAPTER 13

The Psychology of Investing

In this chapter I touch on what is one of the most critical issues in successful futures trading: that of using psychology to your best advantage. There are many issues to consider and, depending on your nature and behaviors, some may be more relevant to you than others. I suggest you read them all and consider them carefully in light of your own self-understanding.

THE BEHAVIOR OF TRADERS

Traders are a strange and wonderful lot indeed. When I made my first trade in the summer of 1968, I had no idea that there are perhaps as many different approaches to the markets as there are traders. I've also discovered that even though traders may tell us they want to make money in the markets, their behavior often tells us otherwise.

243

I've distilled some of my more salient observations of trader behavior into a few pages. I hope you enjoy them, but most of all I hope you benefit from them. Here, then, in no particular order, are my thoughts.

Traders are often too willing to take tips that have no history behind them while they ignore solid trades with a long history of reliability.

Traders work hard to gather reliable information and develop trading systems. They plan their trades. They are methodical in setting a risk point. They have the discipline to follow their systems. Yet all it takes is one urgent call from a broker or one piece of dramatic news, and all their good intentions vanish.

Traders react impulsively to news, not knowing their odds of success, their risk, or the history behind the trades. They lose money on the trade that they took impulsively and yet they fail to learn from the experience. It seems that the human mind is always looking for an "easy shot." When something comes along that seems easy, discipline appears to deteriorate in spite of all intelligent reasons to maintain it.

Traders tend to be a very insecure group of people when it comes to the markets.

What is it that causes traders to err? Lack of knowledge? Lack of capital? Lack of a systematic approach? Yes, at times it is one or all of these. But what it all adds up to is this: Traders tend to wallow in insecurity, no matter how good their trading systems may be. Only the exceptional trader is totally immune to the errors that result from insecurity. Having a solid trading system combined with a disciplined approach can go a long way toward eliminating most trader insecurity.

Traders love forecasts.

Forecasts tend to polarize a person's thinking. They tend to restrict possibilities and give traders tunnel vision. They create a mind-set that is not easily overcome.

Bad price fills are the bane of a trader's existence.

Traders frequently complain about their price fills. While there is certainly an element of truth to the complaints, there is also the fact that the overwhelming majority of traders have no idea about how to place orders effectively or which orders are most suited to their purpose. By merely using the right order at the right time, a trader can save thousands of dollars by saving a few ticks here and a few ticks there.

Those "nasty" floor traders!

Traders are also universal in their dislike and mistrust of floor traders. They accuse them of virtually everything from stealing ticks to fixing prices. Floor traders are just as fallible and human as are all traders. The only difference is that they have more experience and know how to "milk" markets for the few ticks they attempt to extract from their trades.

Traders hate buying on strength and selling on weakness.

A costly lesson I've learned in over 30 years in the futures business is the value of buying on strength and selling on weakness. This is the ultimate way of trading with the trend. Yet traders shy away from this effective strategy because they're always afraid of buying too high or selling too low. The average trader is always trying to find a "deal." While this may work with a street vendor in a flea market, it's not a winning strategy in the futures markets. There are ways to buy at support in bull markets and ways to sell at resistance in bear markets, but most traders don't have the discipline to follow these methods consistently or effectively.

Traders hate taking losses—even small ones.

This is no surprise to you, is it? This is by far one of the worst traits of traders. All too often those little losses, which were not taken when they should have been, turn into account-devouring monsters that can make equity disappear in a matter of days. Many traders would rather allow a small loss of several hundred dollars to turn into a monster than admit to the small loss at the right time.

Traders love to blame everyone but themselves for their losses.

Consider the many times you blamed your broker or the trading floor for your losses. How many times have you blamed the floor for "picking" your stops or the large mutual funds for stopping you out? How often have you blamed your trading advisor or newsletter writers for changing your mind about a trade? Most often we tend to blame everyone but ourselves for losses, but the ultimate responsibility for our trades is our own.

Traders think too much and take too little action.

Thinking is good in many aspects of life, even in trading; however, once you have determined your course of action based on your system or method, you need to *take* action.

Traders are inconsistent.

At times a trader engages in a behavior or behaviors that are clearly in violation of effective trading rules. Yet, in spite of the fact that rules have been broken, the trade or trades result in a profit. This teaches the trader that consistent following of the rules is not necessary. But because the results of inconsistent rule breaking are random, the trader will never know for certain whether breaking the rules will work or not. The inconsistency of results teaches the trader to react inconsistently.

Traders can't accept too many consecutive losses before they begin to doubt themselves as well as their trading systems.

The logic and experience of system testing tell us that some of the best-reading systems are subject to considerable drawdowns as well as strings of losing trades. From my experience I'd have to say that taking as many as seven losses (even up to ten losses) in a row is not unusual. Yet this is precisely what causes traders to abandon their systems or to change them midstream. In order to make a system work for you, you have to give it time and plenty of room. Most traders know this intuitively rather than discursively.

Here is how you may embark or stay firmly on the road to consistent profits. First, examine your trading results by looking at your monthly brokerage statements. Attempt to determine why you made the trades you did. This will let you know at once whether your trades were at all systematic or whether they were based on a whim, emotion, tips, rumors, fear, or greed. If you're like most traders, then you'll find that a relatively small percentage of your trades were the result of a system and that most of your trades were prompted by other factors, most of which were totally unrelated to any definitive system, method, or indicator.

This will alert you to a problem area in your trading. It will let you know, without a doubt, that you are not basing your decisions on a consistent approach. The second step, then, is to fix this problem by looking for a system that has simple, unambiguous rules of application. (See Chapter 14 for a discussion of how to select a trading system.)

MASTERING THE PSYCHOLOGICAL ASPECTS OF COMMODITY TRADING

You can master the psychological end of trading by learning about yourself or by using simple, time-tested, mechanical techniques to overcome the problems. Purists would argue that the latter approach is shallow and not conducive to long-term change. I disagree.

Numerous mechanical techniques can be used to overcome problems of trader discipline. Whether the application of these mechanical methods results in permanent changes is irrelevant. If mechanical methods work, then use them.

What do I mean when I talk about "mechanical methods"? Here are some examples:

1. If too many of your losses are the result of your not using stop losses, don't waste your time trying to figure out why you don't use stops; just have someone enter your stops for you. There are many traders who cannot follow their own systems. To overcome this limitation, simply turn your system over to someone who will implement all the trades for you.

2. How about a method for dealing with overtrading? The answer is simple. Most overtrading comes from either too much contact with the market or attempting to trade too many systems. A mechanical way of dealing with this problem is to eliminate the source or sources of information that stimulate you to make too many trades.

3. Making a verbal contract with your broker can solve other problems. Consider the trader who enters stop losses but who changes them repeatedly as the market approaches

the stop. In such cases, the broker and client can agree that once a stop is entered, it will not be changed unless the system so dictates.

Factors Underlying Successful Trading

While there are many things a trader can do wrong in the markets, there are only a few things he or she can do right. We are all well aware of how important risk management, discipline, and a good trading system are. Yet, without a doubt, they are all useless in the hands of a trader who is psychologically inept or self-destructive. It is unfortunate that traders still believe in the myth that a better system will make them better traders.

The factors in achieving trading success are primarily psychological or behavioral. My experiences have taught me that three factors comprise perhaps 90 percent of the formula for achieving and maintaining market success: detachment, persistence, and a realistic attitude.

Detachment

Many years ago I learned that in order to trade successfully, you have to "not care"—you need to be detached from your work as a trader. At times, being human gets in the way of success by throwing emotional roadblocks in your path. Emotional roadblocks cloud judgment and inhibit success. Just as a surgeon must not become emotionally involved with a patient, a trader must not become emotionally involved with his or her trades, or for that matter, with the idea of success. Keep yourself from caring too much and you'll facilitate success.

Persistence

Clearly, the trader who is a quitter will never succeed, because he or she will not be in the markets when the big moves occur. A truly great trader is willing to come back fighting after a loss or after a string of losses.

Realistic Attitude

Traders must maintain a realistic attitude in order to succeed in the game of high expectations. All too often traders have grossly unrealistic expectations about what they can achieve in the markets. Dreams of striking it rich, of being in on that one trade that makes you fabulously wealthy, are self-destructive and divert your attention from the reality of your goal.

The fact of the matter is that you are far better off trading smaller moves that have a higher degree of accuracy than trading large moves that are not likely to occur and, if they do occur, will take so long to develop that you'll have at least 100 opportunities to make mistakes.

The Majority Is Usually Wrong—Don't Forget It!

There is a strong relationship between the level of market emotion and short-term market turns. When opinions are very bullish, tops are likely; when opinions are very bearish, bottoms are likely.

Remember these general rules about futures trading and market sentiment. They will serve you well!

1. Most futures traders lose money most of the time.
2. Most futures traders make incorrect decisions at major and minor market turning points.
3. When futures traders are in general agreement that a given market is bullish or bearish, they are usually incorrect.
4. The larger the degree of agreement, the more likely it is that a strongly held opinion will be incorrect.
5. Because most futures traders are buyers rather than sellers, they are most likely to be wrong then they are in strong agreement that a market will move down.
6. It is more important to determine the opinions of average traders as opposed to professional traders.

While these are just a few of the important things to remember if you sincerely want to be a successful futures trader, they are by no means the only prerequisites to success.

I urge you to develop and maintain your own list, derived from your experiences as a futures trader, because your own list will be considerably more meaningful to you.

THE PARADOX OF DISCIPLINE AND EMOTION

The past several decades of technological development have rendered an interesting paradox in the world of commodity investing. With computerized systems and lightning-fast communication and advanced economic forecasting, there should be an overwhelming number of market winners. But in reality, over 90 percent of all investors in commodity futures trading are unsuccessful. The reasons for this lie with the individual trader, for it is the individual who stands in his or her own way when it comes to prospering as a trader. The speculator who takes sophisticated market tools and uses them to create losses rather than gains can only look to his or her own limitations. The average investor who feeds the market with losses can blame only a lack of self-knowledge, self-control, and self-discipline.

In spite of overwhelming technological knowledge, the paradox is that most traders still lose money in the futures market. The fact is that knowledge of one's self seems to be more important than the acquisition of so-called facts, news, economic theories, or political motivations. The markets of the 1980s and 1990s have continued to violate the market rules of the 1950s and 1960s. It is therefore essential that any speculator hoping to be successful in such a chaotic marketplace have command of his or her emotional self.

In the chapters on technical analysis, the point was made that chart patterns are little more than a diagram of market psychology. Thus, the various trend lines, reversal patterns, and support and resistance points on a bar chart have no direct relationship to the commodity itself; rather, they reflect the attempts by market traders to cope with forces inside themselves. The rising and falling value of the commodity is a function of what buyers and sellers at any one time and place are willing to pay or receive for it.

Recall the discussion of supply and demand and elasticity of supply and demand. The final act of buying and selling in a marketplace must be performed by people who have examined the situation, considered the variables, studied the charts, and arrived at their conclusions. The information available for study is the same for everyone, yet the conclusions can be worlds apart. The explanation for this phenomenon is contained in Francis Bacon's observation: "Man prefers to believe what he prefers to be true."

What a trader prefers to be true is a function of that trader's inner psychological state. Therefore, an understanding of human psychology and human behavior is just as important as an understanding of market fundamentals, trading systems, chart analysis, and economic theory, for it is human behavior that causes market behavior.

Emotions, Discipline, and the Trader

What is it about trading that causes us to lose our discipline and to commit many of several hundred errors in our trading? A deceptively simple reply is that we are all human. Because we're human, we are also subject to a virtually endless barrage of emotionally based and emotionally charged inputs, all of which tend to cloud judgment and interfere with reason. The greatest enemy of the trader is his or her own emotions!

The role of emotions in the quest for profitable trading has been the topic of many a book and the source of considerable frustration to traders, since the first trader made the first trade. The simple fact is that the most powerful stimulus for an emotional response in a trader is the very act of trading. Because money represents security, power, prestige, survival, and more, it naturally arouses a host of conflicts, wishes, expectations, and fears, all of which are emotionally charged. In short, traders are just as scared by the potential for loss as they are excited by the potential for making money.

The fear of losing everything causes traders to become too conservative in their trading. Hence, they tend not to take chances. They tend to use stop losses that are too small. They tend to shy away from trades that seem to be too risky or at all questionable in terms of their potential. They tend to hold on to losing trades, fearing the reality of taking a loss. Traders who are focused on the profit potential of a trade tend to ignore signals to exit or reverse their positions, imbued as they are with the hope of making money. The desire to make money causes traders to take excessive risks, which are often deleterious to their financial health. In addition to the rather obvious ones cited here, there are many subtle and not-so-subtle emotional responses exhibited by traders.

It would seem that the onset of a counterproductive or loss-producing emotional response would be easy to detect. However, we know that this is not the case. Because traders (in fact, all human beings) have a virtually unlimited capacity to avoid dealing with reality, it is difficult—at times, impossible—for us to recognize the onset of a loss-producing emotional response. But we can learn ways of avoiding those responses.

Learning how to avoid loss-producing emotions is a very complex process that traders have spent fortunes and lost fortunes trying to master. They have attended seminars, read books, visited psychologists and psychiatrists, consulted with futures trading professionals, and pondered long and hard about how to overcome these difficulties. The three lists presented here should prove helpful in your quest to keep losing behaviors to a minimum. I hasten to add, though, that the key ingredient to overall success in the markets is personal awareness.

How Emotional Responses Can Lead to Losses

- Reacting emotionally can cloud judgment, leading to bad decisions.
- Fear of taking a loss can lead traders to hold on to positions too long.
- Greed in the form of expecting or wanting larger profits can lead to overtrading.
- Insecurity can lead traders to seek too many opinions, thereby causing confusion and doubt.
- Confusion and doubt can lead to "nervous" trading (which makes it difficult to trade systematically).
- Lack of discipline can cause a good trading system to become a bad trading system.
- Anxiety caused by the fear of loss can cause a trader to exit positions too soon or to enter them too late.
- Hoping that a losing position will turn profitable causes traders to ride losses.
- Hoping that a winning position will become a bigger winner causes traders to hold trades too long.
- Fearing that a profitable trade will become a losing trade causes premature exit and cuts profits short.

- Insecurity caused by the feeling that other traders know more than you do can cause errors.
- Fear of a market moving to the limit against you can cause you to avoid certain markets.
- Concern about keeping losses small can result in using stop losses that are too small.
- Lack of patience, often caused by fear and insecurity, can lead traders to subvert their own trading systems.
- The inability to withstand a series of losing trades and drawdown causes abandonment of one's system.

Behaviors That Tend to Precede Dysfunctional Trader Responses

- Ignoring or overriding signals from your trading system that are contrary to your current position.
- Riding a loss beyond the predetermined stop loss or exit point.
- Failing to do market "homework" due to negative attitude.
- Succumbing to complete dejection and negative attitude following a series of losing trades.
- Deciding to abandon your trading system for a new one that you hope will perform better.
- Changing the rules of your system or method following a few losses.
- Being unwilling to take trading signals from your system following a series of losses.
- Feeling that if you had more information you'd not have lost money.
- Wanting to ride a profitable trade well beyond its price or time target contrary to your system rules.
- Deciding to pyramid a position by adding more contracts than your original position.
- Spreading your position in order to avoid closing out a losing trade.
- Ignoring any information that does not agree with your current positions.

- Feeling that you will always be a loser in the markets, no matter what you do.

- Feeling that there is nothing you can do wrong in the markets (the feeling that you're invincible).

- Subscribing to many different advisory services.

- Having persistent and unfounded feelings that your broker or floor traders are cheating you.

How to Limit Losing Behaviors and Maximize Winning Behaviors

- Keep written records of all your trades, noting the reasons for entry and exit and their outcome.

- Try to remain isolated from the opinions of others; don't use more than three advisory services at once.

- Avoid listening to the popular press such as business television shows, radio market commentaries, etc.

- Develop a set of specific procedures for your trading that will alert you to deviations from your plans.

- Make certain that you don't overextend yourself in terms of margins and positions.

- Don't try to play someone else's game; in other words, develop your own style.

- Make certain that you can accept and be prepared for a string of losses and drawdown.

- Find a trading system or method that fits your style of trading.

- Try to ride profits and cut losses short as opposed to what most traders do (which is the opposite).

- Once you have researched a trading system you feel comfortable with, use it with discipline.

- Avoid making trading decisions that are not based on input from your systems or methods.

- Trade only within the limits of your financial ability and account size.

- Do not pyramid your positions by adding larger positions as the trend continues in your favor.
- Try not to trade when your personal problems are overwhelming.
- Leave your market work at the office; don't take it home with you.
- Try to avoid hope, fear, greed, indecision, wishes, expectations, remorse, and lack of confidence.
- Deal only with the facts of your system and not the fantasies of your wishes.

While correcting the emotional problems that can afflict the trader is a process that can take many years, consider taking one of these steps to get started:

1. Read a book such as my *Investor's Quotient*, 2nd ed. (Wiley & Sons, 1994).
2. Take a course or seminar in personal development.
3. Keep a close watch on all of your trading-related behaviors. You can do this by keeping a detailed diary of what you trade, why you trade it, and the outcome of the trade. Make sure you write down all your thoughts and actions. Then analyze the results.

Ultimately, paying close attention to your behaviors and actions will yield the results you want, but it will take time and effort. While the application and understanding of trading methods is relatively simple, their implementation can be difficult if your psychological attitudes toward trading are dysfunctional or excessively emotional. If this is the case, then you need to fix your inner self before you can expect to achieve success as a trader.

WINNERS AND LOSERS

It is not possible for me to overemphasize the fact that great traders are great because they have mastered the discipline of trading as well as the mechanical techniques. I've placed great emphasis on discipline, because it is undoubtedly the weak link in the chain of trading behavior. No consistent success is possible without it.

There are many opinions as to what constitutes discipline. My point of view has been tempered and shaped by over 29 years of trading, writing, and advising that have exposed me to every conceivable type of market and every conceivable type of news event. I have developed an arsenal of time-tested suggestions that I will now share with you. Here they are, not necessarily in order of importance.

Find Your Place

One of the most important considerations is for the trader to find his or her place in the vast world of futures trading. There are many things a trader can do, but only a few that can be done at one time. I suggest you find one or more techniques to which you can relate well and with which you feel particularly confident. These are the techniques that you should then use in your trading.

Don't Expect Immediate Results

Many a trader has been sorely disappointed when immediate success was not attainable. Give yourself sufficient time to achieve success. How long will it take, you ask? There is no answer I can give you other than to say, "More than two weeks and less than two years," but this is certainly not a hard-and-fast rule. Some individuals can be successful in several weeks, whereas others are still not capable of achieving consistent success as futures traders even after many years.

Lower Your Expectations

While some books on positive mental attitude will tell you to have great expectations, I caution you against it. Expect to lose at first, but expect that with time you will begin to break even. Expect that with more time you will begin to achieve profitable results.

There are hundreds, if not thousands, of traders who came to the markets with great expectations and a fistful of dollars, but who left the markets beaten, broke, and broken. If anything, you ought to expect failure while hoping that through your efforts you can minimize the failures and maximize the successes.

Play Your Own Game

There will always be those who claim to have better systems, better methods, foolproof indicators, outstanding results, and fail-safe methods. Before you give any of these serious attention, make sure that what you're doing is not intrinsically better.

While there is nothing wrong with attempting to improve on what you are doing, the act of searching tends to distract you from your goal. Don't be sidetracked from your goal. Persevere and ignore the claims as much as you can.

Admit to Your Losses Quickly

I have stated repeatedly throughout my books, articles, and newsletters that the single worst offense a trader can commit is to carry a position beyond its stop loss point. To do so is to violate the essence of futures trading and to expose yourself to all the risks that a futures trader seeks to avoid.

Remember Your Goal As a Trader

I encourage you to have one simple goal every day of your life as a futures trader: Attempt to end each trade with a profit. Place no dollar amount on the profit or it may distract you. To set a goal too high would be unrealistic, and to set a goal too low might be limiting.

Don't Let Good Profits Turn into Losses

Many a good trade has become a bad trade by turning from a profit into a loss due to poor risk management. Preservation of capital is essential to consistent success as a futures trader. Develop a follow-up or trailing stop loss procedure.

Don't Force Trades

If you have seen no opportunity for trades but find yourself idly searching through your screens and charts for opportunities, then you are headed for a disaster. Do not attempt to create an opportunity where one does not exist. Be patient. There will be trades tomorrow or the next day. The market always provides opportunities over time, even though none may exist today. Don't ever force yourself to trade if an opportunity is not readily apparent.

Don't Hesitate

Hesitation is one of the worst enemies of the futures trader. The expression "He who hesitates is lost" is truer in the futures markets than anywhere else. Because futures trading occurs in a circumscribed period of time, every moment you lose in entering or exiting a position is a moment that might cost you money. If you choose to hesitate, then do so with premeditation and calculated caution. Do not hesitate out of fear or indecision.

Keep a Diary

Although I have already elaborated on this topic, I emphasize it here once again due to the great importance it can have in helping you learn from your mistakes, and of course, from your successes. A diary should be kept and should be referred to both at the beginning and the end of each trading day. Use it to learn from what you did or didn't do in past trades.

Act According to Your Systems

Some of the techniques I have discussed in my books are so totally mechanical that your presence is not required, nor are live price quotes necessary. Other methods, however, require your presence and close attention. Act accordingly.

When in Doubt, Stay Out

This is a particularly appropriate expression for the futures trader. Not all indicators or signals will be completely clear all the time. Furthermore, there may be other developments such as news reports or short-term fundamentals that make signals unclear or market response uncertain.

In such cases, my best advice is to stay out of the market. There will always be plenty of trades, and there is no need to enter a trade unless its potential outcome is relatively clear and free from the erratic influence of news or other fundamental events.

Do Your Homework

Too many traders become complacent about their market studies, fail to do their homework, and then wonder why they lose money. If you intend to succeed, then you must do your homework, no matter how simple or complex it may be. Perhaps you have developed a trading system that requires no homework. This is certainly possible. However, you still need to work on your trading diary and you still need to keep in close touch with trading opportunities that may develop during the next trading day.

Monitor Your Performance

Always keep close track of your results on a trade-by-trade and day-by-day basis. Know where you stand at all times, in order to develop effective feedback about the techniques you are using. Unless you know where you stand, you will not have sufficient information about how well your methods are performing, and you will not know when change is necessary. Some traders refuse to monitor their trading results as a form of defense against being distressed by bad results. This is an avoidance technique that can be very costly.

Recognize the Dangers of Pyramiding

Pyramiding is the act of adding increasingly larger units to your position as a market moves in your favor. For example, you may begin by buying one unit and adding two additional units once the trade has moved in your favor. If the trade continues to move in your favor, you may add four new units and then, assuming that it continues in your favor, you might add six or eight units. The essence of pyramiding is that increasingly larger positions are added as the trade moves in your favor. The upside of this methodology is that you will accumulate a very large position consistent with the trend and you will use the capital available in open profits to margin new positions.

The danger of pyramiding is that this is a pyramid clearly built upside down. It is heaviest at the top and rests on only one unit at the bottom. It is therefore subject to violent collapse at the slightest indication of a trend reversal. If you intend to build a pyramid, then do so by establishing your largest position first and following it up with successively smaller numbers of units.

WHAT DO TRADERS REALLY WANT?

You may find that question somewhat amusing or even perplexing. After all, it seems rather obvious that the only thing traders would be interested in is making money. I once thought so as well, but time and experience have taught me otherwise. While it may seem reasonable and logical to assume that the primary goal of traders is to make money, the fact is that there are many other motives that attract traders to the markets.

CHAPTER 14

Trading Strategies and Systems

To many readers, the information presented thus far may have been a first glimpse into an industry that heretofore has been rather mysterious. To some, this brief treatise may have stripped the glitter from the fantasy and reduced trading to a very pedestrian occupation requiring hard work and diligence. Others may have been inspired to pursue further studies of the various components that were discussed in the chapters of this book. All who have read to this point, however, must now realize that a simple understanding of all that has been presented here is insufficient if one wishes to be a successful futures trader.

For this book to be of real benefit, it must now present a plan of action—a strategy by which the reader can, if he or she chooses, become a part of the futures industry. To paraphrase Thomas Huxley, "The great end of (study) is not knowledge but action." Not every reader will choose to be a futures trader, and so other alternatives are also presented. Here are some suggestions to help you put knowledge into action.

DEVELOPING A TRADING STRATEGY

Anyone wishing to become a futures trader will find that there is
an overabundance of help available. On any weekend, somewhere
in the country, some expert is presenting a seminar on a foolproof
trading system. Book after book is available on technical analysis,
options trading, the Elliott wave, cycles...the list goes on.
Hundreds of newsletters provide advice and trading tips. Hotline
phone trading advice is available from dozens of market gurus.
The newcomer to futures trading finds it easy to get too much
help—easy to keep taking in more information and advice.

Just as rock stars have their groupies who follow them around
the country, so commodity trading advisors have their following,
many of whom never trade, but simply seek information. It is not
uncommon to encounter the same individuals at seminar after
seminar who wants to "collect as much information as possible
before I start trading. I want to be sure about what I'm doing
before I take the risk."

For the individual who is serious about trading in the markets, however, there must be a path through this wilderness of
information overload and a way to separate the helpful from the
purely extraneous. It should be obvious to anyone who has read
this far that making money through futures trading is difficult to
the point of being nearly impossible. On the other hand, there are
traders who consistently reap tremendous profits from the futures
markets.

I've already mentioned that approximately 90 percent of all
futures traders lose money while only 10 percent make money.
These figures seem to indicate that the cards are stacked against
anyone who tries to play the game. Yet, if there are indeed futures
traders who consistently make money by trading, then it would
seem that success as a trader might be based on something other
than simply chance.

With that in mind, a prospective trader needs to follow a
thoughtful and well-conceived plan while developing a strategy
for trading. One such plan is outlined here. If followed, this plan
will position a trader to take full advantage of the alternatives that
the futures market has to offer.

HOW TO DEVELOP A SYSTEMATIC APPROACH TO TRADING

In order to develop a systematic approach to trading, I recommend that you take three steps:

Step One: Evaluate the Factors Limiting Your Trading Effectiveness

The characteristic that is most damaging to both occasional and full-time futures traders is an unrealistic view of the task and of their own strengths and limitations. The first exercise that every would-be trader must engage in is to list, in a totally honest and unbiased manner, all of the factors that might adversely affect his or her ability to trade effectively. These factors might be listed under several category headings, such as:

1. Limits on my time.
2. Financial limitations.
3. Equipment limitations.
4. Emotional limitations.
5. Other limitations.

In each of these categories, certain critical questions must be answered, such as:

1. How much time can I give to the market each day (week)?
2. If I can devote time each day, is it during or after market hours?
3. Do I need to buy a computer?
4. Can I afford a computer?
5. Can I afford the exchange fees for real-time quote service?
6. How much can I comfortably allocate to a trading account?
7. Can I take the pressure of intraday trading?
8. Can I ride large losses, or must I settle for small but more frequent losses?
9. Is my family supportive of my undertaking?

Other questions and other categories will occur to each individual who chooses to pursue this exercise. The important thing is to be honest and to let the ideas flow in a brainstorming manner: Simply write down every idea that presents itself without filtering it. Later, evaluate each thought carefully as to its validity.

Step Two: List Your Goals

Again, the key is to be honest. The list may include financial, personal, social, and family goals. They may be long-term or short-term. Financial goals should be listed in terms of dollars or percent return on capital.

After the goals have been listed, they should be reexamined in light of the previous limitations. If any goals are found to be unrealistic, they should be eliminated or modified to match the limitations. It is essential during this step that each goal be practical and achievable. Any deviation from that is a setup for failure.

Step Three: Establish a Trading Approach

At this stage, many decisions must be made. The information to assist you in that decision making is available in the chapters of this book. Once the decisions have been made, however, a tremendous amount of study and preparation are necessary before effective trading can be accomplished. Some of the decisions to be made are:

1. Will I try to day trade?
2. Will I try to scalp small profits or search for big moves?
3. Will I trade only futures, futures and options, or only options?
4. Will I try to diversify into several markets or limit my trading to one or two?
5. Will I approach market analysis from a fundamental or a technical perspective?
6. Will I develop my own trading system or purchase one of the systems on the market?
7. Do I need a chart service?

Many more questions will occur to the serious trader, and each must be answered carefully and thoughtfully. When a carefully considered answer has been written to each question, then a trading strategy will have taken shape—one that is based on a realistic appraisal of all circumstances that could either inhibit or enhance the trader's effectiveness.

A trader who conscientiously completes each step of this plan is much more likely to be among the successful 10 percent than the unsuccessful 90 percent of futures traders, for two reasons. First, a trader who has thoughtfully constructed a trading strategy based on a consideration of personal limitations and the establishment of realistic goals, as well as a careful selection of components and tools, is simply better prepared than most traders. Second, and equally important, that trader has already exhibited the discipline that is absolutely necessary for consistent success. Without discipline, the best plan and strategy will ultimately fail. It is very likely that most of the failures of the 90 percent can be laid at the feet of either poor preparation or poor discipline or both, because they seem to go hand in hand.

Decisions, Decisions, Decisions

In the hope of facilitating a decision for the new trader, or perhaps changing some ideas in an experienced trader, here are some of the things you should consider.

How Much Risk Capital Do You Have?

This is an important first decision, because it will help you decide whether you want to trade futures, options, futures spreads, or all of the above. As a rule, if you have less than $5,000, your chances of making money in futures are slim to none.

Will You Use a Technical or Fundamental Method?

Learn the differences between the fundamental approach and the technical approach to trading. Make a decision. Try to be in one camp or the other, but not in both at the same time. Doing both at first will confuse you. For most traders, technical methods are better because they require less work, less attention, and fewer decisions.

Will You Trade Short-Term, Day Trade, or Position Trade?

Take the time to get in touch with your temperament as a trader. If you have good self-control, discipline, patience, and organization, then you may do well as a position trader. But if you're generally impatient, if you can't wait a long time for market moves to occur, or if you thrive on "action," then short-term or day trading might be best for you.

How Much Time Do You Have?

No matter how you look at it, trading does take time. It's a business that requires study, evaluation, preparation, homework, some thought, and some degree of organization. You can do your work while the markets are closed, or you can follow the markets all day. You make the choice.

There are pros and cons to each approach, but only you can decide the amount of time you can give to the business. This will be an integral decision for you. It will likely precede all other decisions, with the possible exception of how much starting capital you have.

Do You Need a Computer and Tick-by-Tick Data?

For most traders, the answer to both questions is clearly no. Although those who sell data and computerized systems would have you believe otherwise, there is no guarantee that you'll make money trading futures if you have live quotes, a computer, and a computerized trading system.

Do You Need a Chart Service or Newsletters?

In most cases, traders get too much information, and too much information confuses. Be selective. Allow only a small amount of information to affect your decision-making process. Once you have learned the basics, try to go with your own analyses and methods. If you've found a trading advisor, newsletter, or hotline that works for you, then trade with it and don't second-guess it.

Do You Have a Broker You Trust and Who Will Work with You?

The relationship between client and broker has not been given enough attention over the years. If you have an antagonistic or otherwise negative relationship with your broker, then your chances of success will be minimized. You should also consider whether a discount broker or a full-service broker is best for you. Generally, full-service brokers tend to be better for new traders or for those who rely on their brokers for implementing trades consistently or according to a certain methodology.

Do You Know the Vocabulary and the Definitions?

Learn the rules of the markets before you risk a single dollar. Learn the vocabulary, the jargon, the meanings and uses of different types of orders. In short, learn before you try to earn.

When you've made the decisions we've discussed here and you've learned what you need to know, you'll be in a much better position to start trading.

HOW TO CHOOSE A TRADING SYSTEM OR METHODOLOGY

If you have conscientiously completed each step of the foregoing exercise and still honestly feel that you wish to become a trader, it is time to choose a trading system. There are numerous computerized systems on the market that claim profitability. Such claims, of course, must be analyzed carefully.

Many trading systems will work quite well under limited market conditions but fall apart in the long haul as conditions change. Has the system been tested in real time and for a sufficient period of time? Real-time trading, with its accompanying imperfections such as poor fills, bad timing, and unexpected surprises, is totally different from hypothetical trading, which uses historical information that is immune to the quirks and imperfections of the fast-paced market in real time.

In choosing a trading system, be aware that a system does not have to be highly sophisticated, computerized, or complicated. Some of the best trading systems require only a few simple hand computations to generate reasonably accurate buy or sell signals. To be acceptable, however, any trading system must minimally do five things:

1. Provide accurate entry and exit signals.
2. Provide a specific method of entry and exit after generating the signals.
3. Establish a specific objective or reversal point.
4. Establish money management conditions, i.e., stop loss points, amount to risk, etc.
5. Avoid periods of severe drawdown.

Evaluate any trading system according to these guidelines:

1. *Simplicity.* The rules must be simple to understand, simple to follow, and not subject to interpretation.
2. *Accuracy.* Historical accuracy should be 55 percent or more. While it is entirely possible to profit using systems that have a lower percentage of accuracy, it makes things more difficult. Shoot for a higher percentage.
3. *Longevity.* Use a system that has been tested in various markets—bull, bear, sideways, choppy, etc. At least several hundred trades should be included in the test. The fewer the trades, the less likely the results are to be representative of reality.
4. *Drawdown.* Drawdown is defined as the maximum loss in a string of consecutive losing trades. Find a system that has shown reasonable drawdown—no more than 35 percent from its equity peak. Many systems that produce fantastic hypothetical trading records over many years will, upon closer examination, generate periods of severe drawdowns. Most traders cannot emotionally or financially withstand such extended periods of loss.
5. *Consecutive losers.* Most traders cannot accept more than six losing trades in a row. Many profitable systems have shown over 15 consecutive losing trades. Before you trade any system, know the historical facts. A high number of consecutive losers will cause you to abandon your discipline and the result will be a loss.
6. *Study the worst-case scenario, not the best case.* System promoters naturally portray their systems at their best. In reality, many systems deteriorate over time. Hence, you are far

better off looking at a system in its worst light as opposed
to its best light.

ALTERNATIVES TO BEING AN ACTIVE TRADER

Most individuals approaching the futures market will find that the
commitment of time and energy necessary to learn about the markets and to maintain a disciplined trading program is simply too
great. Unfortunately, many will continue to trade on their own,
dabbling, as some call it, and by so doing they will place themselves firmly among the 90 percent of losers.

Others, realizing that such a course of action is much too
risky, and not being of a mind to give away their money but still
being interested in participating in the futures markets, will look
for alternatives to trading on their own. Among the alternatives
available to them are commodity funds, managed accounts, directed hotlines, and broker discretionary trading. Each has its advantages and disadvantages, but the disciplined individual who
approaches the alternatives carefully and with the same degree of
scrutiny used in developing a trading strategy will find each of the
alternatives to be viable and potentially profitable.

Commodity Funds

A recent addition to the world of futures trading is the commodity fund, or limited partnership. Based on the concept of a stock
mutual fund, investors buy units of a commodity fund, which are
then pooled, and the money is traded by a professional trading
advisor or, in some cases, a group of advisors. Most funds are
closed end—that is, once the initial offering is sold out, no more
units are offered publicly. The minimum investment is usually
$5,000, or five $1,000 units. Most funds also qualify for Individual
Retirement Account (IRA) deposits.

There are those who say that commodity funds mark the
coming of age of the futures industry—that funds have opened
futures trading to many who would not have considered investing
in futures previously. Certainly, the funds are a popular investment vehicle.

The popularity of futures funds is derived from four factors:

1. *Low initial investment.* Many people are willing to risk $5,000 in a fund but are not willing to risk $20,000 to $30,000 in a professionally managed account or in their own trading account.

2. *Reasonable limited risk.* Most funds have a clause in the prospectus that stipulates the fund will cease trading and return all assets if the total equity in the fund sinks to 50 percent of its original size. This means there is a reasonable likelihood that each investor will lose no more than half of his or her original investment. When compared to the unlimited risk of futures trading, where the original investment can be lost as well as additional money required to meet a margin call, this characteristic of a fund is very attractive.

3. *Professional management.* The trading advisors for a fund are usually veteran traders with proven track records. An investor in a futures fund can be reasonably certain that the person to whom the money is entrusted is a competent trader with proven expertise. On another level, the general partners of the fund are usually knowledgeable about futures trading and money management and will carefully monitor the progress of the trading that goes on in the fund account.

4. *Diversification.* Because a futures fund pools several million dollars in a trading account, the account can be traded on several markets by several advisors, providing the diversification that would be impossible to obtain if the $5,000 investment were traded in a personal account.

As attractive as futures funds seem, however, there are some disadvantages and some pitfalls that the investor must be wary of. The first disadvantage is that the money is tied up in a fund for a minimum time period, often six months from the time of investment. Thereafter, the money can be taken out only when and if the units can be resold. Thus, a futures fund is not a liquid investment vehicle.

Second, although several of the best-performing futures funds do as well as or better than the best mutual funds, it is not uncommon for a futures fund to lose money rather than to make money. Therefore, a fund must be chosen very carefully, with a sharp eye toward the track record of the advisors. Third, funds can be expensive. Many funds charge management fees up front, thereby reducing the amount of the initial investment. Others charge no management fees but do charge advisory incentive fees as a percentage of profits. Moreover, the amount of commissions charged for each trade varies considerably among funds.

A trader who is considering putting money in a futures fund should approach the choice very cautiously. If the fund has been trading for several months, its performance can be tracked through *Futures Magazine* or *Managed Account Reports*, both of which report on the actual profits or losses of over 120 futures funds. If the fund is new, the track records of each of the advisors should be checked carefully.

Managed Accounts

Another popular vehicle for traders who lack the time or expertise to trade their own accounts is a professionally managed account. With this kind of program, the trader establishes a personal trading account with a broker but signs a limited power of attorney that transfers discretionary trading authority to a selected futures trader, who usually is a registered Commodity Trading Advisor (CTA). All of the trading decisions are made by the CTA, but daily trade confirmations, monthly purchases, and sale summaries are sent to the person in whose name the account was opened.

One advantage of an individual managed account is the liquidity of the investment. The account holder can take money out, add money, request that trading cease, or close the account at any time, with proper notice being given. Another advantage is that the managed account can be monitored closely, allowing the account holder to close the account if he or she does not like the way the CTA is managing it.

Managed accounts do have disadvantages and, as with futures funds, must be approached very cautiously. First, the management fees can be excessive. Some CTAs charge only an incentive fee as a percentage of the profits. This can range from 50 percent down to 10 percent. Others charge a management fee, which is often subtracted from the account each month, whether a profit is made or not.

Second, brokerage commissions vary significantly, from the equivalent of discount commissions to full-service commissions. If a CTA trades frequently, the cost of commissions can add up to a significant drain on the account. Third, the CTA who trades the account may have a trading style that conflicts with the personal nature of the account holder. For example, the CTA may be a very cautious trader, careful to avoid large losses while being content to take small profits on a high frequency of good trades. The account holder, meanwhile, might like to see his or her account traded in a very aggressive manner, willing to sit through large drawdowns in the interest of catching highly profitable trades. Such a match, obviously, will lead to problems between the CTA and the account holder.

A fourth disadvantage of a managed account is that CTAs often require rather large initial investments. Many expect at least $25,000, while some require $50,000 to open an account. A final danger is that the account holder is subject to unlimited risk. A major drawdown can deplete the account and leave the account holder liable for additional losses.

To avoid some of the potential pitfalls of a professionally managed account, the prior performance of a CTA should be evaluated very carefully. Each CTA must provide a disclosure document to any person expressing an interest in a managed account. This document describes the trading strategy to be followed, the markets that will be traded, the minimum investment required, and the fees to be charged.

Additionally, the disclosure details the CTA's track record for at least the past three years and sometimes longer. This track record must be evaluated carefully, as it will reveal a great deal about the trading style of the CTA. The actual percentage of profits can be misleading, as there are two different National Futures Association–approved formulas for constructing a track record, each of which handles equity additions and withdrawals differently, resulting in radically different percentage of gain or loss figures.

Still, the figures should indicate consistent profitability over a reasonable time span. The size of the gains that are acceptable is subject to the judgment of the prospective client. Some individuals may be content with relatively low returns in exchange for small losses, whereas others may want to see gains of at least 100% per year to justify the risk of futures trading.

Just as important as the percentage of gain, then, is the percentage of loss. How many months of gain are there in relation to the months showing a loss? What is the largest loss in a month or a quarter? Is this a loss that would be tolerable? Is the total profitability for the year based on only one or two very profitable months? Or were there consistent profits month after month? In 1987, for example, many CTAs showed extremely profitable years because they happened to be on the short side of the S&P 500 Index in October during the crash. This return was not consistent with their usual performance, and thus should be discounted.

In evaluating a CTA, therefore, one must look at the trading consistency, the profitability over a reasonable span of time, and the size of drawdowns versus the amount of profits. The resulting profile should be consistent with the prospective client's own goals and emotional profile. If the two don't match, then another CTA should be chosen.

Directed Hotlines

A relatively new service offered by some brokers is the directed hotline. With this service, a trader chooses a hotline advisory service he or she likes and then gives the broker the authority to call the hotline and place the trades exactly as recommended. This service works very much like a managed account, but rather than paying a management fee, the client pays a fee for the hotline service.

Many traders who don't have the time to do the necessary market research but still want to be actively involved in trading find that an advisory service, particularly one with a daily hotline recommendation, is an ideal solution. With this kind of service, the trader need only call the hotline number each day to find out which trades are being recommended, then call his or her broker to place the trades.

The advantage of this kind of service is that the trader has ultimate control over his or her account and can choose whether to make a trade and when to cease trading or resume trading. The trader can also select a discount broker, thus saving commission costs. The disadvantage is that many such services can be very expensive, and it may be difficult to find an advisory service that is compatible with the trader's own goals and trading style.

To choose the correct advisory service, a trader must be very careful to thoroughly examine the services being offered. Many hotlines make fantastic claims that, upon closer examination, tend to evaporate. Of critical concern is how specific the recommendations are. Does the hotline recommend what to buy, when to buy, and a price to buy at? Or is the recommendation simply a vague statement open to interpretation and leaving all the decision making to the trader?

A second concern when choosing a hotline advisory is whether the timing of the recommendations permits real-time implementation. An advisory service is no good if the trades are signaled too late for implementation.

Another concern is whether the trader has the time and equipment to follow the recommendations. Some hotlines require order entry and update during the day. Others require real-time price information. Both situations may be unrealistic for a trader who works a very busy daytime job.

Finally, a good advisory service should also provide specific price or time objectives, stop-loss points, and specific follow-up procedures that will leave a trader with alternatives regardless of market conditions. Some services, unfortunately, are excellent at getting a trader into the market but vague and nonspecific about getting him or her out.

When checking the performance record of a hotline, it is important to note certain items:

1. Is the claimed performance based on unrealistic and hypothetical circumstances? Some hotlines, for instance, have been known, in their hypothetical trading, to take extremely large positions, to scale into the market holding losing positions, to purchase or sell extremely large numbers of contracts, or to add more margin to the hypothetical account so as to withstand most losing positions. Such a trading strategy is unrealistic for most small traders, who should not hold more than five to ten positions at any one time.

2. Look closely at the largest single loss, the largest single profit, the average loss, the average profit, and the win–lose ratio to determine whether the hotline matches your preferred style. Some services make most of their

profits on a few big trades while suffering a large number of small losses. Others make many small gains and few small losses. Still others encounter a few large gains and a few large drawdowns.

3. If the performance record is hypothetical, it is important that the amount deducted for commissions and bad fills be realistic. Generally, this should be in the neighborhood of $100 per trade.

4. Is the track record built on trading markets that are too volatile and risky for a small trader?

5. Does the hypothetical performance require a realistic level of margin? If a trader plans to trade an account of $20,000, the hotline cannot recommend trades that would exceed that margin without adversely affecting the performance of the trader's account.

As a final comment, the trader wishing to use the services of a carefully chosen hotline must be prepared to trade his or her account consistently with the recommendations.

Broker-Assisted and Broker-Discretionary Trading

The most common way many small traders experience the market is probably by trading a small account on the recommendation of a broker. Occasionally, a trader will give discretionary authority to a broker to trade the account without seeking approval on every trade.

If a trader chooses this approach, the same rules apply for checking the track record, because there likely will be no published figures to peruse. The trader must have confidence in the integrity of the broker. With broker-assisted and broker-discretionary trading, there is also a potential conflict of interest, because the broker's reward comes from the number of trades made, not the quality of the individual trades.

CHAPTER 15

Making the Futures Market Work for You

What you have read in this book is intended to serve as a very basic introduction to the futures markets and futures trading. I have attempted to achieve several goals in the preceding chapters:

- To introduce the basic concepts underlying futures trading and the futures markets;
- To explain the economic functions of futures trading;
- To explain the roles of speculators, hedgers, commercial interests, and brokers in the futures markets;
- To provide a general understanding of fundamental and technical analysis and to give examples of each; and
- To highlight the various aspects of the futures industry as well as different opportunities available to you as an independent trader, broker, or market analyst.

HOW TO IMPROVE YOUR ODDS OF SUCCESS
AS A TRADER

In order to achieve a thorough understanding of this challenging but rewarding field, I suggest you follow these steps:

1. *Learn more.* Throughout this book I have stressed the value and, indeed, the necessity of education. If you plan to seriously pursue a job in the area of futures trading or if you plan to trade for your own account, you must learn as much as you can. There are literally hundreds of books for beginners and advanced students and many classroom courses you can take.

2. *Get your feet wet.* Once you've taken the time to learn more from books or course work, get involved in futures trading. Open a small account and trade for yourself or work with a broker. Don't risk a great deal, particularly if you can't afford it. Consider the money you put into your account as part of your tuition. If you lose it, you've helped further your education; if you win, you've learned something as well as having something to show for it other than just the learning itself.

3. *Ask questions.* Be sure to ask questions. If you know other traders, use them as resources to learn more. If you open a trading account, ask your broker questions. You'll learn more by asking questions than you will from any book. Best of all, the answers usually won't cost you anything!

4. *Visit a broker's office.* You can learn a great deal by watching brokers do their work. If you have the opportunity to watch your broker work, do so. You'll get to see exactly how orders are entered, time stamped, and reported back to the broker and customers. This will further your understanding of the different types of orders, when they are used, and how to use them.

5. *Visit one of the futures exchanges.* Every futures exchange provides public tours. Take some time to visit the exchanges. The firsthand experience of witnessing the markets in real-time operation will add to your appreciation of how the futures markets work, the role of traders, runners

and exchange officials, computerized price reporting, government regulation, and more. Even after all of my years as a futures trader, I still enjoy an occasional visit to the exchange. If you know someone who can get you onto the trading floor, this is an even more exciting educational thing to do.

6. *Consider taking a job as a runner.* Many successful traders and brokers have started as runners on the trading floor of one or more futures exchanges. The experience has been valuable in spite of the poor salary usually earned by runners. If you have the opportunity to take such a job, you'll learn more in two weeks on the floor than you can in several years of academic studies. This is perhaps the single best way to get an education in the futures industry. If you have the financial means to support yourself while you take a runner's job, then by all means do so!

7. *Subscribe to some newsletters or send for free samples.* See what some of the trading advisors and money managers have to say. More important, see how they say it—learn market vocabulary; become familiar with the issues; and gain an understanding of risks, rewards, methods of analysis, strategies, and more. There are literally hundreds of services, and most of them will provide you with a wealth of information and samples at no cost whatsoever.

8. *Read some of the trade publications.* While such regular reading as the *Wall Street Journal* will keep you informed on current events, it is also helpful to regularly read trade publications such as *Futures Magazine*. It may not be a good idea to take anything you read in these publications too seriously, but it is a good idea to keep informed on industry trends and events.

9. *Do your own research.* If you have some market ideas of your own, don't be afraid to test them. Home computer systems, historical futures data, and analytical software are so reasonably priced nowadays that systems testing is not as expensive a proposition as it was in the past. If you have ideas about trading systems that merit further investigation and development and if you have the funds to pursue this direction, then I encourage you to do so.

These are just a few suggestions that may help you to develop your skills or find employment in the futures industry. How you use this information and what you eventually decide to do is, of course, a matter of individual preference. I do, however, encourage you to consider being involved in futures trading in one way or another.

THE FACTS OF MARKET LIFE

In conclusion, I would like to share with you twenty facts of market life, compiled from my many years of experience as a trader. I believe they will be of great benefit to you. I urge you to read them, analyze them, study them, and think about them.

1. The More You Trade, the Less You Make

The simple fact is that more frequent trading is not necessarily synonymous with more profitable trading. The cost of commissions and the cost of poor order execution on entry and exit all add up. In the long run, they can prove very costly. The idea is not to trade more but to trade better. Know that a good trading system is one that "knows" when to keep you out of the market, not necessarily one that keeps you in the market all the time or one that causes you to trade too often.

2. More Decisions = Less Profit

Because most decisions a trader makes are wrong, the more decisions a trader has to make the more losing decisions there will be. The moral is this: Traders must use simple methods and systems that do not require too many decisions. Furthermore, each decision for a trader can arouse mental conflicts. Mental conflicts increase the probability of making an emotionally based decision as opposed to a logical decision.

3. More Complicated = Less Effective

This cogent point is clearly related to the first two points. In my many years as a trader, I've traded or tested the vast majority of systems that exist. In addition to finding most of them mediocre, I've found that the simple systems seem to work best as well as most consistently. So keep it simple. There are literally hundreds, if not thousands, of trading systems available, often for obscenely large amounts of money. In choosing a system, bear in mind that the complexity of a system is in no way correlated with the value of a system.

4. More Calls to Broker = Less Profit

When you call your broker you often open yourself up to emotional responses that will not serve you well. Call your broker only when you need to place an order, pick up a fill, or ask a valid question. Unless you depend on your broker for recommendations, I suggest you avoid your broker's input, particularly if you trade your own system.

5. Think More, Make Less Money

Too much analysis and thought, once a system has given its signals, is the enemy of successful trading. All too often traders think themselves into losing positions and out of winning positions.

6. Analyze More, Make Less, Lose More

Analysis is fine, but too much analysis can cost you lost opportunities. Find a simple system and use it without too much, if any, second-guessing or analysis. The result will be very much to your liking.

7. More Information In = Less Money Out

With the plethora of books, newsletters, services, systems, computer bulletin boards, and trading courses on today's market (not to mention all of the "free" opinions offered in the media), the odds of being overloaded with information are very high. The danger in being overloaded with information is that you will get confused and you will get too many recommendations. You will begin to doubt your own opinions and ideas.

8. More Emotion = Less Profit

Emotion will make you get in too soon, out too late, in too late, and out too soon. It will cause you to lose sleep over positions and it will cause you to add to positions when you should subtract from them. Yet emotion is the most difficult thing for a trader to control.

9. Care More, Make Less

The more you care, the less you'll make; the less you care, the more you'll make. Care about what? About being right, about making money, about losing, about making a lot, about being wrong. If you care, then you lose your objectivity, and that will lead to losses.

10. Smaller Stop Losses = Less Profits

Most trading systems don't work if the stop losses you use are too small. All markets contain a certain amount of random behavior, expressed as whipsaws, that occurs during the day. Whipsaws stop traders out of otherwise good positions as losses when, in fact, a wider stop loss might have resulted in a profit. Do not use stop losses that are too small. You will guarantee yourself a loss if your stop losses aren't large enough to allow for random market fluctuations.

11. Try Not to Ask "Why" Things Happen

Every market has a significant random element that affects outcomes, and sometimes a cause and effect cannot be discerned. In futures trading, don't always attempt to know why something happens. Knowing why will not necessarily help you, and it may in fact hinder you.

12. What Most Traders Do Doesn't Work

What most traders do in the market doesn't make money. Furthermore, most technical trading systems do not work over the long run. Over the short term they may show some good profits, but over an extended period of time they're losers. Therefore, don't be swayed by what most traders do. Play your own game and choose your own indicators.

13. Commission Costs Make a Big Difference

Don't get suckered into paying $100 commissions and don't pay a percentage or option premium as commission. Keep commissions reasonable!

14. Spreads Work, but Most Traders Don't Use Them

Spreads are very reliable. They often (but not always) involve reduced risk, and they are highly predictable based on seasonals.

Professional traders have used spreads for many years, if you aren't already using them, consider doing so. While the sources of reliable spread information are few, there are a few recognized experts as well as a few valid sources of educational information.

15. Patterns Are the Best Indicators

The more work I do with patterns, the more I realize that patterns are exceptionally valid as indicators and trading methods. As more research is done, I think it will become more evident that patterns are the best indicators available.

16. Live Data and Real-Time Quotes Aren't Necessary

Traders erroneously believe that closer contact with the markets in the form of live, tick-by-tick quotes will make them more money. In fact, the reverse is often true. Traders who are undisciplined are unable to cope with the large influx of information. They begin attending to every tick, watching every market, working with a host of indicators. The end result is that they lose money, not only on the cost of the data, but in their trading as well.

17. Most Traders Can't Accept More Than Three Consecutive Losses Before Losing Their Discipline

It is the nature of all trading systems to lose money at times. Drawdown of equity is a universal problem with trading systems. In addition to dollar drawdown, the number of consecutive losing trades can play on a trader's mind and undermine a trader's discipline. The more consecutive losses a system takes, the less a trader will be inclined to remain disciplined with that system. This lack of discipline can only lead to losses.

18. The Experts' Forecasts Are Unimportant

Forecasts have nothing to do with precise timing, and timing is what will make you money in the futures markets. Forecasts won't do anything for you.

19. How You Place and Use Orders Is Important

Most traders are unfamiliar with the different types of orders they can use. Using the right order at the right time is very important. Frequently it can mean the difference between a profit and a loss. The use of a stop limit order as opposed to a simple stop order, for example, can save you hundreds if not thousands of dollars in the long run, provided you know when to use it. If you aren't familiar with the kinds of orders that are appropriate in specific situations, make it your goal to learn about them.

20. The Vast Majority of Traders Lack Discipline

Discipline in doing your market work and in sticking to a trading system is a very important skill to acquire if you want to succeed as a trader. The underlying reason for most losses is not system related but discipline related. Although an effective trading system can be a great help on the road to success, even the most profitable system will become a losing system if implemented by a trader who lacks discipline.

These, then, are some of the most important facts of commodity life. Understand them, learn them, and use them to come closer to achieving success as a trader. I am certain that you have developed some rules of your own. Add them to the facts I've given you and embark on your road to profits.

APPENDIX I

References and Reading List

Babcock, Bruce Jr. *The Dow Jones-Irwin Guide to Trading Systems.* Homewood, IL: Richard D. Irwin Inc., 1989.

Barnes, Robert M. *Taming the Pits: A Technical Approach to Commodity Trading.* NY: John Wiley & Sons, 1979.

Baruch, Bernard. *My Own Story.* NY: Holt, 1957.

Bernstein, Jake. *The Investor's Quotient I.* NY: John Wiley & Sons, 1980.

Bernstein, Jake. *The Handbook of Commodity Cycles: A Window on Time.* NY: John Wiley & Sons, 1982.

Bernstein, Jake. *How to Profit in Precious Metals.* NY: John Wiley & Sons, 1985.

Bernstein, Jake. *Beyond the Investor's Quotient.* NY: John Wiley & Sons, 1986.

Bernstein, Jake. *New Facts on Futures.* Northbrook, IL: MBH, 1987.

Bernstein, Jake. *Cyclic Analysis in Futures Trading.* NY: John Wiley & Sons, 1988.

Bernstein, Jake. *MBH Seasonal Futures Charts: A Study of Weekly Seasonal Tendencies in the Commodity Futures Markets.* Northbrook, IL: MBH Commodity, 1988.

Bernstein, Jake. *The Analysis and Forecasting of Long-Term Trends in the Cash and Futures Markets.* Chicago: Probus Publishing, 1989.

Bernstein, Jake. *Short-Term Trading in Futures.* Northbrook, IL: MBH Publishing, 1992.

Bernstein, Jake. *The Investor's Quotient, Second Edition.* NY: John Wiley & Sons, 1993.

Bernstein, Jake. *The Compleat Day Trader.* NY: McGraw Hill, 1995.

Bernstein, Jake. *Daily Seasonal Futures Charts.* Northbrook, IL: MBH, 1996.

Bernstein, Jake. *Daily Seasonal Spread Charts.* Northbrook, IL: MBH, 1996.

Bernstein, Jake. *Seasonal Cash Charts and Array Analysis.* Northbrook, IL: MBH, 1996.

Bernstein, Jake. *Weekly Seasonal Futures Charts.* Northbrook, IL: MBH, 1996.

Bernstein, Jake. *Weekly Seasonal Spread Charts.* Northbrook, IL: MBH, 1996.

Bernstein, Jake. *Seasonality.* NY, Wiley 1997.

Bernstein, Jake. *The Compleat Day Trader II.* NY: McGraw Hill, 1998.

Blumenthal, Earl. *Chart for Profit: Point and Figure Trading.* Larchmont, NY: Investors Intelligence, 1975.

Bolton, A. Hamilton. *The Elliott Wave Principle: A Critical Appraisal.* Hamilton, Bermuda: Monetary Research, 1960.

Clasing, H. *The Dow Jones–Irwin Guide to Put and Call Options.* Homewood, IL: Dow Jones–Irwin, 1978.

Contrary Opinion. Hadady Corporation, 1111 S. Arroyo Parkway, Suite 410 0, Pasadena, CA 91109-0490, 1983.

The Dow Jones Commodities Handbook: A Guide to Major Futures Markets. Princeton, NJ: Dow Jones Books, 1983.

Dunn, D. and E. Hargitt. *Point and Figure Commodity Trading: A Computer Evaluation.* West Lafayette, IN: Dunn and Hargitt, 1971.

Gann, William D. *Forty-Five Years in Wall Street.* Pomeroy, WA: Lambert-Gann, 1949.

Gann, William D. *How to Make Profits in Commodities,* rev. ed. Pomeroy, WA: Lambert-Gann, 1951.

Gann, William D. *The Basis of My Forecasting Method for Grain.* Pomeroy, WA: Lambert-Gann, 1970 (originally 1935).

Gann, William D. *Forecasting Grains by Time Cycles.* Pomeroy, WA: Lambert-Gann, 1976.

Gann, William D. *Forecasting Rules for Cotton.* Pomeroy, WA: Lambert-Gann, 1976.

Gann, William D. *Forecasting Rules for Gain-Geometric Angles.* Pomeroy, WA: Lambert-Gann, 1976.

Gold, Gerald. *Modern Commodity Futures Trading,* 7th ed. NY: Commodity Research Bureau, 1975.

Goss, B. A. and B. S. Yamey. *The Economics of Futures Trading.* NY: John Wiley & Sons, 1976.

Hieronymus, Thomas A. *Economics of Futures Trading for Commercial and Personal Profit,* 2nd ed. NY: Commodity Research Bureau, 1977.

Hill, John R. *Stock and Commodity Market Trend Trading by Advanced Technical Analysis.* Hendersonville, NC: Commodity Research Institute, 1977.

Hill, John R. *Scientific Interpretation of Bar Charts.* Hendersonville, NC: Commodity Research Institute, 1979.

Huff, Charles. *Commodity Speculation for Beginners: A Guide to the Futures Markets.* NY: Macmillan, 1980.

Hurst, J. M. *The Profit Magic of Stock Transaction Timing.* Englewood Cliffs, NJ: Prentice Hall, 1970.

Jiler, Harry, ed. *Forecasting Commodity Prices: How the Experts Analyze the Market.* NY: Commodity Research Bureau, 1975.

Keltner, C. W. *How to Make Money in Commodities.* Kansas City: Keltner Statistical Service, 1960.

Kindleberger, Charles P. *Manias, Panics and Crashes: A History of Financial Crisis.* NY: Basic Books, 1978.

Kroll, Stanley and Irwin Shisko. *The Commodity Futures Market Guide.* NY: Harper & Row, 1973.

Lefevre, Edwin. *Reminiscences of a Stock Operator.* NY: American Research Council, 1923. Reprint ed., Burlington, VT: Books of Wall Street, 1980.

Leslie, Conrad. *Conrad Leslie's Guide for Successful Speculating.* Chicago: Dartnell Press, 1970.

McMillan, L. *Options as a Strategic Investment.* NY: New York Institute of Finance, 1980.

Murphy, John. *Technical Analysis of the Futures Market.* NY: New York Institute of Finance, 1996.

Oster, Merrill J. *Commodity Futures for Profit . . . A Farmer's Guide to Hedging.* Cedar Falls, IA: Investor Publications, 1979.

Oster, Merrill J. *Professional Hedging Handbook: A Guide to Hedging Crops and Livestock.* Cedar Falls, IA: Investor Publications, 1979.

Powers, Mark J. *Getting Started in Commodity Futures Trading*, 2nd ed. Cedar Falls, IA: Investor Publications, 1977.

Reinach, Anthony M. *The Fastest Game in Town: Trading Commodity Futures.* NY: Commodity Research Bureau, 1973.

Sharpe, William F. *Investments.* Englewood Cliffs, NJ: Prentice Hall, 1978.

Smith, A. *The Money Game.* NY: Random House, 1967.

Teweles, Richard J., Charles V. Harlow, and Herbert L. Stone. *The Commodity Futures Game—Who Wins? Who Loses? Why?* 2nd ed. NY: McGraw-Hill, 1974.

Williams, Larry R. and Michelle Noseworthy. *Sure Thing Commodity Trading: How Seasonal Factors Influence Commodity Prices.* Brightwaters, NY: Windsor, 1977.

Appendix II

Contracts Traded

U.S. FUTURES CONTRACTS TRADED

Grains & Oilseeds

Barley
Minneapolis Grain Exchange (MGE)

Corn
Chicago Board of Trade (CBOT)
MidAmerica Commodity Exchange (MidAm)

Oats
Chicago Board of Trade (CBOT)
MidAmerica Commodity Exchange (MidAm)

Rice
Chicago Board of Trade (CBOT)

Soybeans
Chicago Board of Trade (CBOT)
MidAmerica Commodity Exchange (MidAm)

Soybean Meal
Chicago Board of Trade (CBOT)
MidAmerica Commodity Exchange (MidAm)

Soybean Oil
Chicago Board of Trade (CBOT)
MidAmerica Commodity Exchange (MidAm)

Wheat
Chicago Board of Trade (CBOT)
Kansas City Board of Trade (KCBT)
MidAmerica Commodity Exchange (MidAm)
Minneapolis Grain Exchange (MGE)

White Wheat
Minneapolis Grain Exchange (MGE)

Interest Rates

2-Year U.S. Treasury Notes
Chicago Board Options Exchange
(CBOT)

5-Year U.S. Treasury Notes
Chicago Board Options Exchange
(CBOT)

10-Year U.S. Treasury Notes
Chicago Board Options Exchange
(CBOT)

30-Day Federal Funds
Chicago Board Options Exchange
(CBOT)

Brady Bond Index
Chicago Board Options Exchange
(CBOT)

EuroDollar
Chicago Mercantile Exchange (CME)

Flexible 10-Year T-Notes
Chicago Board Options Exchange
(CBOT)

Flexible U.S. T Bonds
Chicago Board Options Exchange
(CBOT)

LIBOR
Chicago Mercantile Exchange (CME)

Municipal Bond Index
Chicago Board Options Exchange
(CBOT)

Treasury Bills
Chicago Mercantile Exchange (CME)

U.S. Treasury Bond
Chicago Board Options Exchange
(CBOT)

Stock Index Futures

S&P 100 Index
Chicago Board Options Exchange
(CBOE)

S&P 500 Index
Chicago Mercantile Exchange (CME)

Meat and Dairy Products

Butter, Cheddar Cheese
Chicago Mercantile Exchange (CME)

Feeder Cattle
Chicago Mercantile Exchange (CME)

Fluid Milk
Chicago Mercantile Exchange (CME)
Coffee, Sugar & Cocoa Exchange Inc.
(CSCE)

Lean Hogs
Chicago Mercantile Exchange (CME)

Live Cattle
Chicago Mercantile Exchange (CME)
MidAmerica Commodity Exchange
(MidAm)

Live Hogs I
Chicago Mercantile Exchange (CME)
MidAmerica Commodity Exchange
(MidAm)

Milk
Coffee, Sugar & Cocoa Exchange Inc.
(CSCE)

Non-Fat Dry Milk
Coffee, Sugar & Cocoa Exchange Inc.
(CSCE)

Pork Bellies
Chicago Mercantile Exchange (CME)

Shrimp
Minneapolis Grain Exchange (MGE)

Currencies

Australian Dollar
Chicago Mercantile Exchange (CME)
Philadelphia Board of Trade (PBOT)

British Pound
Chicago Mercantile Exchange (CME)
Philadelphia Board of Trade (PBOT)

Canadian Dollar
Chicago Mercantile Exchange (CME)
Philadelphia Board of Trade (PBOT)

Deutsche Mark
Chicago Mercantile Exchange (CME)
Philadelphia Board of Trade (PBOT)

Euro FX (European Currency Unit)
Chicago Mercantile Exchange (CME)

French Franc
Chicago Mercantile Exchange (CME)
Philadelphia Board of Trade (PBOT)

Italian Lira
Philadelphia Board of Trade (PBOT)

Japanese Yen
Chicago Mercantile Exchange (CME)
Philadelphia Board of Trade (PBOT)

Spanish Peseta
Philadelphia Board of Trade (PBOT)

Swiss Franc
Chicago Mercantile Exchange (CME)
Philadelphia Board of Trade (PBOT)
New York Board of Trade (NYBOT)

Energy

Crude Oil
New York Mercantile Exchange
(NYMEX)

Electricity
New York Mercantile Exchange
(NYMEX)

Gasoline
New York Mercantile Exchange
(NYMEX)

Heating Oil
New York Mercantile Exchange
(NYMEX)

Natural Gas
Kansas City Board of Trade (KCBT)
New York Mercantile Exchange
(NYMEX)

Propane Gas
New York Mercantile Exchange
(NYMEX)

Unleaded Gasoline
New York Mercantile Exchange
(NYMEX)

Western Natural Gas
Kansas City Board of Trade (KCBT)

Metals

Gold
Chicago Board of Trade (CBOT)
MidAmerica Commodity Exchange
(MidAm)
New York Mercantile Exchange
(COMEX)

Palladium
New York Mercantile Exchange
(NYMEX)

Platinum
MidAmerica Commodity Exchange
(MidAm)
New York Mercantile Exchange
(NYMEX)

Silver
Chicago Board of Trade (CBOT)
MidAmerica Commodity Exchange
(MidAm)
New York Mercantile Exchange
(COMEX)

Indexes

CRB Index
New York Board of Trade (NYBOT)

Eurotop 100 Index
New York Mercantile Exchange
(COMEX)

FT-SE-100 Stock Index
Chicago Mercantile Exchange (CME)

Goldman Sachs Commodity Index
Chicago Mercantile Exchange (CME)

Major Market Index
Chicago Mercantile Exchange (CME)

Mexican IPC Stock Index
Chicago Mercantile Exchange (CME)

Mexican Peso
Chicago Mercantile Exchange
(CME)

Mini Value Line
Kansas City Board of Trade (KCBT)

NASDAQ 100 Index
Chicago Mercantile Exchange (CME)

Nikkei 225 Stock Average Index
Chicago Mercantile Exchange (CME)

Russell 2000 Stock Price Index
Chicago Mercantile Exchange (CME)

S&P 500/BARRA Growth Index
Chicago Mercantile Exchange (CME)

S&P 500/BARRA Value Index
Chicago Mercantile Exchange (CME)

S&P MidCap 400 Index
Chicago Mercantile Exchange (CME)

S&P 500 Stock Index
Chicago Mercantile Exchange (CME)

VLA5 Value Line/A
Kansas City Board of Trade (KCBT)

VLC5 Value Line/G
Kansas City Board of Trade (KCBT)

Value Line
Kansas City Board of Trade (KCBT)

Foods

Cocoa
Coffee, Sugar & Cocoa Exchange Inc.
(CSCE)
New York Board of Trade (NYBOT)

Coffee
Coffee, Sugar & Cocoa Exchange Inc.
(CSCE)
New York Board of Trade (NYBOT)

Frozen Concentrated Orange Juice
Citrus Associates of the NYCE Inc.

Orange Juice
New York Cotton Exchange (NYCE)
New York Board of Trade (NYBOT)

Potatoes
New York Cotton Exchange (NYCE)
New York Board of Trade (NYBOT)

Sugar
Coffee, Sugar & Cocoa Exchange Inc.
(CSCE)
Minneapolis Grain Exchange (MGE)

Other Products

Anhydrous Ammonia
Chicago Board of Trade (CBOT)

Diammonium Phosphate
Chicago Board of Trade (CBOT)

Lumber
Chicago Mercantile Exchange (CME)

Oriented Strand Board
Chicago Mercantile Exchange (CME)

Plywood
Chicago Mercantile Exchange (CME)

INTERNATIONAL FUTURES EXCHANGES TRADED

Grains & Oilseeds

Azuki Beans
Tokyo Grain Exchange (TGE)

Barley
Budapest Commodity Exchange (BCE)
China-Commodity Futures Exchange, Inc. of Hainan (CCFE)
Commodity Exchange of Ljubljana (LCE)
London International Financial Futures Exchange (LIFFE)
Shenyang Commodity Exchange
Winnipeg Commodity Exchange (WCE)

Beans
Beijing Commodity Exchange (BCE)
China-Commodity Futures Exchange, Inc. of Hainan (CCFE)
China Zhengzhou Commodity Exchange (CZCE)
Chubu Commodity Exchange (C-COM)
Dalian Commodity Exchange
Hokkaido Grain Exchange (HGE)
Kanmom Commodity Exchange (KCE)
Kasai Agricultural Commodities Exchange (KACEX)
Nagoya Grain & Sugar Exchange (NGSE)
Shanghai Cereals and Oils Exchange
Suzhou Commodity Exchange
Tianjin United Futures Exchange
Tokyo Grain Exchange (TGE)

Bread Wheat
Mercado A Termino De Buenas Aires S.A.

Canola
Winnipeg Commodity Exchange (WCE)

Castorseeds
The OTC Exchange of India. (OTCEI)

Corn
Beijing Commodity Exchange (BCE)
Bolsa de Mercadoris & Futuros (BM&F)
Bolsa de Cereales de Buenos Aires
Budapest Commodity Exchange (BCE)
Changchun United Commodities Futures Exchange
China Zhengzhou Commodity Exchange (CZCE)
Dalian Commodity Exchange
Guangdong United Futures Exchange
Kanmon Commodity Exchange (KCE)
Mercado A Termino De Buenas Aires S.A.
Shanghai Cereals and Oils Exchange
Tokyo Grain Exchange (TGE)

Crude Palm Kernel Oil
Kuala Lumpur Commodity Exchange (KLCE)

Crude Palm Oil
China-Commodity Futures Exchange, Inc. of Hainan (CCFE)
Kuala Lumpur Commodity Exchange (KLCE)

Feed Peas
Winnipeg Commodity Exchange (WCE)

Flaxseed
Winnipeg Commodity Exchange (WCE)
Hokkaido Grain Exchange (HGE)

Maize
Commodity Exchange of Ljubljana (LCE)
The South African Futures Exchange (SAFEX)

Oats
Winnipeg Commodity Exchange (WCE)

Peanut Kernel
Beijing Commodity Exchange (BCE)
Shenyang Commodity Exchange

Potato Starch
Chubu Commodity Exchange (C-COM)
Hokkaido Grain Exchange (HGE)
Kanmon Commodity Exchange (KCE)
Nagoya Grain & Sugar Exchange (NGSE)

Rape Seed (Canola)
Winnipeg Commodity Exchange (WCE)

Red Beans
Kanmon Commodity Exchange (KCE)
Hokkaido Grain Exchange (HGE)
Kasai Agricultural Commodities Exchange (KACE)
Nagoya Grain & Sugar Exchange (NGSE)
Tokyo Grain Commodity Exchange (TGCE)
Manila International Futures Exchange (MIFE)

Red Corn
Mercado A Termino De Buenos Aires S.A.

Rice
Beijing Commodity Exchange (BCE)
Dalian Commodity Exchange
Guangdong United Futures Exchange
Shanghai Cereals and Oils Exchange

Rye
Winnipeg Commodity Exchange (WCE)

Sorghum
Shenyang Commodity Exchange

Soybeans
Beijing Commodity Exchange (BCE)
Bolsa de Mercadoris & Futuros (BM&F)
Bolsa de Cereales de Buenos Aires

China Zhengzhou Commodity Exchange (CZCE)
Chubu Commodity Exchange (C-COM)
Changchun United Commodities Futures Exchange
Dalian Commodity Exchange
Guangdong United Futures Exchange
Hokkaido Grain Exchange (HGE)
Kanmon Commodity Exchange (KCE)
Kasai Agricultural Commodities Exchange (KACEX)
Manila International Futures Exchange (MIFE)
Mercado A Termino De Buenas Aires S.A.
Nagoya Grain & Sugar Exchange (NGSE)
Shanghai Cereals and Oils Exchange
Tianjin United Futures Exchange
Tokyo Grain Exchange (TGE)

Soybean Meal
Beijing Commodity Exchange (BCE)
Changchun United Commodities Futures Exchange
Dalian Commodity Exchange
Guangdong United Futures Exchange
Tianjin United Futures Exchange

Soybean Oil
Beijing Commodity Exchange (BCE)
Dalian Commodity Exchange
Kanmon Commodity Exchange (KCE)

Sweet Potato Starch
Nagoya Grain & Sugar Exchange (NGSE)

Sunflower Seed
Budapest Commodity Exchange (BCE)
Bolsa de Cereales de Buenos Aires
Mercado A Termino De Buenas Aires S.A.

Wheat
Agricultural Futures Market Amsterdam
Beijing Commodity Exchange (BCE)

Bolsa de Cereales de Buenos Aires
Budapest Commodity Exchange (BCE)
Changchun United Commodities
Futures Exchange
China Zhengzhou Commodity
Exchange (CZCE)
Dalian Commodity Exchange
London International Financial
Futures Exchange (LIFFE)
Mercado A Termino De Buenas Aires
S.A.
Shanghai Cereals and Oils Exchange
Sydney Futures Exchange (SFE)
The South African Futures Exchange
(SAFEX)
Winnipeg Commodity Exchange
(WCE)

White Beans
Hokkaido Grain Exchange (HGE)

Interest Rates

1-Day Interbank Deposit
Bolsa de Mercadoris & Futuros
(BM&F)

30-Day Interbank Deposit
Bolsa de Mercadoris & Futuros
(BM&F)

90-Day Accepted Bank Bill
Sydney Futures Exchange (SFE)

90-Day Bank Accepted Bill
New Zealand Futures & Options
Exchange (NZFOE)

90-Day Bankers Accepted Bills
Sydney Futures Exchange (SFE)

1-Month BUBOR Futures
Budapest Commodity Exchange, Ltd.
(BCE)

1-Month Euromark
London International Financial
Futures Exchange (LIFFE)

1-Month HIBOR Futures
Hong Kong Futures & Options
Exchange, Ltd. (HKFE)

3-Month BIBOR
Belgium Futures and Options
Exchange (BELFOX)

3-Month BUBOR Futures
Budapest Commodity Exchange, Ltd.
(BCE)

*3-Month Canadian Bankers' Acceptance
Futures (BAX)*
Montreal Exchange (ME)

3-Month CD Interest Rate
Korean Futures Exchange (KOFEX)

3-Month DIBOR
Irish Futures and Options Exchange
(IFOX)

3-Month ECU
London International Financial
Futures Exchange (LIFFE)

3-Month Euromark
London International Financial
Futures Exchange (LIFFE)

3-Month Euroyen
Tokyo International Financial
Exchange (TIFFE)

3-Month Eurodollar
Tokyo International Financial
Exchange (TIFFE)

3-Month HELIBOR
Helsinki Securities and Derivatives
Exchange, Clearing House

3-Month HIBOR Futures
Hong Kong Futures & Options
Exchange, Ltd. (HKFE)

3-Month KILBOR
Malaysia Monetary Exchange (MME)

3-Month MIBOR
MEFF Renta Fija (MEFF-F)

3-Month PIBOR
Marche a Terme International de
France (MATIF)

3-Month Short-Sterling
London International Financial
Futures Exchange (LIFFE)

3-Month STIBOR
OM Stockholm

2-Year Notional Mortgage Bond
OM Stockholm

2-Year Swedish Government Bond
OM Stockholm

3-Year Government Stock
New Zealand Futures & Options
Exchange (NZFOE)

3-Year Notional Government Bond
MEFF Renta Fija (MEFF-F)

3-Year Treasury Bonds
Sydney Futures Exchange (SFE)
New Zealand Futures & Options
Exchange (NZFOE)

5-Year BTP
Mercato Italian Futures (MIF)

*5-Year Government of Canada Bond
Futures (CGF)*
Montreal Exchange (ME)

5-Year Irish Gilt
Irish Futures and Options Exchange
(IFOX)

5-Year Gilt
London International Financial
Futures Exchange (LIFFE)

5-Year Malaysian Government Securities
Kuala Lumpur Commodity Exchange
(KLCE)

5-Year Notional Bond
Mercato Italian Futures (MIF) 10-year
notional bond

5-Year Notional Mortgage Bond
OM Stockholm

5-Year Notional Swedish Bond
OM Stockholm

10-Year AUS Bond
Sydney Futures Exchange (SFE)

10-Year BTP
Mercato Italian Futures (MIF)

*10-Year Government of Canada Bond
Futures (CGB)*
Montreal Exchange (ME)

10-Year Government Stock
New Zealand Futures & Options
Exchange (NZFOE)

10-Year Japanese Govt Bond GB
Singapore International Monetary
Exchange Ltd. (SIMEX)

10-Year Omr Swap
OM Stockholm

10-Year Notional Government Bond
MEFF Renta Fija (MEFF-F)
Mercato Italian Futures (MIF)

10-Year Notional Swedish Bond
OM Stockholm

10-Year Treasury Bonds
Sydney Futures Exchange (SFE)

20-Year Irish Gilt
Irish Futures and Options Exchange
(IFOX)

All Ordinaries Index
Sydney Futures Exchange (SFE)

Austrian Government Bond
Austrian Futures & Options Exchange
(OTOB)

Belgian Government Bond
Belgium Futures and Options
Exchange (BELFOX)

BONO E-5
MEFF Renta Fija (MEFF RF)

BONO E-10
MEFF Renta Fija (MEFF RF)

BONO E-30
MEFF Renta Fija (MEFF RF)

BTP
London International Financial
Futures Exchange (LIFFE)

Bund
London International Financial
Futures Exchange (LIFFE)

CAC 40
Marche a Terme International de
France (MATIF)

Canadian Bankers' Acceptances –
1 Month
Montreal Exchange (ME)

Canadian Bankers' Acceptances –
3-Month
Montreal Exchange (ME)

CIBOR
Guarantee Fund for Danish Options &
Futures (FUTOP)

Clearing OTC Government Bonds
Helsinki Securities and Derivatives
Exchange, Clearing House

CT2 Mortgage Bond
OM Stockholm

CT5 Mortgage Bond
OM Stockholm

Dutch Government Bond
European Options Exchange (EOE)

ECU
London International Financial
Futures Exchange (LIFFE)

EURIBOR
MEFF Renta Fija (MEFF RF)

EuroDollar
London International Financial
Futures Exchange (LIFFE)
Singapore International Monetary
Exchange Ltd. (SIMEX)

EuroLira
London International Financial
Futures Exchange (LIFFE)

EuroMark
London International Financial
Futures Exchange (LIFFE)
Singapore International Monetary
Exchange Ltd. (SIMEX)

EuroSwiss
London International Financial
Futures Exchange (LIFFE)

EuroYen
London International Financial
Futures Exchange (LIFFE)
Singapore International Monetary
Exchange Ltd. (SIMEX)

French Treasury Bond
Marche a Terme International de
France (MATIF)

General Market Price Index
Bolsa de Mercadoris & Futuros
(BM&F)

Government of Canada Bond
Montreal Exchange (ME)

IFOX Interest Rate Swaps
Irish Futures and Options Exchange
(IFOX)

IMM Forward Rate
OM Stockholm

Individual Share
Sydney Futures Exchange (SFE)

Italian Government Bond - BTP
London International Financial
Futures Exchange (LIFFE)

Japanese Government Bond - JGB
London International Financial
Futures Exchange (LIFFE)

JGB
London International Financial
Futures Exchange (LIFFE)

German Government Bond - Bund
London International Financial
Futures Exchange (LIFFE)

KLIBOR
Kuala Lumpur Commodity Exchange
(KLCE)

Long Gilt
London International Financial
Futures Exchange (LIFFE)

Long-Term Danish Government Bond
Guarantee Fund for Danish Options &
Futures (FUTOP)

Medium-Term Danish Government Bond
Guarantee Fund for Danish Options &
Futures (FUTOP)

Medium-Term French Government Bond
Marche a Terme International de
France (MATIF)

*Medium-Term German Government
Bond - Bobl*
London International Financial
Futures Exchange (LIFFE)

MIBOR E-90
MEFF Renta Fija (MEFF RF)

MIBOR E-360
MEFF Renta Fija (MEFF RF)

Mortgage Bond
Guarantee Fund for Danish Options &
Futures (FUTOP)

New Zealand Dollar
New Zealand Futures & Options
Exchange (NZFOE)

Notional Bond (GLOBEX)
Marche a Terme International de
France (MATIF)

Notional Guilder Bond
Financial Futures Market Amsterdam
(FTA)

Notional T Bills
OM Stockholm

SB5 Mortgage Bond
OM Stockholm

Short Sterling
London International Financial
Futures Exchange (LIFFE)

Spanish Government Bond (Bonos)
London International Financial
Futures Exchange (LIFFE)

U.S. Dollar
Tokyo International Financial
Exchange (TIFFE)
New Zealand Futures & Options
Exchange (NZFOE)

VIBOR
Austrian Futures & Options Exchange
(OTOB)

Stock Index Futures

All Ordinaries Share Price Index
Sydney Futures Exchange (SFE)

Boilvar/US Dollar Exchange Rate Futures
Bolsa de Valores de Caracas

Hang Seng Index Futures
Hong Kong Futures & Options
Exchange, Ltd. (HKFE)

Hang Seng 100 Futures
Hong Kong Futures & Options
Exchange, Ltd. (HKFE)

Hang Seng Properties Sub-Index Futures
Hong Kong Futures & Options
Exchange, Ltd. (HKFE)

HKFE Taiwan Index Futures
Hong Kong Futures & Options
Exchange, Ltd. (HKFE)

IBC Stock Index Futures Contract
Bolsa de Valores de Caracas

Red-Chip Futures
Hong Kong Futures & Options
Exchange, Ltd. (HKFE)

Selective Stock Price Index IPSA
Santiago Stock Exchange (SSE)

Stock Futures
Hong Kong Futures & Options
Exchange, Ltd. (HKFE)

TAC3m Interest Rate Future Contract
Bolsa de Valores de Caracas

U.S. Dollar Interbank Exchange Rate
Santiago Stock Exchange (SSE)

Textiles

Broad Wool
Sydney Futures Exchange (SFE)

Cotton
Bolsa de Mercadoris & Futuros
(BM&F)
The OTC Exchange of India (OTCEI)

Cotton Yarn
China Zhengzhou Commodity
Exchange (CZCE)
Chubu Commodity Exchange
(C-COM)
Nagoya Textile Exchange (NTE)
Osaka Textile Exchange (OSE)
Tokyo Commodity Exchange
(TOCOM)

Dried Cocoon
Chubu Commodity Exchange
(C-COM)
Maebashi Dried Cocoon Exchange
(MDCE)
Manila International Futures
Exchange (MIFE)
Toyahashi Dried Cocoon Exchange
(TDCE)

Fine Wool
Sydney Futures Exchange (SFE)

Greasy Wool
Sydney Futures Exchange (SFE)

Hessian
The OTC Exchange of India (OTCEI)

Jute Goods (Sacking)
The OTC Exchange of India (OTCEI)

New Zealand Wool
New Zealand Futures & Options
Exchange (NZFOE)

Raw Jute
The OTC Exchange of India (OTCEI)

Raw Silk
Kobe Raw Silk Exchange (KRSE)
Yokohama Raw Silk Exchange
(YRSE)

Staple Fiber Yarn
Chubu Commodity Exchange
(C-COM)
Nagoya Textile Exchange (NTE)
Osaka Textile Exchange (OSE)

Staple Fiber Yarn-Dull
Nagoya Textile Exchange (NTE)

Wool
New Zealand Futures & Options
Exchange (NZFOE)
Sydney Futures Exchange (SFE)

Woolen Yarn
Chubu Commodity Exchange
(C-COM)
Nagoya Textile Exchange (NTE)
Osaka Textile Exchange (OSE)
Tokyo Commodity Exchange
(TOCOM)

Meat and Dairy Products

Chilled Carcass Beef
The South African Futures Exchange
(SAFEX)

Feeder Cattle
Bolsa de Mercadoris & Futuros
(BM&F)

Live Cattle
Bolsa de Mercadoris & Futuros
(BM&F)
Sydney Futures Exchange (SFE)

Live Hogs I
Agricultural Futures Market
Amsterdam
Budapest Commodity Exchange (BCE)

Live Hogs II
Budapest Commodity Exchange (BCE)
National Average Beef Index
The South African Futures Exchange
(SAFEX)

Piglets
Agricultural Futures Market
Amsterdam

Currencies

British Pound
Singapore International Monetary
Exchange Ltd. (SIMEX)

Deutsche Mark
Commodity Exchange of Ljubljana
(LCE)
Singapore International Monetary
Exchange Ltd. (SIMEX)

Italian Lira
Commodity Exchange of Ljubljana
(LCE)

Japanese Yen
Commodity Exchange of Ljubljana
(LCE)
Singapore International Monetary
Exchange Ltd. (SIMEX)
Tokyo International Financial
Exchange (TIFFE)

Jumbo U.S. Dollar/Guilder
European Options Exchange (EOE)

Korean Wan
Korean Futures Exchange (KOFEX)

Rolling Forex
Hong Kong Futures & Options
Exchange, Ltd. (HKFE)

Spanish Peseta/Deutsche Mark
MEFF Renta Fija (MEFF-F)

Spanish Peseta/U.S. Dollar
MEFF Renta Fija (MEFF-F)

U.S. Dollar
Bolsa de Mercadoris & Futuros
(BM&F)
Commodity Exchange of Ljubljana
(LCE)
Tokyo International Financial
Exchange (TIFFE)

U.S. Dollar/British Pound
Manila International Futures
Exchange (MIFE)

U.S. Dollar/DMark
Manila International Futures
Exchange (MIFE)

U.S. Dollar/Guilder
European Options Exchange (EOE)
Financial Futures Market Amsterdam
(FTA)

U.S. Dollar/Japanese Yen
Manila International Futures
Exchange (MIFE)

U.S. Dollar/Korean Wan
Korean Futures Exchange (KOFEX)

U.S. Dollar/Peso
Santiago Stock Exchange (SSE)
Manila International Futures
Exchange (MIFE)

U.S. Dollar/Swiss Franc
Manila International Futures
Exchange (MIFE)

Energy

Brent Crude Oil
International Petroleum Exchange of
London (PE)

Crude Oil
International Petroleum Exchange of
London (IPE)
Singapore International Monetary
Exchange Ltd. (SIMEX)
Sydney Futures Exchange (SFE)

Gasoil
International Petroleum Exchange of
London (PE)
Singapore International Monetary
Exchange Ltd. (SIMEX)

Gasoline
Guangdong United Futures Exchange
International Petroleum Exchange of
London (IPE)
Nanjing Petroleum Exchange
Singapore International Monetary
Exchange Ltd. (SIMEX)

Heating Oil
Sydney Futures Exchange (SFE)

High Sulfur Fuel Oil
International Petroleum Exchange of
London (IPE)
Singapore International Monetary
Exchange Ltd. (SIMEX)

Light Sweet Natural Crude Oil
New Zealand Futures & Options
Exchange (NZFOE)

Natural Gas
New Zealand Futures & Options
Exchange (NZFOE)
Sydney Futures Exchange (SFE)

NSW Base Load Electricity
Sydney Futures Exchange (SFE)

NSW Peal Period Electricity
Sydney Futures Exchange (SFE)

NZ Electricity
New Zealand Futures & Options
Exchange (NZFOE)

Propane Gas
Sydney Futures Exchange (SFE)

Unleaded Gasoline
International Petroleum Exchange of
London (IPE)
Sydney Futures Exchange (SFE)

VIC Base Load Electricity
Sydney Futures Exchange (SFE)

VIC Peak Period Electricity
Sydney Futures Exchange (SFE)

Metals

Aluminum
Beijing Commodity Exchange (BCE)
China Zhengzhou Commodity
Exchange (CZCE)
Guangdong United Futures Exchange
London Metal Exchange (LME)
Nanfang Non-Ferrous Metals
Exchange
Shanghai Metals Exchange
Shenyang Commodity Exchange
Shenzhen Metal and United Futures
Exchange
Tokyo Commodity Exchange
(TOCOM)

Aluminum Alloy
London Metal Exchange (LME)

Antimony
Shenzhen Metal and United Futures
Exchange

Copper
Beijing Commodity Exchange (BCE)
Guangdong United Futures Exchange
London Metal Exchange (LME)
Nanfang Non-Ferrous Metals
Exchange
New Zealand Futures & Options
Exchange (NZFOE)
Shanghai Metals Exchange
Shenyang Commodity Exchange
Shenzhen Metal and United Futures
Exchange

Gold
Belgium Futures and Options
Exchange (BELFOX)
European Options Exchange (EOE)
Bolsa de Mercadoris & Futuros (BM&F)
Hong Kong Futures & Options
Exchange, Ltd. (HKFE)
Kuala Lumpur Commodity Exchange
(KLCE)
New Zealand Futures & Options
Exchange (NZFOE)
Singapore International Monetary
Exchange Ltd. (SIMEX)
The South African Futures Exchange
(SAFEX)
Tokyo Commodity Exchange (TOCOM)
Vancouver Stock Exchange

High Grade Aluminum
London Metal Exchange (LME)

Lead
London Metal Exchange (LME)
Shanghai Metals Exchange
Shenzhen Metal and United Futures
Exchange

Magnesium
Shenzhen Metal and United Futures
Exchange

Nickel
London Metal Exchange (LME)
Shanghai Metals Exchange
Shenzhen Metal and United Futures
Exchange

Palladium
Tokyo Commodity Exchange (TOCOM)

Platinum
Tokyo Commodity Exchange (TOCOM)

Primary Aluminum
London Metal Exchange (LME)

Silver
European Options Exchange (EOE)
New Zealand Futures & Options
Exchange (NZFOE)
Tokyo Commodity Exchange (TOCOM)
Toronto Futures Exchange (TFE)

Special High Grade Zinc
London Metal Exchange (LME)

Tin
Kuala Lumpur Commodity Exchange
(KLCE)
London Metal Exchange (LME)
Shanghai Metals Exchange
Shenzhen Metal and United Futures
Exchange

Zinc
London Metal Exchange (LME)
Shanghai Metals Exchange
Shenzhen Metal and United Futures
Exchange

Indexes

10-year Norwegian Government Bond
Oslo Stock Exchange (OBX)

All Ordinaries Index
Sydney Futures Exchange (SFE)

ATX Stock Index
Austrian Futures & Options Exchange
(OTOB)

BEL 20 Index
Belgium Futures and Options
Exchange (BELFOX)

BIFFEX
London Commodity Exchange (LCE)

Bovespa Stock Index
Bolsa de Mercadoris & Futuros (BM&F)

CAC 40 Stock Index
Marche a Terme International de
France (MATIF)
Marche des Options Negociables de
Paris (MONEP)

CECE Index (CEX)
The Austrian Futures & Options
Exchange (OTOB)

Czech Traded Index (CTX)
The Austrian Futures & Options
Exchange (OTOB)

Dutch Top 5 Index
Financial Futures Market Amsterdam
(FTA)
European Options Exchange (EOE)

EOE Index
OM London (OMLX)

EOE Stock Index
European Options Exchange (EOE)
Financial Futures Market Amsterdam
(FTA)

Eurotop 100 Index
European Options Exchange (EOE)
Financial Futures Market Amsterdam
(FTA)
New York Mercantile Exchange
(COMEX)
OM London (OMLX)

Finnish Options Index –FOX
Helsinki Securities and Derivatives
Exchange, Clearinghouse

FT-SE-100 Stock Index
London International Financial
Futures Exchange (LIFFE)

GEMx Index
OM London (OMLX)

Hang Seng Index
Hong Kong Futures & Options
Exchange, Ltd. (HKFE)

Hungarian Traded Index (HTX)
The Austrian Futures & Options
Exchange (OTOB)

IBEX 35 Stock Index
MEFF Renta Variable (MEFF-V)

Ibovespa Futures
Bolsa de Mercadoris & Futuros (BM&F)

IPSA Index
Santiago Stock Exchange (SSE)

KFX Stock Index
Guarantee Fund for Danish Options &
Futures (FUTOP)

MSCI Hong Kong Index
Singapore International Monetary
Exchange Ltd. (SIMEX)

MSCI Taiwan Stock Ox3e I
Singapore International Monetary
Exchange Ltd. (SIMEX)

MSCI Taiwan Stock Index
Singapore International Monetary
Exchange Ltd. (SIMEX)

Major Market Index
European Options Exchange (EOE)

Nikkei Index
Singapore International Monetary
Exchange Ltd. (SIMEX)

Nikkei 225 Index
Osaka Securities Exchange (OSE)

Nikkei 300 Index
Singapore International Monetary
Exchange Ltd. (SIMEX)

Nikkei Stock Average
Singapore International Monetary
Exchange Ltd. (SIMEX)

NYSE 40 Index
New Zealand Futures & Options
Exchange (NZFOE)

OMX Index
European Options Exchange (EOE)
OM London (OMLX)

Polish Traded Index (PTX)
The Austrian Futures & Options
Exchange (OTOB)

Russian Traded Index (RTX)
The Austrian Futures & Options
Exchange (OTOB)

Rubber Cash–Settled Index
RSA Commodity Exchange (Rubber
Association of Singapore)

Swedish OMX Index
OM Stockholm

Toronto 35
Toronto Futures Exchange (TFE)

TSE 300 Spot
Toronto Futures Exchange (TFE)

Toronto 100 Stock Index
Toronto Futures Exchange (TFE)

Foods

Arbica Coffee
Bolsa de Mercadoris & Futuros
(BM&F)
Tokyo Grain Exchange (TGE)

Black Pepper
The OTC Exchange of India (OTCEI)

Cocoa
China-Commodity Futures Exchange,
Inc. of Hainan (CCFE)
Kuala Lumpur Commodity Exchange
(KLCE)
London International Financial
Futures Exchange (LIFFE)

Cocoa No. 8
London Commodity Exchange (LCE)

Coffee
Bolsa de Mercadoris & Futuros
(BM&F)
China-Commodity Futures Exchange,
Inc. of Hainan (CCFE)
Indonesian Commodity Exchange
Board (Badan Pelaksana Bursa
Komoditi)
Marche a Terme International de
France (MATIF)
Manila International Futures
Exchange (MIFE)
Singapore Commodity Exchange Ltd.

Conillion Coffee
Bolsa de Mercadoris & Futuros
(BM&F)

Copra
Manila International Futures
Exchange (MIFE)

Crystal Sugar
Bolsa de Mercadoris & Futuros
(BM&F)

Potato Index
The South African Futures Exchange
(SAFEX)

Potatoes
Agricultural Futures Market
Amsterdam
Marche a Terme International de
France (MATIF)
London International Financial
Futures Exchange (LIFFE)
London Commodity Exchange (LCE)
The OTC Exchange of India (OTCEI)

Raw Sugar
London Commodity Exchange (LCE)
Kasai Agricultural Commodities
Exchange (KACE)
Tokyo Grain Commodity Exchange
(TGCE)

Refined Sugar
Kanmon Commodity Exchange (KCE)
Nagoya Grain & Sugar Exchange
(NGSE)

Robusta Coffee
London International Financial
Futures Exchange (LIFFE)
London Commodity Exchange (LCE)
Bolsa de Mercadoris & Futuros
(BM&F)
Tokyo Grain Exchange (TGE)

Sugar
Bolsa de Mercadoris & Futuros
(BM&F)
Kanmon Commodity Exchange (KCE)
Kasai Agricultural Commodities
Exchange (KACEX)
Marche a Terme International de
France (MATIF)
Manila International Futures
Exchange (MIFE) Wheat
Nagoya Grain & Sugar Exchange
(NGSE)
Tokyo Grain Exchange (TGE)

Turmeric
The OTC Exchange of India (OTCEI)

White Sugar
London International Financial
Futures Exchange (LIFFE)
London Commodity Exchange (LCE)

Other Industrials

*International 1 Ribbed Smoked Sheet –
RRSS 1*
RSA Commodity Exchange (Rubber
Association of Singapore)

*International 3 Ribbed Smoked Sheet –
RSSS 3*
RSA Commodity Exchange (Rubber
Association of Singapore)

Rubber
Beijing Commodity Exchange (BCE)
China-Commodity Futures Exchange,
Inc. of Hainan (CCFE)
Indonesian Commodity Exchange
Board (Badan Pelaksana Bursa
Komoditi)
Kobe Rubber Exchange (KRE)
Kuala Lumpur Commodity Exchange
(KLCE)
Singapore Commodity Exchange Ltd.
Tokyo Commodity Exchange (TOCOM)

Rubber - RSS3
Kobe Rubber Exchange (KRE)

Technically Specified Rubber 20 – TSR
RSA Commodity Exchange (Rubber
Association of Singapore)

Financial Futures and Options

All Share Index
The South African Futures Exchange
(SAFEX)
Bleached Hardwood Kraft Pulp Index
Finnish Options Exchange Ltd. (FOEX)

BIFFEX (Dry Freight Futures)
London International Financial
Futures Exchange (LIFFE)

BTC
Commodity Exchange of Ljubljana
(LCE)

De Beers
The South African Futures Exchange
(SAFEX)

Droga Portoroz
Commodity Exchange of Ljubljana
(LCE)

Equity Options
Anglo American
The South African Futures Exchange
(SAFEX)

Eurotop
London International Financial
Futures Exchange (LIFFE)

FTSE 100
London International Financial
Futures Exchange (LIFFE)

FTSE 250
London International Financial
Futures Exchange (LIFFE)

Financial Index
The South African Futures Exchange
(SAFEX)

HKFE Taiwan Index Futures
Hong Kong Futures & Options
Exchange, Ltd. (HKFE)

HKFE Taiwan Index Options
Hong Kong Futures & Options
Exchange, Ltd. (HKFE)
Hang Seng China-Affiliated
Corporations Index Futures (Red-Chip
Futures)

Hang Seng 100 Futures
Hong Kong Futures & Options
Exchange, Ltd. (HKFE)

Hang Seng 100 Options
Hong Kong Futures & Options
Exchange, Ltd. (HKFE)

Hang Seng Index Futures
Hong Kong Futures & Options
Exchange, Ltd. (HKFE)

Hang Seng Index Options
Hong Kong Futures & Options
Exchange, Ltd. (HKFE)

Industrial Index
The South African Futures Exchange
(SAFEX)

KID
Commodity Exchange of Ljubljana
(LCE)

KRKA
Commodity Exchange of Ljubljana
(LCE)

LEK
Commodity Exchange of Ljubljana
(LCE)

Liberty Life
The South African Futures Exchange
(SAFEX)

Luka Koper
Commodity Exchange of Ljubljana
(LCE)

Mercator
Commodity Exchange of Ljubljana
(LCE)

Mining Index
The South African Futures Exchange
(SAFEX)

OBX Index
Oslo Stock Exchange (OBX)

Petrol
Commodity Exchange of Ljubljana
(LCE)

Pivovarna Lasko
Commodity Exchange of Ljubljana
(LCE)

R150 Long Bond
The South African Futures Exchange
(SAFEX)

R153 Long Bond
The South African Futures Exchange
(SAFEX)

R157 Long Bond
The South African Futures Exchange
(SAFEX)

R162 Long Bond
The South African Futures Exchange
(SAFEX)

Rand/U.S. Dollar
The South African Futures Exchange
(SAFEX)

Richemont
The South African Futures Exchange
(SAFEX)

Sasol Ltd
The South African Futures Exchange
(SAFEX)

Short-Term Interest Rate
The South African Futures Exchange
(SAFEX)

SKB Banka
Commodity Exchange of Ljubljana
(LCE)

Terme Catez
Commodity Exchange of Ljubljana
(LCE)

The South African Breweries
The South African Futures Exchange
(SAFEX)

Other Products

Anhydrous Ammonia
Bleached Hardwood Kraft Pulp Index
Finnish Options Exchange Ltd. (FOEX)

Gur
The OTC Exchange of India (OTCEI)

Lumber
Oriented Strand Board

Plywood
Beijing Commodity Exchange (BCE)
China-Commodity Futures Exchange,
Inc. of Hainan (CCFE)

Shanghai Commodity Exchange
Shenyang Commodity Exchange
Suzhou Commodity Exchange

Polypropylene
Beijing Commodity Exchange (BCE)

Polyvinyl Chloride
Beijing Commodity Exchange (BCE)
Shanghai Commodity Exchange
Suzhou Commodity Exchange

Sodium Carbonate
Beijing Commodity Exchange (BCE)

Wood
Shenyang Commodity Exchange

Glossary

Arbing. See Arbitrage.

Arbitrage. The simultaneous purchase of one commodity against the sale of another to profit from distortions in usual price relationships. Variations include simultaneous purchase and sale of different delivery months of the same commodity, or of the same commodity and delivery month on two different exchanges, or the purchase of one commodity against the sale of another commodity. *See also* Spread.

Arbitraging. See Arbitrage.

Back month. A calendar month that is active and more than 90 days from the current trading month.

Example:

Active Months	Mar	May	Jun	Jul	Dec
Current Month	Mar				
Back Months	Jul	Dec			

Sometimes the term is used to signify a month in which futures trading is taking place with a maturity other than current spot.

Example:

Active Months	Mar	May	Jun	Jul	Dec
Current Month	Mar				
Back Months	May	Jun	Jul	Dec	

Bar chart. A graph of horizontal bars or vertical columns comparing characteristics of two or more items or showing differing proportions of those items. Bar charts are used in technical analysis to track price ranges and movements.

Basis. The difference between a cash price at a specific location and the price of a particular futures contract.

Bottom. Lowest price reached during a market cycle.

Call option. An exchange-traded option contract that gives the purchaser the right, but not the obligation, to enter into an underlying futures contract to buy a commodity at a stated strike price at any time prior to the option's expiration date. The grantor of the call has the obligation, upon exercise, to deliver the long futures.

Example: The buyer (traded)

Option	Strike Price	Expire Date	Trade Price
October 12:			
Long 1 Mar Sugar #11 @1200		March 9	1.20

On the dates of October 12 and March 9 of the next year, the March futures market trades at 1400. The buyer exercises the right to be long (the futures) at 1200 (option strike price):

Futures Market Transaction			
	Long 1	Mar Sugar #11	@1200
		Mar Sugar #11	@1400
Buyer paid		Points	+200 gain
option premium		Points	−120
		Net Points	80 gain*

*Less commission and fees upon ultimate sale of the futures.

Carrying charges. Costs incurred in warehousing the physical commodity, generally including interest, insurance, and storage.

Cash settlement. A finalizing mechanism in which a contract is satisfied with a cash value calculation. Cash ,may be given in lieu of the actual commodity, or it may be required in addition to physical delivery of a commodity (for example, when commodity quality necessitates a premium or a discount). In finalizing a financial product, such as an index or foreign exchange product, cash settlement is necessary because the contract represents a value rather than a physical product.

Clearinghouse. An agency connected with a commodity exchange through which all futures contracts are reconciled, settled, guaranteed, and later either offset or fulfilled through delivery of the commodity, and through which financial settlement is made. It may be a fully chartered separate corporation rather than a division of the exchange itself.

Commodity fund. Investment pool, observed as a limited partnership, formed to speculate in commodity futures and options. Each participant (investor) will have his or her original investment increased (reduced) by his or her proportional share of income and trading profits (expenses and trading losses).

Crush spread ("crushers"). This position entails long soybean futures contracts and short soybean oil and soybean meal futures contracts in fixed proportions. It is called a crush spread because this replicates the positions taken by soybean processors when hedging the later purchase of inputs and sale of products.

Cyclic analysis. Analysis that uses various seasonal factors as a basis to determine trends and prices.

Delta. A percentage value of the amount that an option premium can be expected to change for a given unit change in the underlying futures contract.

The factor takes into consideration the time remaining to an option's expiration, the volatility of the underlying futures contract, and the price relationship.

Factors are available from brokerage firms offering option trading. They change on a daily basis. Your broker can give you the delta factor on any option.

Demand. The quantities of a commodity that potential buyers would want to purchase at different prices given current conditions (e.g., prices of related goods, expectations, tastes, etc.). The quantity of commodity demanded is inversely related to price.

Discretionary trading. Customer accounts in which specified employees of a brokerage firm may execute trades without explicit authorization for every individual transaction.

Dollar value (or cash value). The monetary value of the full amount of a commodity or financial instrument represented by a futures contract. This is the price per unit times the number of units.

Examples:

| Grain futures: | $5.00/bu X 5,000 bu = $25,000 or |
| T Bond or T Note future: | 87 16/32 X $100,000 = $87,500. |

Elasticity of demand (supply). The percentage change in quantities demanded (supplied) for a given percentage change in price. Inelastic
demand (supply) indicates relatively small changes in quantities
compared to the price change. Elastic demand (supply) indicates
relatively large changes in quantities compared to the price change.

Elliott wave. Theory of cyclical movements of prices. Follows certain indicators that predict and confirm price movements.

Exercise price. The predetermined price level(s) at which an underlying
futures contract or actual commodity contract may be established
upon exercise of the option. For futures options, the exchange sets a
price in line with the previous day's settlement price for the underlying futures. From that price, exercise prices at exchange-deter-
mined intervals above and below are established. Options may be
traded at these exercise prices. Each successive day, new prices may
be established in addition to those currently trading or available for
trading if the futures market fluctuations warrant it.

Expiration date. The last day that an option may be exercised into the
underlying futures or actual commodity contract. If not exercised or
assigned, the option ceases to exist.

Fibonacci ratios. Ratios of cyclical market movements to one another that
are used to establish price objectives concerning the likely movements in the next cycle.

Fill-or-kill order. An order that must be offered or bid immediately at a
given price and canceled if not executed. The standard abbreviation
is FOK. Also known as Immediate Order, FOK.

Example:

Buy 1 Dec COMEX Gold @ 400.00 Fill or Kill

May also be written as:

B 1 Z COMEX GLD @ 400.00 FOK

Floor manager. A brokerage firm employee responsible for overseeing and
coordinating the activities of all the trading floor personnel of the
firm: runners, phone clerks, traders, and assistants.

Floor supervisor. See Floor manager.

Foreign currency future. A contract requiring the later purchase and sale of
a designated amount of money issued by a foreign bank. (A March

Swiss franc contract would call for the delivery of 125,000 francs during a specified period in March.)

Full carrying charge market. A situation in the futures market when the price difference between delivery months reflects the full costs of interest, insurance, and storage.

Futures contract. An agreement to later buy or sell a commodity of a standardized amount and standardized minimum quality grade, during a specific month, under terms and conditions established by the federally designated contract market upon which trading is conducted, at a price established in the trading pit.

Futures option. An option contract, exercise of which results in the holder and writer of the option exchanging futures positions.

Good-till-canceled order. An order to buy or sell at a fixed price that remains open until executed or canceled by the customer.

Example:
Buy 1 Dec COMEX Gold @ 420.00 Good-Till-Canceled

May also be written as:
B 1 Z COMEX GLD @ 420.00 GTC
Note: Provision may be made to cancel automatically on a given day.

Example: An order entered on March 10
Buy 1 Dec COMEX Gold @ 420.00 Good-Till Mar 15

Hedging. The initiation of a position in a futures market that is intended as a temporary substitute for the sale or purchase of the actual commodity. The sale of futures contracts in anticipation of future sales of cash commodities as a protection against possible price declines, or the purchase of futures contracts in anticipation of future purchases of cash commodities as a protection against the possibility of increasing costs.

Initial margin. Cash or securities required as a good faith deposit to establish a specific new position in the futures or option market. An initial margin amount is set by the respective exchange. *Note:* Initial margin is not a partial payment of the purchase.

Intercommodity spread. The purchase and sale of two different, but related, commodities with the same delivery month and trading on the same exchange.

Intermarket spread. The purchase and sale of the same commodity on two different exchanges.

Example:

Chicago Board of Trade (CBT)

Long 5 Mar Silver (1,000 oz. each)

New York Commodity Exchange (COMEX)

Short 1 Mar Silver (5,000 oz.)

Interest rate future. A contract reflecting the value (and usually the later purchase or sale) of debt instruments (as T Bond, T Bill, EuroDollar Deposit, or Municipal Bond Futures).

Intramarket spread. The purchase of a commodity and sale of the same commodity of a different contract month or of a different commodity of the same or a different month, both contracts of which are trading on the same exchange.

Example:

Chicago Board of Trade

Long 5M May Wheat

Short 5M July Wheat

Limit order. An order with some restrictions, such as price, time, or both, on execution. Restrictions are set by the client.

Example: Time limit

Buy 1 Apr Gold @ 400.00 Opening Only

May also be written as:

B 1 J GLD @ 400.00 Opening Only

Example: Price limit

Buy 1 Apr Gold @ 390.00

May also be written as:

B 1 J GLD @ 390.00

Limited partnership. Business organization with full flow-through of the consequences to the partners. Limited partners' liabilities are limited to their investment plus any debt they have agreed to be charged for. Limited partnerships must have one or more general partners whose liability is unlimited.

Liquidity. Refers to the least cost at which one can enter and then close out a position.

Local (broker). A floor broker who may trade for customers but primarily for his or her own account, continuously buying and selling for quick profits.

Maintenance margin. The monetary value to which the original margin requirement may depreciate and still be considered a satisfactory margin to carry the established position. A minimum is specified by the governing exchange, but it may be the policy of an individual firm to set a minimum higher than the governing exchange's. *Also known as* Variation allowance.

Example:

Initial Requirement I Contract	$4,000.00
Allowable Market Fluctuation (negative)	-1,000.00
Maintenance Level for the Contract	$3,000.00

Note: The rule of thumb is maintenance at 75% of the original requirement.

Managed accounts. Customer accounts in which all trades are determined by a trading advisor or fund manager.

Margin. An amount of money deposited by both buyers and sellers of futures contracts to ensure performance of the terms of the contract (the delivery or taking of delivery of the commodity or the cancellation of the position by a subsequent offsetting trade). Margin in commodities is not a payment of equity or a down payment on the commodity itself, but rather is a performance bond or security deposit.

Margin call. A call from a clearinghouse to a clearing member, or from a brokerage firm to a customer, to bring margin deposits up to a required minimum level.

Market analyst. An individual who follows all important factors potentially affecting the price of the commodity or financial instrument in question. Market analysts typically distribute analyses of past market movement and forecasts of future developments.

Market order. An order to buy or sell a specified number of contracts for a specified commodity month at the best price available at the time the order reaches the trading ring.

Example:

Buy 5M May Wheat Market

May also be written as:

B 5M K WHT MKT

As long as the execution price represents the best offering at the time of execution and the price received was traded approximately at the time the order entered the trading ring, any price is acceptable.

Market-if-touched order. A contingency order given with a limited price instruction, that when the market reaches the required price level, it becomes a market order to trade at the next best trading price. This term is also known by the standard abbreviation MIT.

Example:

Buy 1 Dec Gold @ 320.00 Market if Touched

May also be written as:

b I Z GLD @ 320.00 MIT

This buy order is placed below the marker and is not to be executed unless and until the market reaches 320.00. At that point, the order becomes a market order and is executed at the best available price. The 320.00 price level cannot be guaranteed.

Note: This order can be given as a sell order as well. The significant difference between an MIT order and a Stop order is its location for execution relative to current prices.

Market-on-close order. An instruction to buy or sell at the best price available during the closing period of the market on a given day.

Example:

Sell 5M May Wheat Market on Close

May also be written as:

S 5M K WHT MOC

Market-on-the-open order. An instruction to buy or sell at the best price available during the opening period of the market on a given day.

Example:

Sell 5M May Corn Market on the opening

May also be written as:

S 5M K Crn Mkt opening only

Execution can take place only during the exchange-specified opening period. If the market trades in the range of 330 to 335 during that time, any price in that range can be the trade price. Trade price need not be the first price traded nor necessarily be guaranteed to be the best price in that range.

Minimum fluctuation. The smallest increment or gradation of price movement possible in trading a given contract. *Also known as* Minimum price fluctuation, Point, Tick.

Example:

Commodity	Basis Point Minimum Fluctuation	Dollar Value
Wheat	1/4 per bushel	$12.50
Ginnie Mae	1/32 of a dollar	31.25
Gold	10¢ per ounce	10.00
Cattle	21/2¢ per pound	10.00
Sugar #11	1/100¢ per pound	11.20

Moving average. A method for averaging near-term prices in relation to long-term prices. Oldest prices are dropped as new ones are added.

Example:

Closing prices day	1	2.00
	2	2.01
	3	2.02
Average (6.03 divided by 3) =		2.01

As a new day is added, the oldest is dropped.

Closing prices day	2	2.01
	3	2.02
	4	2.03
Average (6.06 divided by 3) =		2.02

Note: Moving averages are not restricted to day measurements. Any constant unit measure can be applied, and the average can be from as few as two units to whatever number of units the user wishes.

Naked option. A short option position whereby the seller does not possess any position in either options or futures that will satisfy exercise of the short option position.

One-cancels-the-other order. An order designating both sides or the same side of a trading range with different months, markets, commodities, prices, etc. When the condition of one is reached and executed, the other is canceled.

Example:

Buy 5M July Soybeans   575 or

5M August   579 One Cancels Other

May also be written as:

B 5M N BNS 575 OR 5M Q BNS 579 OCO

This order may be executed by buying either July or August soybeans. Once either month has been purchased, the other is automatically canceled by the broker. The choice of month traded is left to the broker, who is guided by the dictates of market conditions.

Open interest. The total number of futures contracts of a given commodity that have not yet been offset by opposite futures transactions nor fulfilled by delivery of the commodity; the total number of open transactions. Each open transaction has a buyer and a seller, but for calculation of open interest, only one side of the contract is counted.

Option writer. The seller in an option trade that creates an option contract. The terms *short* and *grantor* are synonymous with *writer* and *seller*.

Or-better order. See Limit order.

Oscillator. Type of technical analysis tool used in predicting price movements.

Out trade. A trade that does not compare in the clearing process.

Out-trade clerk. An employee of the clearinghouse charged with helping to resolve problems with unmatched trade confirmations (out trades). The clearinghouse will not recognize a trade (or thus give a trader the desired position) without a matching confirmation enabling the creation of the contra position.

Pit. An area of the exchange floor designated for executing orders for a given commodity.

Point and figure chart. A chart constructed to detail a continuous flow of price activity without regard to time. Plotting direction is determined by a preset number of price changes in sequential order.

Premium. The additional payment allowed by exchange regulations for delivery of higher-than-required standards or grades of a commodity against a futures contract. In speaking of price relationships between different delivery months of a given commodity, one is said to be "trading at a premium" over another when its price is greater than that of the other. In financial instruments, a dollar amount by which a security trades above its principal value.

Price order. See Limit order.

Put option. An exchange-traded option contract that gives the purchaser the right, but not the obligation, to enter into an underlying futures contract to be short the commodity at a stated strike price at any time prior to the expiration of the option. The grantor of the put has the obligation, upon exercise, to deliver the short futures contract.

Pyramiding. Adding contracts to an existing position as it becomes profitable.

Quote board. Mechanism for displaying current prices on commodity futures contracts. The quote board is situated so as to be easily seen from most positions on the trading floor.

Regression. Method of statistical analysis that measures quantitative correlations between different variables. One method used to weigh hedges (hedge ratios).

Relative strength indicator. Technical analysis tool that attempts to indicate when the market has moved excessively in one direction and is likely to be reversed by a technical reversal.

Round trip. See Round turn.

Round turn. The combination of an initiating purchase or sale of a futures contract and the offsetting sale or purchase of an equal number of futures contracts of the same delivery month. Commission fees for commodities transactions cover the round turn.

Scalper. An active trader who attempts to profit on small price changes by buying and selling on the short term (current trading day); a floor trader who trades only his or her own account and creates liquidity by buying and selling continuously.

Seasonality. Condition of being affected by or occurring during a particular period of the calendar year. This factor determines a repeatable pattern influencing supplies and prices.

Example: Price Behavior

Commodity	Price	
	High	Low
Wheat	December	August
	May	September
Cotton	July	November
		December

Short selling. Generally, selling something that is not already owned. In futures, a short position not closed out requires the short seller to make delivery of the underlying asset.

Spot month. The near month or current month in which futures trading is still possible and notices can be issued to the long position holder advising that delivery is about to be made. Depending on the commodity, delivery may be the physical commodity or cash settlement in lieu of the commodity.

Example: On the Chicago Board of Trade for October Silver

Last Trading Day	The fourth last business day of the month
First Notice Day	Last business day of month preceding the delivery month.
Last Notice Day	The next-to-last business day in the delivery month

Spread. The purchase of one futures contract and sale of another, in the expectation that the price relationships between the two will change so that a subsequent offsetting sale and purchase will yield a net profit. Examples include the purchase of one delivery month and the sale of another in the same commodity on the same exchange, or the purchase and sale of the same delivery month in the same commodity on different exchanges, or the purchase of one commodity and the sale of another (wheat vs. corn or corn vs. hogs), or the purchase of one commodity and the sale of the products of that commodity (soybeans vs. soybean oil and soybean meal).

Standardization. The uniformity of terms and contract specifications of the futures markets to effectively interface with the cash (spot) markets, enabling the transfer of economic risk and recording control (clearance).

Stochastic-random. Finance theorists believing in the efficient market hypothesis hold that futures prices move in a random fashion (stochastic process).

Stock index. A group of stocks selected as representative of the stock market or some industry sector. Changes in the value of the stock index are a way of measuring the changes in the stock market.

Stock index future. A contract reflecting the value of a selected group of common stocks. Currently, all stock index futures are broad-based indexes reflecting movements of the overall market. These contracts can be used to hedge against or speculate on market moves. There is no physical delivery against any stock index futures. All are cash settlement contracts.

Stop order. See Limit order.

Straddle (futures). Similar to a futures spread, a strategy entailing long and short positions in related futures contracts.

Straddle (options). A strategy that entails the purchase (sale) of both calls and puts is known as a long (short) straddle.

Strike price. See Exercise price.

Supply. The quantities of a commodity that potential sellers would order for sale at different prices given current conditions. The quantity of commodity supplied is positively related to price.

Tick value. The change in the dollar or cash value of the contract when a futures price changes by the minimum possible price fluctuation (one tick). The tick value is the dollar price equivalent of one tick times the number of units in the futures contract.

> *Examples:*
>
> In most grain futures, 1/40/bu X 5,000 bu = $12.50
> In 6,000 futures, 100/oz X 100 oz = $10.

Top. Highest price reached during a market cycle.

Trade checking. The process of reconciling trade confirmations reflecting transactions that have been executed in the trading pits.

Trading range. Range of prices over which market action has been taking place during the time frame under study.

Volume. The number of contracts that changed hands during a given period of time.

Volatility band. Range of prices around current market levels that are within the likely trading range.

Whipsaw. Term used to describe what has happened to traders who have had stop orders executed as a result of volatile market swings. The traders' intentions were for the stop orders to be executed on market movements indicative of a sustained trend.

Index